FROM NORTHERN RHODESIA TO ZAMBIA

Recollections of a DO/DC
1962-73

Mick Bond

Gadsden Publishers

Gadsden Publishers

P O Box 32581, Lusaka, Zambia

Copyright © Mick Bond, 2014

All rights reserved. No part of this publication may be reproduced, stored in a retrieval system or transmitted, in any form or by an means electronic, mechanical, photocopying, recording or otherwise, without the prior permission of the publisher.

ISBN 978 9982240901

Printed by Lightning Source UK

CONTENTS

Acknowledgements	iv
Foreword	v
Abbreviations	vi

Chapter

1	WHY AND HOW I WENT TO NORTHERN RHODESIA	1
2	MPOROKOSO, 1962-64: DOMESTIC AND SOCIAL LIFE	13
3	MPOROKOSO, 1962-64: THE WORK	29
4	MPOROKOSO, 1962-64: AROUND THE DISTRICT	49
5	CHINSALI, 1953-64: LUMPA CHURCH BACKGROUND	71
6	CHINSALI, 1964: THE LUMPA CONFLICT	85
7	CHINSALI: THE AFTERMATH, INDEPENDENCE AND FAMILYLIFE	111
8	BANCROFT AND CHINGOLA, 1965-66	135
9	MONGU, 1966-67	147
10	MY LUSAKA & KITWE EPISODES, 1967-73	163
11	CONTRASTS AND RETROSPECT, SEEN FROM 2012	179

APPENDIX 1
    MPOROKOSO: MY FIRST VILLAGE-TO-VILLAGE TOUR REPORT   197

APPENDIX 2
    RULES OF LUMPA CHURCH AND SOME OF LENSHINA'S HYMNS   227

APPENDIX 3
    STRUCTURE OF GOVERNMENT ADMINISTRATION AT LOCAL LEVEL – 1995 RECOMMENDATIONS   231

Acknowledgements

I am most grateful for permission from John Hudson, MBE, of Lusaka and his publishers Bookworld to quote, in my Chapters 1, 5 and 6, from his book *A Time to Mourn*. My ex-colleague Peter Moss has allowed me to quote his recent email messages in my chapter 6, and I thank him for this.

I am also indebted to my late mother-in-law who had the affection and good sense to keep **all** my wife's letters written to England during our elevenyears in Northern Rhodesia/Zambia – only recently discovered (!), they have served excellently in correcting our memories of details and reminding us what we actually were thinking at the time.

Foreword

My wife and I lived and worked from 1962 to 1973 in Northern Rhodesia and Zambia i.e. through its period of Independence. Apart from my two three-night stopovers in Lusaka on behalf of Newcastle University, neither of us returned to Zambia until 2012, when we had a delightful month revisiting many parts of the country. We then came across so many Zambians who, hearing that I had once been a District Commissioner at the time of Independence, kept saying "You are a living part of our history, a part we know nothing about! You must tell us what it was like."

This modest account of our work and life half a century ago is, then, primarily intended for Zambian readers who recognise a gap in their understanding of that significant period in their country's history. By its nature this account can do no more than describe events from the perspectives of one expatriate couple, but a couple who immediately developed a great love for the country and its people.

Mick Bond, July 2014

Abbreviations used frequently

DC: District Commissioner
D/M, S/D/M: District Messenger, Senior D/M
DO: District Officer
DS: District Secretary
LDA: Learner District Assistant
N/A: Native Authority
PA: Provincial Administration
PC: Provincial Commissioner
P&DG: Provincial & District Government (PA's successor)
PMO: Provincial Medical Officer

1. WHY AND HOW I WENT TO NORTHERN RHODESIA

Let me start with some answers to a few very basic background questions. Why had I gone to the then Northern Rhodesia in the first place, in 1962? And, in essence, how did the British Colonial Service operate in pre-independent colonies and protectorates?

When I was fourteen, at home in southern England, we had a lodger staying with us for a month. He was studying at London University on a postgraduate course in Colonial Administration, preparatory to going out as a young District Officer to what was then Nyasaland. Talking with him often, I became fascinated by his descriptions of what he imagined the work would involve. Of course it was coloured by all the concepts of imperialism and British arrogant superiority of which we have long since come to be embarrassed or ashamed – but one cannot change history. Above all it seemed to be a job of immense variety and responsibility, playing one's part in ensuring good (if at times paternal) government, maintaining law and order, and pushing local development on all fronts, for the benefit firstly of the local population – and only coincidentally to satisfy any British interests. I then decided, at that tender age, that this was a most attractive career for me to pursue.

My education from 1947 to 1956 was at the City of London School, a day public school with a good reputation both for its academic achievements (e.g. for its tally of scholarships gained to Oxbridge) and for religious tolerance. About one third of the boys there were Jewish, and any sign or thought of anti-semitism amongst the majority of us was so exceptional as to lead to disgrace – more potent than punishment. Looking back, I suppose the subconscious acceptance of human equality regardless of religious beliefs, as practised at the school, was extended to the realms of racial equality, even though at that age I had no African acquaintances.

After school (I was Head Boy in my final year) I did the obligatory two year period of National Service in the Army. I did my basic training in, and was soon commissioned into, the famous Black Watch (Royal Highland Regiment) as a Second Lieutenant, and thoroughly enjoyed my time in pre-Wall Berlin and then in Edinburgh. It was often said that National Service turned boys into men; it certainly taught young officers the ethics of responsibility and basic administrative concepts. Then I went up to Jesus College, Cambridge, to read Classics for three years. Although I must have forgotten a lot of the Greek and Latin of my schooldays, I am sure my approach to both my studies and the inimitable social life there was that much more mature for the two years spent in the Army.

Throughout my time in the Army and at Cambridge my aspirations to join the Colonial Service did not change. In this period we experienced, of course, Harold Macmillan's famous speech on the "Winds of change sweeping across Africa," the nationalist calls for independence, and Britain's acceptance of the need to move from an Empire to a Commonwealth. While I still felt mentally committed to a career in what would be left of the Colonial Service, there was now an increasing desire to pursue it with the aim of helping to achieve as smoothly as possible the morally unchallengeable and inevitable transition to independence; in other words, to accept it as a 'suicide career' from the start, from which who knows where the experiences would lead. It was more a matter of fact, than just a joke, that a classical education had been regarded as the natural academic background for administrators in the Foreign and Colonial Services, although that was not the only reason I chose to read Classics at Cambridge. Wendy, who read English at Girton College, knew my clear career intentions when in 1961 she agreed to marry me, and equally I knew she would be the right partner for the kind of life ahead (had I married somebody else, I might well have changed tack and tried the Foreign Office – and had a very different life and family!).

By the time I was actually interviewed at the Colonial Office in 1960 the number of dependencies was dwindling further. Nigeria, Kenya, Nyasaland and Tanganyika were no longer options, and there remained Northern Rhodesia and various Pacific islands. I remember being much impressed by the 1961 Reith Lectures of Dame Margery Perham, the historian and Director of the Oxford Institute of Colonial Studies, entitled "The Colonial Reckoning". They were reassuring at the time, and still retain their reputation, in weighing dispassionately both the positive and the less worthy aspects of Britain's record as a colonial power. Even though now fully in support of moves to independence for all the dependencies, I did not feel on balance that we had that much to be ashamed of in our recent colonial history –

certainly not when compared with the Belgians, Portuguese, French or Germans.

I was accepted onto the postgraduate course in Colonial Administration at Cambridge in 1961-62, continuing to be a member of Jesus College. This was the last course of its kind, as it was clear to all except an ostrich that the days of the Colonial Service as such were severely numbered. We did come across one such ostrich: an elderly white-haired old hand visited us from the Colonial Office and, in order to encourage us perhaps, talked about the "magnificent career ahead of you all, young men!" We were sure we knew better.

The twenty three of us on the course were all, except one, destined for Northern Rhodesia, if we passed. The exception was Prince Stephen of Toro, brother of Princess Bagaya who was at Girton College with Wendy, reading Law, and who later became first an international fashion model and later still Foreign Secretary of Uganda under Idi Amin. Stephen would have entered the Ugandan Civil Service, but we all lost touch with him. There were some ten others who were doing a parallel course in Tropical Agriculture before going out as Colonial Agricultural Officers to various other dependencies (mostly in the Caribbean); we did not socialise much with them. The course Director, Mr Hugh McCleery, a former Provincial Commissioner (PC) of Tanganyika, was full of reminiscences from the past but not so strong on advising us on what the future would be like in the rapidly changing pre-independence scene. There was also a parallel 'senior' or refresher course; Jack Fairhurst, District Commissioner (DC) in Lusaka, was on this course and was very helpful to us.

So far as I can now recall, the contents of the course were: Language, Law (we would become junior Magistrates ex-officio), Colonial History, some Anthropology, basic Tropical Agriculture and Agricultural Economics, Land Surveying and the elements of construction. The Rev. Quick, an ex-missionary, came every week from South Wales to teach us ciBemba: this was regarded as the most difficult and structured of the eight main languages of Northern Rhodesia, and if we could master that we could more easily pick up one of the others, depending on where we were posted. I certainly concentrated more on the language than on the other subjects and came top of the class in that. In the vacations we had two placements: one was for a week with a Rural District Council to understand all the complexities of the UK's Local Government system, and for this I was placed at Oxted in Surrey; the other was to sit on the bench at Bow Street Magistrates' Court in London and see the law in action.

Apart from the above, the course did **not** really provide us with a clear idea of what our day-to-day duties, responsibilities and activities would be – not even the bare bones of office/personnel management or accounts, etc.! Those of us who had done National Service as officers had some experiences to call on, but the others had not. Some of our group, however, had already served for a year or two in Northern Rhodesia as Learner District Assistants (LDAs, a lower form of life than even Cadets) and with that experience had come in as non-graduates. It was from them, from Jack Fairhurst, and even more from Valentine Musakanya and Lazarus Mwanza (high-flying local graduates, destined for high office soon), that we novices really learnt what the country and the jobs were like. For three years I had taken the monthly *Africa Digest*; from this journal I had built up a very large card-index of all the personalities and events (political, economic and social) in every African country, including Northern Rhodesia, which was very informative – Valentine was most impressed!

Wendy and I were married in Cambridge on 7th April 1962, and on our return from honeymoon for the final term of the course Valentine and another course member came to join us in our rented terrace house. Valentine's wife, Flavia, had left Cambridge at this stage to return home to give birth to their third child, so Valentine would have been on his own. Thus we became close friends at an early stage with not just any African officer from Northern Rhodesia but the one who in two years' time would be Zambia's top civil servant. And Wendy started married life catering for three men, not just a husband. She recalls with amusement how, when she delivered an early morning cup of tea to Valentine in his bed, he'd hastily pull a vast law book from under his pillow to pretend he had been studying and, when challenged, said that if he kept it under his pillow he might absorb its contents while he slept.

Why and How I Went to Northern Rhodesia

We all passed the course, and were now District Officer Cadets. In June we heard of our postings. I shall only mention the colleagues whom we would meet again later. We were posted to Mporokoso, Valentine to Isoka, Max Keyzar to Abercorn and Neil Morris to Luwingu, all in the Northern Province; Lazarus Mwanza to Lundazi and Jim Lavender to Chadiza, both in the Eastern Province; Malcolm Mitchell to Choma, Richard Pelly to Kalomo and D'Arcy Payne to Livingstone, all in the Southern Province. It was noted that all of us were to go to fairly remote districts, at some distance from the capital or the Copperbelt.

Malcolm and Judy Mitchell married during our final term, as did another couple; Richard and Ruth Pelly who left such matters to the last moment and were actually honeymooning on the boat as we left the UK. I cannot recollect any problems as we made all our preparations for leaving (packing and the farewells), so we must have been very well organised! Our parents took our impending departure most calmly in the circumstances; after all, we were off 6,000 miles into the (to them) unknown for at least three years. This is especially true of Wendy's family, while my parents had had several years to prepare themselves for it.

Flying was out of the question, as we all had our total worldly possessions packed in large wooden crates and tin trunks, ready to start a new life. On 5th July 1962 we sailed from Southampton on the Union Castle liner "Transvaal Castle" for the fourteen day cruise to Cape Town, calling on the way at both Madeira and Las Palmas (the Canaries). On the ship with us was a District Officer (DO) and his wife, who had completed one three-year stint (in Luwingu) and was returning for another tour; this indicates that travelling by ship was the norm in those years, and not just the unavoidable route for first-timers with all their crates.

At Cape Town, with its magnificent backdrop of Table Mountain, we had to endure a lot of formalities to clear our goods through customs. Then, as a matter of family duty, Wendy and I had to meet and spent much of the day with my grandfather's niece and family who lived there. I can recall them driving us through the lovely city and saying: "You see, we're not so backward here; we've even got traffic lights." But it was my first exposure to aspects of apartheid which remain more vividly: their use of the term 'boy' for their servants, the almost total absence of any Africans in any of the areas they took us through, and then my faux-pas at the station as we left because I tried to go through an empty gate and was stopped because its label said "Niet-Blanks" – non-whites only!

A three-day train journey followed, taking us through wonderful and varied scenery – a twisting climb up to the high veldt, across the Little and Great Karoo semi-deserts, through the towns of Kimberley and Mafeking with their Boer War connotations, and then along the length of Bechuanaland Protectorate (now, of course, Botswana) to Bulawayo, and then with a change of train to Livingstone. The meals on board all seemed to be of something called stockfish, plain boiled at first and later curried, but perhaps our memory has been led to an exaggeration by some unpalatable experience. I was not to set foot in either South Africa or Southern Rhodesia again until they had achieved Independence – after 1990 and 1980 respectively – keeping my passport and conscience 'clean'.

We crossed the iconic bridge, with a brief glimpse of the Victoria Falls for the first time. D'Arcy Payne met us all at Livingstone station, hassled us with a load of immigration and other bureaucratic paperwork, and took off the Mitchells and others who were posted to the Southern Province. Arriving at Lusaka on 22nd July, we had our luggage all conveyed to a Public Works Department store and were housed for four nights in the main Government Rest House in the capital, at Longacres. We had reached our country of destination!

A brief period of intense socialising and shopping followed, with a lot of generous help from 'old colonial hands.' There was a reception for all our group and wives at Government House (now State House) where we met the Governor, Sir Evelyn Hone, his Deputy, Richard Luyt, and several current Ministers. I also met there Mr Gaminara, with whom my father had been at school and whom he had alerted as to our arrival; he was the Chief Secretary (i.e. the no.3), who in 1964 would train and hand over to our friend Valentine in the role of Secretary to the Cabinet. We were entertained to lunch one day by the Minister of Native Affairs (sic), Mr Thomas and wife, a charming couple who were most informal and interesting. This was effectively the most important Ministry, as it ran the Provincial Administration. At the time I just accepted, with some surprise, the colonial connotations of 'native affairs' – it would soon change – but at least it emphasised that local African interests were deemed to be paramount. We also had lunch with Len Bean, the Permanent Secretary of the Ministry and therefore quasi-no.4 in the Government. Mr Bean apparently warned our DC Mporokoso, ahead of our arrival, that Wendy was a "Girton blue-stocking", which was unfair to say the least, but indicated the systemic sexism of the colonial civil service. I only met him once after that, in Chinsali (see p.105). We Cadets all had to spend most of a morning being shown around the Secretariat offices (the civil service hub) to fill in forms or to be introduced to important people; and one afternoon was taken up with touring around the houses of various important characters to sign their visiting books – it was all exhausting and fairly confusing.

On the shopping and other practical sides Pam Fairhurst was most helpful to our wives. She introduced them to Lusaka's main shopping street, the dual-carriageway Cairo Road, whose name conjures up Cecil Rhodes's arrogant ambition of extending Britain's imperial sway all the way from the Cape to Cairo. We had to open a bank account, buy up an enormous bulk-order of goods at Kee's (to go 'free-baggage') and acquire a paraffin fridge and four 44-gallon drums of paraffin, ready for life in the rural area. Wendy also had a chance to go inside LegCo, the Legislative Assembly, to listen to a debate, which she found fascinating. And she managed to visit the hospital, where a check gave her a 95% chance of being pregnant, as we had suspected.

On my birthday, 26th July, we thankfully left Lusaka on the penultimate leg of our journey. It had been a time of having to dash madly around, meeting so many people (most of whom, though important, we should never see again), and trying to absorb from these meetings how the machinery of central government worked and how it would or should impact on our future work. We flew first to Ndola, with Neil and Fiona Morris who were bound for Luwingu, and then by an old Dakota to Kasama. This second flight took us over the Congo 'Pedicle', the Luapula river and Lake Bangweulu; it also gave us our first understanding of what "miles and endless miles of tree-tops" really means!

From Northern Rhodesia to Zambia

From the day we left Britain until late in 1963 I kept a day-by-day diary. I am so glad that I did, as I can now be confident that much of this account is accurate and not distorted by the tricks of memory over the years. How stupid of me not to have continued with a diary during my later days in Zambia! But it was only in 2012 that I rediscovered this totally forgotten diary, together with various other documents of relevance.

It is from my newly-found diary that I am reminded what occurred when we arrived in Kasama. We were met by the DC Kasama and his wife and a Kasama LDA, and taken straight to the Government Rest House. Here we met our own DC, Ian Macdonald and his wife; she was going off to the UK the next day to put their children into schools, so we didn't get to know her. He, with his moustache and keen eyes, seemed to me very military and efficient, but pleasant enough, and I was sure I would get on well with him. In the evening we went for drinks with the Provincial Commissioner for Northern Province, Peter Clarke and his wife, and met most of the other members of the Provincial Administration in Kasama. This was a much smaller, friendlier and more informal group than we had met in Lusaka, and naturally they had more immediate interest in and for us. The next day, Ian Macdonald drove us the 175 kilometres to Mporokoso.

* * * * * * *

The above account of why, and how, we went to Africa only touches slightly on how the Colonial Service operated, with reference to our mad round of social meetings in Lusaka. Let me go back a little in history – but without recounting how or why Britain acquired an Indian Empire, colonies, protectorates, etc.!

Lord Lugard (1858-1945) is generally regarded as one of the most influential of Britain's past colonial administrators. With an Indian Army birth and background, he came to Africa in 1888 to command an expedition against the Arab slave trade in Nyasaland. Next, he was responsible for Uganda becoming a British Protectorate in 1894. Then he became Commissioner of the Nigerian Hinterland, and later the High Commissioner of Northern Nigeria (1897-1907), both areas being Protectorates. After a spell as

Governor of Hong Kong he returned to Nigeria to achieve the amalgamation of the two Protectorates and to become the first Governor-General of Nigeria (1914-19).

In Uganda and in Nigeria there were well-established African monarchies and local civil services, e.g. the Kabaka of Buganda, the Sultan of Sokoto, the Emir of Kano, etc. Unlike other colonial powers which tended to sweep aside the local systems, Lugard employed these local rulers as the channels of government, giving to the expedient of indirect rule the status of an orthodox philosophy. Thereafter Lugard and indirect rule have become virtually synonymous, and his concepts were quickly adopted or introduced in most African dependencies, especially in East and Central Africa (except the colony of Southern Rhodesia).

How was indirect rule applied in Northern Rhodesia? How did it still operate there sixty years after Lugard, and essentially up to the time of Independence?

In Central Africa, villages were usually inhabited by families who shared a common language, ancestral and tribal origin, and customs. Each village would have a headman – his would usually be the name by which the village was known. Villages were grouped under tribal chiefs, who were often related to one another in a royal clan; where there were several chiefs in a tribe, one would be the Senior Chief; and the largest tribal groupings had two or three Senior Chiefs plus a Paramount Chief. Since this pattern of African rural society had existed for centuries, it made sense for the Protectorate's colonial administrators to use the chiefs as the basic local government authorities through whom they could operate indirect rule. They officially recognised the chiefs as 'native authorities' and paid them small salaries. As such, the chiefs were permitted, and indeed encouraged, to make local regulations, to raise money by local levies, and to spend it on local services; thus they were also in charge of 'native treasuries'. Chiefs also continued to preside over their local courts, now referred to as 'native courts', administering customary law in both civil and criminal cases so long as their ideas of justice were not repugnant to those of the British system.

For administrative purposes the country was divided into districts (41 plus 9 sub-districts in 1962), and these were grouped into eight provinces. A rural district would typically have a population of around 60,000. Provincial and District Commissioners were the senior government officers and the representatives of the Governor in their respective province or district. They and their staff constituted the Provincial Administration (PA). A DC was usually supported by one or two District Officers (or one plus a Cadet like myself). I shall try to describe later, in Chapter 3, the main responsibilities and powers of a DC and his team, but in the barest summary one could say there were two aspects: one was to coordinate the operations of all branches of Government in the district, the other was to supervise the operations of its 'native authorities' and 'native courts' – the pattern of indirect rule.

Despite what one might today think of colonialism, most of the individual DCs and DOs were conscientious and hard-working. They had to learn the relevant local languages, and were expected to become familiar with local customs and history. They spent much of their time touring villages by bicycle or on foot, in two-way exercises of getting a clear picture of the villagers and their living conditions and of informing them of any Government policies or regulations which they should know about. They really cared for the well-being of the people in their districts and, within the constraints of very limited resources, tried all kinds of development measures to improve the socio-economic lives of their areas.

A district headquarters was called a Boma, a kiSwahili word meaning an enclosure (often used to keep cattle in at night). Most administrative posts in the earliest colonial days had been enclosed like small forts, for safety reasons. Gradually, over the decades, the term 'Boma' came to be used for the small rural townships which developed around these posts, as much as for the DC's headquarters. Conspicuous at every 'Boma' were the fifteen or more District Messengers in their distinctive uniforms. John Hudson, in his book *A Time to Mourn*, admirably encapsulates their roles as follows.

> *The duties and authority of the [D/M] group were much wider than their title suggests. Just as DCs had to be versatile jacks-of-all-trades to handle their wide range of responsibilities (which included the maintenance of law and order, court cases in their capacity as magistrates, road and building maintenance, development projects, local government*

functions through the native authorities, and co-ordination of the activities of specialised government officials), so the District Messengers had powers of arrest, acted as interpreters, and were sent out on bicycles to deal with almost anything in the district that might need attention, including the hire and supervision of local villagers to build or repair roads and bridges. And they were the effective 'eyes and ears' of the DC. They accompanied DOs on their tours of villages and on visits to chiefs' headquarters, missions and other centres. As the officers wore uniform only on rare ceremonial occasions, District Messengers also served to identify them to the local people. In general, District Messengers were highly regarded by the people; in many instances the arrival of a single Messenger could calm down an unruly gathering or stop a brawl.

For the first half of the twentieth century, although economic and social progress in rural districts was painfully slow, the situation was generally peaceful and local people seemed reasonably content with the combined authorities of the PA and their chiefs. But from the mid-1950s nationalist movements emerged all over Africa and gathered strength, demanding more representation in a colonial country's government and a swifter progress towards complete independence. In Central Africa the situation was exacerbated by the formation of the Federation of Rhodesia and Nyasaland in August 1953. This ill-conceived creation by Britain was intended to act as a compromise, or middle way, between a fully independent majority-ruled state and the European-dominated territories of South Africa, Angola and Mozambique. But from the start it was realised by both nationalists and liberal-minded Europeans in the two northern Protectorates that Southern Rhodesia would be the dominant partner in the Federation – economically, electorally and militarily. In 1960, while all three territories had roughly the same number of African residents (around 2.8 million each), Southern Rhodesia had over three times as many Europeans as Northern Rhodesia; the Federation seemed a mechanism for starving the northern partners (especially of the income from the copper mines, Northern Rhodesia's main economic asset) for the benefit of the Europeans in the south. Notably, most of the Federal Government's responsibilities (as distinct from those of the individual territories), such as European Agriculture, European Education and European Health, were of little relevance and virtually no benefit to the northern Protectorates. In Northern Rhodesia's Northern Province there were only two very small hospitals and two little primary schools for Europeans, and in Mporokoso District not a single place under Federal control. But on the Copperbelt and on the line of rail the existence of Federation-funded institutions, alongside the clearly racialist electoral system in which only handfuls of Africans had the vote, added fuel to the fire of the nationalists in their growing campaign for Independence.

Officers of the PA generally recognised that Independence in Northern Rhodesia was an ultimate objective. They felt they had to prepare the country for it, and, like myself, now realised they were in that sense in a 'suicide career.' In the meantime, however, it was part of their duty to maintain law and order, and they found it difficult – even impossible – to tolerate the increasing instances, in the late 1950s and early 1960s, where nationalist militants created unrest and acted criminally. The unrest and rebellion against the colonial Government reached a climax in 1961, when illegal gatherings, intimidation of non-party members, disrespect for the native authorities, road blocks, stoning of vehicles and burning of schools became all too frequent. This was the period known as *cha-cha-cha*. Those responsible were caught and imprisoned. But this reaction, though justifiable, was very unpopular and only went to sever the former good relations between the PA and local people. The tension was only eased and normal relationships resumed when, in 1963, the Federation was dissolved and a credible timetable was announced for the final steps towards Independence.

That, briefly, is a summary of the operation of indirect rule, the Federation and the political situation prior to our arrival in 1962. I trust it also gives sufficient background on the PA and on the role of the DO or DC for my retrospective accounts of our activities in later chapters to make some sense. My detailed day-by-day diary to which I have referred also gives an insight into the daily work of a young officer at the end of the colonial era, and I shall give some extracts from it in due course.

2. MPOROKOSO, 1962-64: DOMESTIC AND SOCIAL LIFE

Mporokoso quickly became *ku mwesu* (at ours, our home). This was where we were to spend our first two years in Africa, the first two years of our married life, and for me my first paid employment (apart from National Service). We immediately fell in love with Mporokoso, as a station and as a District, and that intense feeling was probably enhanced because it was our first posting and we were learning so much all the time. For the next fifty years we would retain vivid nostalgic memories of it; it is certainly true that today we still have clearer recollections of people and events and scenery from our time there in 1962-64 than from any of our subsequent postings. And we often feel they were the happiest two years of our lives.

Mporokoso was a small bush station or Boma. In the pioneer days of the 1900s, bomas tended to be established at around 160 kilometres (or 100 miles) from each other, and Kasama, our nearest town and the Northern Province's headquarters, was slightly more than that distance away. Kasama had electricity and a few telephones, shops and a bank and hospitals (one for Africans and a tiny Federal cottage hospital for Europeans). We had none of those amenities.

In Chapter one I described our first journey to Northern Rhodesia up to the point where we arrived at Mporokoso with our first DC, Ian Macdonald. What were our initial impressions, who were the other residents, what was the set-up and normal routine?

It would be fair to remind oneself that these were still the days of the colonial regime, albeit with the prospects of Independence in a few years' time. Class divisions, too, still existed in the 1960s among Europeans: as I had become used to in the British Army (in National Service), there was still an old-fashioned distinction of the 'officer class' and 'other ranks'. Again, the acts of lawlessness committed by nationalist militants which I have mentioned in the previous pages occurred nowhere more than in this Northern Province. Many serving officers including Ian Macdonald and John Hudson had experienced the road-blocks, arsons and killings of what was called the *cha-cha-cha* campaign of 1961, only a year before our arrival – quite frightening for any Europeans living on bush stations. It was, then, hardly surprising that the combination of colonialist/class attitudes and the recent period of violence meant that a latent feeling of 'them and us' still pervaded much (but not all) of our working and social lives – to begin with.

When we first arrived the European officers at the Boma were: the DC (Ian Macdonald, now a grass-widower as his wife had left to take their children back to schools in the UK), the DO Cadet 1, one year my senior (Jeremy Collingwood and his wife Margaret), the SBO (Special Branch Officer: John Cochrane, a bachelor), and the Game Officer, when he wasn't tramping through his beloved Reserves (the bearded, irascible and teasing Leslie Allen and his wife Jean). With our arrival as DO Cadet 2 the number rose to eight in total!

At the Catholic Mission across the airstrip were Fathers Deslauriers and Carrière, French-Canadian White Fathers, always dressed in long white soutanes. Three kilometres away was Kashinda Mission and clinic of the London Missionary Society, with initially two couples – Rev. Ernest and Kathie Cruchley with two young boys, and the senior and more elderly Rev. Ken and Mildred Francis. Completing the European population in the District but further afield were: Father Ladouceur and another White Father at Kalabwe Mission (thirty kilometres west), Father Bedard and another at Kapatu Mission (106 kilometres south-east), and Paul Mathis the fish trader at Sumbu. The non-African population could be rounded off by the inclusion of the 'coloured' Road Foremen and a Mechanic – Paddy McCormack at Bulaya, and Ken Munson and Fred Leese in Mporokoso – if they were not regarded as quite 'one of us' in those days I think it was not so much their mixed blood as that they were not of the 'officer class'! And there was the redoubtable Turkish store-keeper, Mr Memmish at Nsama.

We gradually built up easy friendships with the main African civil servants and their wives. Lloyd Ponya was an AAA, which I am now embarrassed to say meant 'African Administrative Assistant' or 'almost one of us'; Lloyd was on leave when we arrived and shortly after he returned he died. Dryden Yikona was the quiet and very industrious Medical Assistant in charge of the Clinic/Dispensary. He was very good to me when I had a bad dose of malaria, even accompanying us in the back of a landrover to Kasama Hospital; and he attended to Wendy and Alastair. Bethuel Kapota was the

Mporokoso, 1962-64: Domestic and Social Life

District Agricultural Officer (his wife was Joy) – a large, competent and very industrious officer who was usually out on tour somewhere. Frank Sichangwa was a Senior Clerical Officer (Rosemary was his wife); Frank was highly intelligent, was frequently used as an interpreter in the DC's court cases, and even in 1962 clearly deserved promotion; in 1964 he went to University College, Salisbury (Harare), and when I next met him I was PDO in Mongu and he was DS (District Secretary) Sesheke. Patrick Chifungo was another Senior Clerical Officer (his wife was Blandina); sadly I heard in 1966 that he had committed suicide. Washington Malama (Esther was his wife) was the elderly Accounts Clerk, and in my first month I sat at his elbow and learnt book-keeping and trial balances from him; he retired to Chinsali in 1965. Ignatius Chewe was the junior Accounts Clerk (wife, Victoria).

Other people, non-civil-servants, whom we saw fairly frequently included: Eleazar Namweleu and his sister Ethel from Lupungu, our servant James's village five kilometres away (see also pp. 18 below); Binneys Kaite, the District Scoutmaster and teacher from Chiwala (see p.16); and Mr Mudolo, a teacher who came to Wendy for private (free) English lessons.

I remember, too, many of our smart District Messenger force – probably around sixteen in all. In their distinctive blue uniforms with red facings and (normally) slouch hats, they were the first characters any visitor to the Boma would meet. John Hudson has concisely described their functions and importance (see pp 10-11). All the Senior D/Ms were ex-askaris (soldiers) who had served with either the Northern Rhodesia Regiment, or the KAR (King's African Rifles), in Abyssinia 1941, Libyan Desert 1942, Burma 1944, or Malaya 1952-4 ; they wore their rows of medal ribbons with pride. I can still recall most of their names. There was Head D/M Alan Chilufya, who usually accompanied the DC (I inherited him when we had both been posted to Chinsali in 1964); Second D/M Folo Lubushya (he accompanied me on my first village-to-village tour); Senior D/M Clement Musonda, Prison Head Warder; S/D/M Moses Lubansa (I seem to have travelled a lot with him around the District); S/D/M Andrew Ponde – the smartest and best-looking of the lot (he accompanied me on my second and third village-to-village tours). As an inexperienced young Cadet I learnt a lot of useful tips about the District and what was expected of me, from these seasoned characters. I can also recall the names and faces of many of the ordinary D/Ms, some of them with amusing names: Sylvester Chanda, Buxton Chitimbwa, Nothing Wamiya, Paul Chasaya, Substone Chiinga, Sixpence Mulenga, John Chomba, etc.

Geographically, and to a large extent socially, Mporokoso was divided by the grass airstrip. The most frequent user of this was a man who later became our good friend, the 'flying doctor' Derek Braithwaite (Provincial Medical Officer), calling in to see and pay his staff at the small clinic before flying on to Chocha (for Kaputa). Visiting VIPs also used it. But it was a comfort to have it there for any emergency too, and we always kept it well maintained. By convention, housing was referred to as 'low-, medium- or high-density', i.e. large, medium or small. On the north side of the airstrip were the Government offices and the low-density (= European, with the one exception of Lloyd Ponya) staff houses. Immediately on the south side were some medium-density houses for the African middle-ranking civil servants, plus a Catholic Mission, a small clinic and, later, a new prison. Behind this row were the D/Ms' lines, high-density

Mporokoso in 1962

Mporokoso, 1962-64: Domestic and Social Life

houses of other Boma employees and, further on, the Primary School with its staff housing on site. To the side of this area small stores lined the road which led west to the next Boma at Kawambwa. Yes, even those few sentences imply correctly that, apart from the few storekeepers and Mission staff, all the residents in the township were Government employees.

I shall digress briefly here to describe the layout of Mporokoso on the north side of the airstrip. West of the Kasama-Kawambwa road was the DC's house, dating from 1901. This was obviously the largest and had a guest-wing for the fairly frequent visits of civil servants from elsewhere. It had a lovely and well cared-for front garden and a great view westwards. Some 500 metres from it, across a grassy wilderness, was the Boma garden from which we could often get fresh vegetables, and a *mushitu* (grove of tall trees at the source of a stream) in which a swimming pool had been created. At the rear of the house was an *insaka* (shelter) beside a tennis court – an amenity most old-style DCs had constructed at their Bomas for free, using the available prison labour (Chinsali had a golf-course instead).

Next to the DC's house and alongside the road was the Boma itself, i.e. the District HQ offices. The building was old, thatched, full of bats in the roof and with its ceilings sagging under the weight of accumulated bat droppings which gave it a pungent aroma. Behind it was the thatched prison. This was a semi-open prison, in that the exercise yard was merely enclosed by a spindly hedge. Secure? A prisoner once ran away; the others immediately ran after him, caught and hauled him back and beat him. "You don't do that here: it'll give us all a bad name!" Of course, regular wholesome meals could make a spell in prison very welcome for some unemployed and undernourished villagers. Prisoners chopped firewood for residents of the low-density houses; thereby they considered themselves part of the Boma community, and were treated as such in all those households. A new Boma and new prison were built during our first nine months, and the old buildings were demolished.

On the east side of the road there was a lovely avenue of tall blue gum trees for one hundred metres. The first large plot on this side was where the new Boma was built in early 1963, its open-square design intentionally built around a beautiful spreading tree. There followed seven houses, all facing the airstrip. The largest and oldest of these (built in 1904), conventionally reserved for the senior DO, was occupied in 1962-63 by the Collingwoods and later by ourselves. Next was the Government Rest House, for visiting civil servants not staying with the DC. Then there was the Game Officer's house, followed by Lloyd Ponya's, John Cochrane's (SBO), a house empty at first but later occupied by a Police Officer; and finally ours.

Beyond this was just thick bush and a gravel pit. This two-bedroomed little house, the first proper home of our own in married life, was all we needed. It had a productive pawpaw tree at the side. Within the first few days, on recommendations from other officers, Wendy had taken on a cook (Black Mpundu) and a house-servant (James), and a young lad, Jimmy, to do the gardening. Fairly soon they had created a vegetable garden at the back and made a chicken house. It took rather longer to get the front garden looking reasonable, within its semi-circular driveway – an unnecessary amenity as we didn't have or need (and couldn't afford) a car for our first three years, and went locally on foot or by bicycle.

All the buildings on the station were single-storey (the English equivalent term, bungalow, was never used), and nearly all had corrugated iron roofs which could make quite a din when the rains were heavy. I should also explain that all civil service staff houses included basic hard furniture such as beds and mattresses, tables and chairs, provided by the Public Works Department; soft furnishings such as curtains and bedding one provided oneself. This system was justified by the fact that in colonial days expatriate officers could expect to be moved every year or two to another station. Of course, on a bush station there was no electricity and no telephone. We all had paraffin fridges and tilley lamps and little 'pixie' oil lamps for the rooms. Cooking was on a wood-burning stove (Wendy became so used to this and the timings it demanded that she was completely thrown when, years later, she had to cook on an electric model). Older houses obtained hot water from a 'Rhodesian boiler' behind the house; this was a 44-gallon drum supported by bricks over a fire, with pipes leading into the house. Yes, we did at least have running water, though it was intermittently dark brown – and failed to reach our house at the far end of the pipeline after our first child was born! At the end of every garden was a small two-roomed house for one servant and his family – in our case, Black Mpundu.

Mporokoso, 1962-64: Domestic and Social Life

Mail and meat came once a week from Kasama on the bus; groceries, newspapers and other supplies arrived once a month from Lusaka. This meant that we had to wait some three weeks before we received responses from parents to our letters, and maybe a month before we heard of an event on the wider world's stage such as the Cuban crisis, the Beatles, or the infamous James Bond. But we didn't feel deprived of anything of real, non-material, value.

The details of daily life I have described were new experiences for us but, with guidance from some of the older hands, we adapted very rapidly. Having servants was a novelty for us – if paternalistic, it gave employment. Even today some Zambians, brought up in an urban environment, might also find our pattern of living in a rural township strange and difficult to adjust to at first.

Changes inevitably occurred over the next two years among the small European group. Ian Macdonald left in November 1962 and we were not to meet him again (in 1964 he was put in charge of the arrangements for Independence Day itself in Lusaka). He was replaced as DC by Alan McGregor; Alan was younger than Ian, more liberal-minded and easier for us to get on with both socially and at work. He was replaced in 1964 by the lively Angus McDonald, only a few years older than ourselves, whom I was to meet again in both Chinsali and Lusaka – the fourth consecutive "Mac" to be DC in Mporokoso! Our lonely Irish SBO bachelor, John Cochrane, got posted to Mpika in mid-1963: I never really got to know his successor, Mr Mwanza, well enough. A uniformed Police Officer, Harry Schneeman, was posted here in November 1962 but, strangely, with only a couple of constables and no separate police station building; it was only after Harry's arrival, we all said, that any crimes occurred! The Collingwoods were sent to Abercorn (later called Mbala), always regarded as a plum posting, in early July 1963. Their replacements, Max and Ursula Keyzar, had been with us on the Cambridge Course; but they too left in May 1964. I think the Allens moved at about the same time to Mpika, the only other Northern Province station with a Game Officer, where Leslie was able to exchange Sumbu and Mweru Marsh for North Luangwa and Lavushi Manda Game Reserves. Harry too left in early 1964. So by the time we were moved to Chinsali in July 1964 Angus the DC was probably the only European officer left on the station.

We certainly enjoyed a full social life, as my diary entries reveal – read today, they give a fascinating insight into our activities and impressions of the first fifteen months of our time in Africa, and I do wish I had continued it for longer! The diary makes it clear that we were entertaining to dinner, or being entertained by others of just the small European officer group at least once a week, and much more frequently to tea or drinks. Such social interacting was so vital in a small and relatively isolated community.

The successive bachelor-DCs were especially generous in their hospitality and, of course, invited all the few Europeans along when they had visiting civil servants to stay with them, the wives often contributing puddings. There was, I think, an unspoken recognition that the three bachelors could otherwise be lonely on such a bush station; we often used to go for early evening walks with John Cochrane across the airstrip to see building progress on the Mission's new Blind School, or down to the Boma garden. At weekends we might go to the nearby Kapumo Falls which was a good picnic spot. The swimming pool was another attraction and in the hottest season we would certainly make frequent use of it after work or at weekends. Sited beside a *mushitu* it was just a rectangular unlined pit with a diving board – not very sophisticated, but it served our needs. Harry Schneeman took to keeping pigs, and when he butchered the boar we all helped in transforming every part of it into a delicacy; when he left Wendy and I inherited his piglets.

Monopoly and bridge were quite common evening entertainments. Sometimes the White Fathers came across to one of us; I recall Father Deslauriers tucking his arm through his rosary to play games of rounders with vigour on the airstrip. On Saturday afternoons tennis (in whites) on the court behind the DC's house was virtually compulsory; the best silver teapot was brought out for interval refreshments, and the wives took it in turn to bake a cake. Ernest Cruchley often cycled over from Kashinda to join us for tennis, and when his wife Kathie came she would sometimes teach the other wives how to cut their men's hair.

We were experiencing the last years of the British colonial way of life. Such routines as Saturday tennis teas, mentioned above, were just some of the manifestations of that dying way of behaviour which Wendy and I found old-fashioned, amusing if harmless, and distinctly un-African. And in spite of the impressions the previous paragraphs will have given, we were also breaking the old racial and class barriers in socialising, and much credit should go to Margaret Collingwood for having started this movement before we arrived. The DCs hosted several parties which included all the senior African staff and their wives, and we danced. Wendy put on a hilarious New Year's Eve party in our small house, to which all the same civil servants and their wives came. Some couples came to meals with us on other occasions. Senior Chief Nsama and Chief Shibwalya Kapila also felt able to drop in on us casually a couple of times each and we had easy chats with them over either tea or beers without a hint of awkwardness on either side (Shibwalya Kapila as an ex-teacher was happy to converse in English – or, for my language benefit, to switch in and out of ciBemba in a teasing fashion – while with Nsama we had to stick to ciBemba).

Margaret Collingwood had been assigned by the DC's wife the duty of running the Girl Guides. Wendy had been earmarked, willy-nilly, for running the Women's Welfare. This was not one of her strengths; in fact, she thought it was a crazy idea as she had herself been a Girl Guide for years whereas Margaret had not, while she (Wendy) felt quite ignorant of needle-work and other domestic skills. But the colonial practice is interesting: the DC's wife told other wives what they should do, as part of the overall running of Boma life. However, Wendy threw herself into the role, and used to trot across the airstrip every weekday afternoon to the house in the Messengers' lines assigned for these Welfare activities; she loved the company, and her ciBemba rapidly improved. Through that means she came to know all the African officers' wives very well, on a social basis, and they would often call across at our house. She also used to cycle out to Kashinda to help with record-keeping at the Mission's maternity clinic there. She ran some Adult Education classes, too, on her own initiative, at what became an extremely popular night school.

We thoroughly enjoyed local school plays and concerts, and I found myself coaching the senior boys and girls at the Primary School for their sports day and, later, for fixtures against two other large schools in the District (Nsama and Vincent Bulaya). I also became involved, at arm's length, with the scouts and on three occasions we went off to watch them in camp at the nearby Kapumo Falls. I had never been a scout myself but I was keen to encourage the teacher from Chiwala, Binneys Kaite, who was the local District Scoutmaster – and our 'flying doctor' friend, Derek Braithwaite, was the Divisional Commissioner of Scouts. We were always given a fantastic welcome at these camps, and the ingenuity of their games and activities was inspiring.

The foregoing might only be a superficial summary of the social side of our lives. But it was never possible to divorce our work interests from the socialising, nor did we wish to. In most of our get-togethers we were also 'talking shop' without feeling any reason to apologize for doing so. Our work was our life; our life was the work. We observed no fixed maximum hours, and never felt off-duty – and some might say this attitude has stayed with me for the rest of my working life. We felt responsible through our work for the well-being of all 65,400 inhabitants of the District and everything which affected their lives from the cradle to the grave. One might with generosity forgive those older colonial types who had allowed this sense of all-inclusive responsibility to be so warped that they regarded themselves as 'little white Gods.'

It is with hindsight that I now appreciate how good our DCs were in maintaining the domestic and social morale of the younger expatriate officers. Every so often they would let us go off, using a Government landrover, for a long weekend break either to one of the District's many beauty-spots or to the hospital and cinema in Kasama or, annually, to the Copperbelt for visits to a dentist and for Christmas shopping. We were granted an opportunity for the last in late 1963 when we went to Mufulira and Kitwe; this gave us the chance to drive through Luapula Province and, crossing the Chembe pontoon, through the Congo 'Pedicle'. This was usually troublesome: Congolese soldiers, police and immigration/customs staff had received no pay for months, so it was hardly surprising that border officials should extort whatever they could from those having to travel through their domain – especially from affluent-looking Europeans; one could obtain no receipt for anything paid to them on entering the 'Pedicle', and often had to pay again to officials at the exit point too. I wonder whether the situation has now improved!

Mporokoso, 1962-64: Domestic and Social Life

One notable event in early September, 1962, was a visit by the Governor-General of the despised Federation of Rhodesia and Nyasaland, Lord Dalhousie, with his wife and entourage and accompanied by the PC. He was calling at every station in Northern Rhodesia (and possibly Nyasaland too), more by way of a farewell tour than as a belated attempt to hear and understand what residents of the two northern Protectorates thought of the Federation. Later, I heard some hilarious tales from some of my ex-Course colleagues of how his visits had been received in other Districts – e.g. stuck in canoes for hours in the Kalabo swamps. After meeting all the station's officers, he and his party were taken for a week's shooting safari in the Sumbu Game Reserve, led by our Game Officer whose comments afterwards were unrepeatable. According to my diary record, our wives "took to the handsome ADC" (Aide-de-Camp) while John Cochrane was "smitten with the Lady-in-Waiting – a great lass."

Also in September we made our first visit to Lupungu Church with our servant, James. We walked the five kilometres in the heat. Eleazar Namweleu (see p.15 above, and below) preached, in ciBemba of course, for less than an hour: "I kept it short for your sakes," he said! The African custom of men and women sitting separately was also a new experience for us, and we found the backless log benches hard. We were given an enthusiastic welcome, and presented with a Bemba Bible. We made a second visit to a service at Lupungu Church on Christmas Day, with James and his wife, Daviness. Wendy, now six months pregnant, found the five kilometres walk tiring in the heat; but it was a worthwhile exercise both to support James and to become more familiar with the local people and their church customs. James's full name was James Mwaba Bowa Nonde; Bowa was his football nickname, and as *bowa* means mushroom it said something about his performance on the pitch – but he was universally popular.

Eleazar was not only a Church Elder and a great lay preacher. He was also the senior *kabilo* (traditional adviser/counsellor) to Chief Mporokoso. He was an old muBemba who spoke perfect high-class old-style ciBemba, with clear diction and beautifully rounded phrases interwoven with metaphors and proverbs in which the language is so rich; he was a joy to listen to, and I seriously attempted to emulate his style. He quite often used to drop in on us for tea when he was on his way back from his Chief's to Lupungu. For some of us his great moment came on 15th August 1963, soon after Chief Mporokoso had died. Paramount Chief Chitimukulu had come himself to a meeting of Bemba elders in our courthouse, to get his nominee made the next chief. But Eleazar, we understood, persuaded all the elders that "we here are 'sons of Mwamba': **we** decide, and our Chief will come from the Mwamba side of the royal clan, not Chitimukulu's." When he emerged with a smiling face from the meeting the crowd outside went wild with joy at his success, and carried their nominee off on their shoulders to his village. Chiti left, alone and defeated.

In early January, 1963, I went down with malaria, despite regularly taking the right pills, and my temperature went up to a worrying 104°. So the good Dryden Yikona, our local Medical Assistant, spoke on the police radio (with Wendy's help) to Dr Braithwaite in Kasama, explaining the symptoms and treatment, and Dr Braithwaite said that if my temperature wasn't down in two days after more injections I was to be brought to the hospital in Kasama. Mr Yikona even insisted on accompanying us in the back of the landrover. By this stage in our stay at Mporokoso I knew the roads through the District so well that, apparently, although lying prone I could tell Wendy precisely where we were on the journey by feeling the twists in the road and the bumps as we crossed the little bridges. After nine days I recovered sufficiently to come home. For many years after leaving Africa I used to get mild recurrences of malaria, for no obvious reason and in no possible contact with a mosquito.

Wendy was due to give birth to our first child in March 1963, towards the end of the rainy season. The DC, by now Alan McGregor, was adamant that there should be no risks of a tricky birth (with many miles of muddy roads to the nearest doctor!), and packed her off to Kasama in very good time, on 16th February – a move which turned out to be well justified in the event. It was arranged that she should stay with Mo and Clive Curnow until the baby arrived, and I stayed the weekend there too. We hadn't met them before but they turned out to be a very friendly couple. He was the Provincial Mechanical Engineer. By an extraordinary coincidence Wendy discovered that she had taught Mo's class in a London school while working as a supply teacher in 1961! A small world. On my last day with Wendy before

Mporokoso, 1962-64: Domestic and Social Life

leaving her we went off for a picnic together and chose the Mpika road as we hadn't previously been that way. After fifty kilometres we reached Nkolemfumu and immediately went to greet the Chief. We had a very gracious reception and short chat with him, explaining that we were just passing through. Then we went beyond the *musumba* (Chief's headquarters), to the ferry at Chibubutu, where a little summer house overlooked the river Lukulu. It was a gorgeous spot, with a broad sweep of the river in front, the flooded marshes on the other side, and the ferryman plying to and fro to add interest to the scene. I then left Wendy in Mo's tender care and returned on my own to Mporokoso.

On 15th March my DC allowed me to visit Wendy in Kasama for the weekend. She had been moved from Mo's into Dr Trant's next door. Dr Trant was a wonderful lady of about eighty, deaf, Irish, and a great character. She kept a monkey who objected to other women, a dog, three cats, rabbits and chickens. As she was on night duty and thought the baby would be arriving soon, she insisted on Wendy coming under her roof for the final days. Wendy obviously had great trust in her, which was a good thing. While in Kasama that time we were invited to lunch with the Hudsons, who had only just arrived in Kasama; he, John Hudson, was filling in as DO there before going off very soon to be DC Isoka. I recorded in my diary that they were a **very** pleasant couple.

At 3 o'clock on the morning of 21st March 1963 Wendy produced Alastair James Bond! I was told over the police radio at 8 o'clock and set off driving immediately for Kasama, where I went straight to the hospital. I saw him first and then Wendy. When she saw him properly she said: "Thank God he's a boy with a nose like that!" But he'd arrived and he was ours, a He and no longer an It, and I was very relieved and as happy and proud as any father. Dr.Trant had delivered Alastair and said Wendy had behaved wonderfully. Mrs.Clarke, the PC's wife, insisted that I stay with them, which I did, and I popped in to see Wendy a couple more times. Both the PC and his wife had been so generous to me and good to Wendy.

I can recall one amusing addition to the above account. Regarding that drive to Kasama on 21st March, two years later in Chinsali a policeman came up to me. "Do you remember me, sir?" "I'm not sure." "You gave me a lift to Kasama on the day your child was born, sir, and I'll never forget how fast you drove – the wheels never touched the road!"

Our memories of Kasama have perhaps been mixed. For our first three years it was our nearest town, our only conception of bright lights, the source of supplies and amenities we did not have at hand, and our Provincial Headquarters. But it was not a place where we should have wished to live in the 1960s, probably because so many Europeans there still retained a colonial outlook. One example of this was the ladies' attitude to Wendy. When she was expecting Alastair they were all very kind, helpful and friendly. But when later she came for her post-natal check, with the baby tied on her back in the African fashion, they cut her dead – even crossing the road to avoid this "betrayer of European standards"!

It was our servant James who introduced Wendy to the *impapa*, the cloth in which an African baby is carried on the mother's back. He explained to her that the word actually means a skin. In the old days women had carried their babies in animal skins, but the word, now used for the cloth, conveys the idea that the baby is somehow inside the mother's skin – good bonding for both mother and baby. A baby had to be four weeks old before it was carried in this way, or its neck would not yet be strong enough. Wendy's *impapa* was the same as everybody else's in those days – bright blue. It took her some time to get the technique correct, but she persevered. Ian Macdonald, like most of his European contemporaries, would not have approved of adopting this African style, but he had left by then. Of course, the practice opened up so many doors for her: every local woman would greet her the more warmly, stop and get into a long conversation (which improved her ciBemba) – and insist on adjusting the *impapa* for this unconventional *musungu* (European).

Our domestic life obviously changed somewhat with a baby, but our social life did not. Wendy had already become utterly at ease with a wood stove: although it did make the kitchen very hot, it was so versatile for many jobs – drying clothes in the rain, boiling buckets of Terry nappies, heating flat-irons and producing constant hot water. But our water came out in a trickle, often thick and brown. We pretended that the resulting peach colour of Alastair's nappies was just the latest fashion! Then, as a remedy, Wendy took to cycling over to Kashinda where they had a good supply of clean water, with a nappy bucket on her handle-bars and Alastair on her back. One evening as she was returning late after lengthy conversations, she became aware of the huge overhanging trees as she negotiated the sandy track and remembered that nobody had yet found the owner of the large cat prints seen in that location – and leopards can climb trees!

On 30th May 1963 the Governor, Sir Evelyn Hone, visited Mporokoso with Lady Hone and the PC, Peter Clarke. Alan McGregor, our bachelor DC, had at one time been ADC (Aide-de-Camp) to Sir Evelyn, and had used that connection to persuade him to come and open our new Boma building. The design and precise siting of it had been one of the first things Alan had authorised when he had arrived in November 1962, and we had thereafter watched its construction with growing interest. Alan had been keen to have its open-square layout built around a beautiful old tree with spreading branches and a uniform shape. After inspecting the D/M guard of honour, the Governor presented Senior Chief Nsama with a Certificate of Honour and a medal in recognition of "outstanding loyalty to his Native Authority and consistently wise leadership of his people." He then officially opened the new Boma building, and after lunch at Alan's went on to open the Mission's new Blind School.

The White Fathers' Blind School was a wonderful institution and, as I have already mentioned, we took a simple delight in our first few months in walking across the airstrip to watch the progress in its construction. River blindness, trachoma and other eye problems were prevalent in the northern parts of the District. Once the school was built, the Fathers toured the villages to collect children to fill it, often finding them hidden away in dark huts by shamefaced parents. Some twenty percent of the children were albinos. These were likely to have a progressive visual impairment caused by lack of pigmentation, but we had no idea why the albino gene should be so prevalent in this region; wearing sunglasses seemed to be some help for them. The school's attitude was cheerfully bracing; in a matter of days a group of children was taken to swim in the nearby gravel pits, and very soon the football-with-a-bell-in-it was rejected by the boys in favour of a 'proper' ball. Their first musical instruments were made from used tins –

flattened into percussion rattles, beaten as drums, filled with dried peas, etc. And how they could sing! By the time of the Governor's visit they were adept at arranging themselves into giant pyramids, dancing to their own music, running races, and already reading braille. We have so many happy memories of the school and of Father Carrière who ran it. He even conned a gullible business company into giving him a film projector, saying it was for the blind children (!) but adding, when challenged, "We like to expose them to every modern experience" – that one was really for the benefit of the Boma!

The name of Sir Evelyn Hone, the last Governor of Northern Rhodesia, is still well known throughout Zambia, enshrined in the Evelyn Hone College of Applied Arts and Commerce in Lusaka.

3. MPOROKOSO, 1962-64: THE WORK

What did I actually do? What did I find were the multifarious tasks and the range of responsibilities of a DO or DC, to which I have alluded in Chapter 1? From my recently found diary I can give a fairly accurate analysis of what my tasks as a young DO Cadet amounted to. One interesting comment in my diary at the end of my very first day of work was, after describing the introductions to other staff and the general assignments given to me by the DC:

> *The set-up is quite simple …… I got the impression from the start that much of the office routine and procedures and the general administration are just like in the Army, so I think I'll get it straight pretty soon.*

On the official work side, the day started at 07.30 Mondays-Saturdays, with the DC inspecting the parade of D/Ms and, in consultation with the Head Messenger, allocating them their duties for the day – or week, for those being sent off to distant parts of the District on their bicycles; these might need to draw an imprest, in order to hire and pay local gangs for bridge/road repairing jobs, etc.

The first main regular responsibility the DC gave me was to look after the Boma accounts, and this quickly taught me a lot about how the PA had to operate in a bush station. Initially I sat at the elbow of the elderly accounts clerk, Washington Malama, and soon I was able to do weekly checks of his double-entry bookkeeping every Saturday morning, and monthly trial balances of the station's financial position. The job also entailed, of course, running the monthly pay parade for all D/Ms and junior Boma staff, so I quickly got to know everybody. If, as mentioned above, a D/M had hired villagers for some work, he had to account for the cash spent from his imprest with receipted pay-sheets, and these had to be checked. Given their low wages, the Boma staff were incredibly honest. And, amazingly, the hard cash we needed came in a steel specie box sent monthly from the bank in Kasama by the bus without, so far as I can recall, any guard! I handed over these duties to another Cadet in late 1963 after 15 months.

As I shall describe in more detail later, the District was populated by people of three tribes, under six chiefs. So there were six Native Authorities and three Native Authority Treasuries. It immediately became another of my duties to do the monthly checks of their draft trial balances and the completion thereof. This work I shared with the senior Cadet, Jeremy Collingwood, although I did the majority. It normally entailed visits to the N/A headquarters at Chishamwamba (Bemba), Nsama (Tabwa) and Mukupa Kaoma (Lungu). Even the basics of accounts and trial balances were not matters on which we had been given any guidance on the Cambridge Course, but we learnt fast – on the job, and Washington Malama was a great teacher!

The other important responsibility of a Native Authority's work was in its Court. As the principle of indirect rule implied, Native Customary Law was upheld and its application encouraged so long as it was not incompatible with English legal ethics. The more serious cases would be referred upwards to the DC's court. So, again in duties shared with Jeremy, I had to do monthly checks on all the Native Court records and particularly on the efficient collection of the fines they had imposed, etc. We were doing this in our capacity as junior Magistrates. This work was also carried out at the N/A headquarters.

Our judicial system, often regarded later by Zambians as one of the best legacies of British colonial rule, was in general fine and worthy of pride. But its operation in a rural Boma with very few legally qualified officers would, these days, raise eyebrows if not be seen as totally unacceptable. Starting out as Cadets, we were ex-officio Magistrates Class 4 (the most junior rank), and our judicial powers were accordingly restricted. We had to pass a Law examination within three years to become confirmed as DOs, and by the time an officer became a DC he would, I think, become a Magistrate Class 2 with greater powers. Our DC, Ian Macdonald, frequently heard cases in the Boma's small courthouse; Jeremy, the senior DO Cadet, was keen on law and was often involved as prosecutor in the days before we had a police presence. So you had a situation where PA officers made arrests (themselves or through their D/Ms), and then both prosecuted and judged the cases – and were in charge of the District's prison too! In my first two years I only prosecuted or defended in four cases, and I did not enjoy that part of the work. But issuing writs of summons or warrants of arrest seemed to be a more frequent duty I undertook, certainly until we had some police on the station.

With hindsight it is remarkable how this cosy atmosphere of a couple of colleagues sharing wide judicial powers was tolerated. If the situation was rarely abused, that says something for the general integrity of the officers. Many apocryphal anecdotes circulated in the PA as amusing cautionary tales. One was that an inexperienced young DO said to a convicted prisoner: "I'm sorry, but I think the only sentence I am allowed to give you is the death sentence." It was when he sent a message to the PC asking for advice as to whether he should carry out the execution by hanging or shooting the convict that a miscarriage of justice was rectified. Another tale concerned a DC and DO who, having killed an impala in the Game Reserve, had fallen out over shares of the meat. The Game Officer found out that a DO had some meat and persuaded the DC to convict the DO. The DC said in court that, to set an example, he would fine the DO £20. The DO next day summoned the DC to court and, saying "This is the second such case to come before this court in as many days, and such illegal hunting must be stopped," fined the DC £40.

Associated with the magisterial side of the work, I suppose, was the regular weekly inspection of the Prison on Saturday mornings, another job I shared with Jeremy on a roster basis. One of our Senior D/Ms, Clement Musonda, was the Head Warder and other junior D/Ms took their turns in doing warder duties. The inspection normally involved a parade of warders and prisoners, male and female separately, and listening to any complaints; as I have hinted elsewhere, prison life with its regular good meals was seen as no great hardship for many villagers, and I cannot recall ever receiving a complaint. We would check their food, and the cleanliness of the cells and toilets. Most weeks we would have to supervise the caning of those sentenced to corporal punishment, administered by the Head Warder while the victim lay face down on a bench; the good Dryden Yikona, Medical Assistant, was always in attendance to apply iodine to the wounds. I was responsible for overseeing the transfer from the old to the new prison on

From Northern Rhodesia to Zambia

18th September 1962, and my diary entry was:

> *I got the stores moved into the new prison which is now completed, checked all the keys, and then moved in all the prisoners in time for their evening meal. It's a wonderful place, and they should enjoy it (which sounds silly!). The messengers are quite envious, I think, of the facilities there.*

Very many minor manual jobs were carried out around the Boma by squads of prisoners in their white uniforms, marched along by messenger-warders, and they always seemed cheerful and full of friendly greetings. I noted in my diary, too, a time when we were really held up on completing some minor project because "we only have a total of ten prisoners at present!"

Behind the Boma buildings we still had an emergency prison known as 'the cage'. This had been constructed for, and had been much used during, the *cha-cha-cha* period of disturbances in 1961 to which I have referred earlier (p.12). We had to use this once during my time in Mporokoso, for a few days in early April 1963. Riots had broken out at Chief Mukupa Katandula's *musumba* (headquarters), primarily in objection to the Tabwa Native Authority's beer tax orders and the summonses arising therefrom. Harry, our new Police Officer, had been confronted with road blocks and a crowd of around 150 armed with spears and axes, and the DC (Alan McGregor) decided to call in a Mobile Police Unit. While he and they went to sort out the problem, I had to get 'the cage' ready with blankets and food to receive any prisoners they might bring in – 190 in the end were arrested and eventually taken off to Kasama. As important was my task of keeping communications open. Apart from the frequent messages over the police radio at the Boma, both from Kasama and from the DC at Mukupa Katandula, and the lack of D/Ms to relay messages locally, I had to organize emergency repairs along the Kawambwa road with the help of the District Roads Capitao and using gangs of our current prisoners. It was the end of the rainy season, and the road was in poor shape; but it was essential that the Mobile Unit should be able to get through swiftly and back again, as well as the vehicles with their own cages to carry prisoners. Wendy became involved, too, organizing soup kitchens for the prisoners as they were brought in and visiting the women prisoners in our 'cage' where she kept them occupied with needlework.

The Police Radio was the station's means of our twice-daily contact with Provincial HQ and other Districts. The announcement over the radio of our son's birth (see p.25) meant that this news was conveyed to every Boma in the country, leading to immediate congratulatory telegrams from some of our Cambridge Course colleagues! It was mostly manned and dealt with by our SBO (Special Branch Officer), John Cochrane, and the DC. But we Cadets would also take our turns to man it, maybe a couple of times a week, and John gave us on-the-spot guidance for this. Even our wives were instructed in how to operate it – and its essential little generator – in case they had to look after the fort while all their menfolk were away dealing with some emergency. In the aftermath of the 1961 *cha-cha-cha* period the DC and SBO still did not rule out the possibility of further anti-Government troubles.

During some conversation with the DC and Jeremy in my first fortnight I had rashly quipped Jeremy about the need to be adaptable over some issue. The DC latched onto my remarks and said, "Well, you seem to have a practical flair, so I'd like you to supervise all the building works in the District." On the one hand this entailed assisting the DC in overseeing the building programme of all the Government departments. On the other hand it involved the greater task of inspecting the progress on all constructions being carried out by the three main Native Authorities, approving and arranging the payments to them of Government subsidies for the completed works (mostly staff housing, school buildings and local amenities), and preparing with them their estimates and plans for the following year.

During our time there we had three major exercises to undertake on a District-wide basis. All the Boma staff were involved in these. The first was the preparation for the elections on 30th October 1962. For most of the preceding month I toured around much of the District with Patrick Chifungo (Senior Clerical Officer) and my cook, Black Mpundu, to explain what the elections were for. The exercise was called "Your Vote is Secret". The Government's Information Department had a van which brought two films on the voting procedure and how to mark the ballot paper, plus a model of a typical polling station. Patrick did most of the detailed oral explanations of the voting system as my command of ciBemba was not yet adequate for the extraordinarily complex technicalities of this election, but I had a try. The films had a supposedly catchy little calypso song, whose first verse I can still remember:

> *Oh listen to me, yes listen to me;*
> *We have a song for this territory.*
> *In October we'll have elections;*
> *Yes, we are going in the right direction.*

Yet that journey to universal adult suffrage had barely begun.

This was the second set of elections held during the time (1953-63) of the despised Federation of Rhodesia & Nyasaland. In the first, in 1959, Harry Nkumbula's Northern Rhodesia African National Congress won several seats in the Protectorate's Legislative Council, while Kenneth Kaunda's Zambia African National Congress boycotted the elections, regarding the franchise as racially biased. I do not want to describe in detail the political or constitutional turmoil of the next few years. But the outcome was that in 1962 the British Colonial Secretary, Iain Macleod, accepted the proposals of Sir Roy Welensky, Federal Prime Minister, for a Northern Rhodesia Legislative Council of 45 members: 15 elected by a largely African electoral roll ('lower roll'), 15 by a largely European roll ('upper roll'), 14 by both rolls together ('national' seats), and 1 to be elected by Asians. It was intended to "provide a chance for Africans to form a Government while preserving the influence of Europeans". But the upper and lower rolls were defined in terms of the income and property held by the voter, and the race of the voter also came into account. So it still had a racial bias, and a very limited suffrage. Those few Africans in the District who qualified by income to vote (so few that we only had three polling stations in the whole District!) could presumably understand the calypso song in English!

I presided at the Mukupa Kaoma polling station, for which I used the bottle store. All went very quietly on election day, with all the eligible voters lining up in a quiet and orderly queue (I just had to arrest one young man for impersonation). The national results of these elections were: Kaunda's UNIP (formerly ZANC), 14 seats with 60% of valid votes; the mainly European United Federal Party, 16 seats but with only 17% of total votes; Nkumbula's ANC held the balance of power with 7 seats; 8 'national' seats were not filled as no candidate for them gained the required 10% of both African and European voters. Simon Kapwepwe, whom I should come across later, won the Northern lower roll seat, which covered half the Northern Province. Of some personal interest to us was the win by John Mwanakatwe of the Northern Rural upper roll seat – for a constituency which covered the whole of Northern and Luapula Provinces combined – with 86% of the meagre 1,600 electorate. John was Flavia Musakanya's uncle, had visited us on the Cambridge Course, and at Independence was to become Zambia's first Minister of Education. Now he was the only African and UNIP candidate to win an upper roll seat. John popped in to see us briefly for tea during his canvassing tour, renewing the friendly conversations we had had with him in Cambridge. On the Copperbelt and in Central and Southern Provinces there were reported to have been various scuffles between UNIP and ANC supporters at party political meetings. But in Mporokoso, and indeed throughout the Northern Province, UNIP by then had almost total support (Kapwepwe received an astonishing 97.2% of the 3,951 valid votes cast in his constituency), and anyone who favoured ANC didn't say so in public.

The next major exercise was to run a Census over the whole District, in June 1963, and Alan McGregor (the DC) put me in charge of this. The Native Authorities had their registers of taxable householders, but I am not sure whether a full national census had ever previously been run. With advice from others, I first had to decide whom to recruit as the census enumerators who would interview every single household in a given area, plus the team leaders who would coordinate and check their work. Naturally I chose Primary School teachers as the sixteen team leaders; many of the enumerators were senior Secondary School boys on holiday from their schools in Kasama (our District then had no Secondary School). Again we were helped on the publicity side by a film van of the Information Department from Kasama, which toured the main centres over the week preceding the census. During the census period itself, 3rd-19th June, I myself went out every day (with a few overnight stops) touring round to see the progress and especially to give interim payments to all the team members, and this was a wonderful way for me to get to know all corners of the District and to meet many people. I have no record of any major problems encountered on those visits. Amazingly I have recently come across all my handwritten plans for the exercise, listing the names and educational qualifications of all the team leaders and enumerators, the day-by-day journeys and loads of vehicles to get them to and from their census areas, plus drivers' duties, names of D/Ms and Native Authority Kapasus who would accompany each team, and expenditure estimates for paying wages plus daily subsistence and cycle allowances to all those involved; the latter came to a modest total of £1,994!

I still have the details of the Census results. Here are extracts in rounded figures:

	Mporokoso	N.Province	National total
Male, over 21	11,000	98,800	748,500
Male, under 21	19,900	170,000	943,100
Female, over 21	13,500	120,600	770,200
Female, under 21	21,000	173,600	949,400
Born in N.R.	64,600	555,900	3,173,000
Born elsewhere	800	7,100	238,200
Totals	65,400	563,000	3,411,200

One indication from the above is the large proportion of adult males who were away working on the Copperbelt, a feature to which we were now accustomed. Another is the small number of people in Mporokoso born outside Northern Rhodesia.

The next exercise for which the DC asked me to take the lead was to prepare for and run the January 1964 elections over the whole District. The first task was to use the detailed Census figures I had and to plan constituency and polling area boundaries. The District was to have two constituencies, north and south, and the polling areas had each to have roughly the same numbers of potential voters – subject to variations for geographical remoteness, etc. The Federation had now been dismantled, and these were to be the first elections on a full adult suffrage basis ("One Man, One Vote" was the obvious slogan) leading to a period of Internal Self-Government before full Independence. My proposals for polling areas and polling stations were accepted, and the next stage was to mount the necessary campaign for the Registration of Voters. This took place from 9th September to 7th October 1963, and my appointments and training of the staff required, and the subsequent touring to supervise their progress and pay them, followed fairly closely my methods on the Census. We had a total of 25,523 registered voters in the whole District – compared with the paltry 1,200 of the more racially biased and very limited suffrage elections of 1962. The elections took place, smoothly, on 20th January 1964. People were excited, but the days of anti-colonial demonstrations were over; they were content to have at last been given the vote. Enthusiasm for these elections was so great that voter turnout nationally was 94.8% for the main roll and 74.1% for the reserved roll – incredibly high by the standards of British elections!

There were two voter rolls for the Legislative Council: a main roll (African) that elected 65 seats, and a reserved roll (European) that elected 10; Asians and other minor ethnic groups could choose which roll to be part of. Kaunda's United National Independence Party (UNIP) won, taking 55 of the common roll seats, and he became Prime Minister. The overall national results were:

Party	Main roll			Reserved roll			Total seats
	Votes	%	Seats	Votes	%	Seats	
UNIP	570,612	68.8	55	6,177	34.8	0	55
ANC	251,963	30.3	10	165	0.9	0	10
Nat'l Progressive Party	-	-	0	11,157	62.8	10	10
Independents	3,662	0.4	0	35	0.2	0	0
Invalid/blank votes	4,178	0.5	-	224	1.3	-	-
Total	830,415	100	65	17,758	100	10	75

One aspect of our preparations for Independence was the modification of the old colonial system of indirect rule, and the introduction of a Local

Government system based roughly on the British model. Alongside the work on registering voters, the DC and I spent a lot of time in September 1963 in negotiating with the six chiefs and the staff of the three Native Authorities on our plans to create a new Rural Local Council, to involve them plus elected local politicians. We favoured having just one such Council for the District, and initially Senior Chief Nsama of the Tabwa tribe accepted this in principle. Then, after wider consultation with his people, he asked for a separate Council for the Tabwa as they feared the Bemba would dominate one combined Council. That would leave Chief Mukupa Kaoma with a problem, as the smaller Lungu tribe would be even more likely to be dominated by the Bemba without the counterweight of the Tabwa. In the end, the new Government itself decreed that each rural District should only have one Council.

Our District Council met for the first time in December 1963. Alan (DC) and I attended the first meeting, to ensure that the members had a reasonable understanding of their responsibilities and of basic points of committee procedures, and over the next few months intervened less and less. In March 1964 Wendy and I went to stay for a week at Mungwi, the local staff training centre twenty five kilometres east of Kasama. Here the DO in charge, Frank Schofield, had for a long time been organising and running courses for Native Authority staff, e.g. clerks, treasurers, Kapasus. Now that so much Native Authority work had been taken over by the District Councils he had started courses for elected councillors, e.g. how to propose a motion, what committees were for, general procedures and an idea of how they themselves might fit into Government's general scheme of finance and policy-making for the whole territory. My role at Mungwi was to help him in this work, particularly with our Mporokoso councillors; I found it great fun, and it gave me a chance to discuss local issues more thoroughly with our local politicians.

Before the District Councils were established all the chiefs were concerned that, with Independence, their traditional authority would be greatly diminished. A Rural Local Council would be a democratic body, which might undermine their position. In fact, such difficulties had been to some extent anticipated. As early as late 1962 a national House of Chiefs was established, and on

Mporokoso, 1962-64: the Work

21st December 1962 there were elections to this House from every Province. I was privileged to attend the election at Mungwi (my first visit there) of the four to represent all the Northern Province chiefs in this new national institution, and drove the two nominated from our District to the meeting. I was very happy with a fair result – Chiefs Chikwanda and Kopa from Mpika District, Mukupa Kaoma and Shibwalya Kapila (my favourites) from ours; i.e. two Bemba, one Bisa and one Lungu, which broadly worked out as 'proportional representation' as well as getting the most educated and articulate elected. Only the chiefs of the several minor tribes in Isoka District were dissatisfied, feeling they were left out.

Then there were the local UNIP politicians. Our dealings with them changed greatly over those two years. To our first DC, Ian Macdonald, they were obviously people who had only recently served a prison sentence he had given them for their part in the 1961 *cha-cha-cha* disturbances. Our Special Branch Officer, John Cochrane, was constantly keeping an eye on them and what they were up to. But Wendy and I carried no 1961 baggage, and to us they were friendly and we conversed easily with them. They might even have considered me a soft touch as increasingly over our second year they seemed to come to me rather than seek an audience with the DC himself. I well remember their constituency party chairman, John Mundibile, always smiling. He would often turn up at our house, with a colleague or two, and we would naturally give them tea and cakes or biscuits; we got the impression that these were their first experiences of simple European hospitality, and perhaps our attitude disarmed them from some of their nationalist anti-authority stances. But while I was friendly and listened carefully to their requests and complaints, I remained an impartial civil servant and would not appear to favour or support the party. I could argue amicably with John. In the 1962 elections he had sat in my polling station at Mukupa Kaoma as the candidate's polling agent, and had behaved himself impeccably. According to my diary he came several times to me during the 1963 Registration of Voters campaign, wanting me to change polling area boundaries or the location of polling stations; with more Census evidence than he had, I never conceded to his demands but he always left in a good mood, defeated but aware he'd had a fair hearing. John would doubtless have reported on me to his party superiors; with hindsight I think it possible that from these discussions I gained a reputation as a liberal which, years later, rendered me politically acceptable to the Zambian Government, though at the time even subconsciously I had no such motive.

As to my thoughts on the national and local political situation in 1963, I can draw on the record of a letter I wrote at the time to my parents-in-law, in which I attempted to describe to them how the situation affected us in Mporokoso, in the lead-up to the first full-suffrage national elections which brought in Internal Self-Government.

I first explained how in 1961 the British Government sent out Lord Monckton and his team to review the Federation. Theirs was a very fair and thorough review, and they came to the conclusion that Federation was imposed in 1953 against the wish of the majority of the inhabitants, and that now there was a pathological hatred of the Federation and anything Federal. It was seen as fundamentally racist. But the Monckton Commission Report was put in the waste paper basket because the Tories who sent out the Commission didn't agree with its verdict. Britain then created a muddle for itself (and us) by the involvement of two different Cabinet Ministers, Maudling and Sandys; one represented the Colonial Office and therefore held the age-old colonial view that "in a difference of opinion the aspirations of the indigenous people shall be paramount", the other represented the Commonwealth Relations and therefore the Federation which was a member of the Commonwealth. Neither could do their job properly in Central Africa without directly opposing the other, clearly. So Rab Butler was then put in charge of the whole situation – quite an astute move. He recognised the right of each country to secede from the Federation, and we then saw it as merely a matter of giving the Federation a decent burial. That, I thought, would be fairly complicated because of how to share the national debt, apart from the split up of Federal services (health, European education, European Agriculture, railways, aviation, customs, post, etc.). But in a rural district like Mporokoso the only Federal items which impinged at all on our lives were the postal services and stamps, and customs duty payable on gifts sent to us from the UK.

I went on, in my letter, to describe the rise of the nationalist parties, Kaunda's break with Nkumbula, and the outcome of the 1962 elections. UNIP and ANC had formed a coalition to gain power from the detested European UFP who formed the last government. But I saw this as an unhappy alliance; Kaunda and Nkumbula seemed really to dislike each other, and to have to persuade their followers to be more peaceful and stop their inter-party fighting.

In my analysis of the situation in Mporokoso I said we found three very different strata of feeling: news of the national leaders, who were now tasting the weight of responsibility for the first time, the branch leaders of the parties, and the villagers themselves. The leaders seemed to play things both ways: they realised that they still needed many Europeans for their money and experience and technical knowledge, but of course they couldn't admit that to their followers, so they continued to say "all Europeans must go," and that when Independence came everyone would be richer, wiser, free, have a wonderful standard of living and so on. The villagers very often believed this at its face value, the branch leaders exploited it because they thought they would soon be running the Boma, while the leaders knew that money doesn't grow on trees and had much more sense. I saw one obvious advantage in UNIP being effectively the only party present in the District: if the local leaders did anything silly they would get a rocket from us in the Boma **and** from their party chiefs, so they didn't know where they stood.

Since the 1961 *cha-cha-cha* the District had been reasonably peaceful. Since we arrived there had been a couple of incidents of arson; schools were burned down because they were supposed to be expressions of Government (European) power, and the Boma had to step in smartly both to get the offenders and to prevent the offenders being lynched by the angry parents of the schoolchildren. On these occasions it was noticeable that the real offenders kept in the background. I went on in my letter to paint a theoretical picture as follows.

> *A local thug tells some youngsters to go and burn a school, all in the grand cause of UNIP, "Kaunda says so" etc.; if they refuse, even on these worthy arguments, the thug threatens to burn down their*

*houses (most houses, remember, are thatch with mud and wattle walls, so it takes only a minute to burn them down; conversely it doesn't take long to build a new one, but a house is a family home). So the youngsters do the job, the thug gets the credit from his superiors and fades away. We arrive and investigate. Nobody will say who's really responsible because they fear reprisals, but we pursue enquiries. The thug comes back and tells the youngsters to own up or their houses really **will** be destroyed. So they admit, come before the magistrate and plead guilty. In all fairness, if a man pleads guilty and no other evidence can be produced, the magistrate can do nothing but convict him, though he knows the man is not principally responsible. All made worse, of course, because the District Commissioner as DC wants to hammer the thugs but when acting as magistrate within the courtroom he must obey the rules of law; hence he tries either not to get involved until he hears the case in court or lets another DC hear it.*

In 1962-63, new branches of UNIP were being registered everywhere – every third village seemed to have one. Their regional officials and constituency officials held meetings frequently and occasionally processions; sometimes the leaders tried to incite the crowd to hatred if not violence, but our D/Ms were always there to see they stuck to the conditions of the meeting which the DC laid down as Regulating Officer. They usually claimed to get an attendance of about 4,000, but rarely was it more than 500 in fact, and mostly women and children. After the new UNIP/ANC coalition Government took over, the local leaders were obviously not sure what line they should take. When they condemned the Boma, we could reply that as always we were acting for the Government which was now their party anyway so "why attack your own party?" Most villagers didn't understand anyway. The branch leaders could still chant "Whites go home. Federation must go," etc., and burn their identity certificates (a colonial-imposed system) but after that they needed to think of new ideas. One of their new lines was: "UNIP isn't complete power yet, but will be when we can get rid of ANC; then all our promises will come true." So on the Copperbelt there was the friction between the two parties. Around Mporokoso they merely talked about it; the people were all so friendly by nature and the Europeans were so few that we had no personal fears; everybody greeted us and nobody seemed to bear the slightest malice by themselves

After the above diversion on the political scene, I should now complete the picture of what a young Cadet might be expected to do by listing some of the minor or one-off tasks I undertook, with great enjoyment. Several of these were vaguely related to my responsibilities for the Boma's accounts and/or with working alongside the three Native Authorities. For example, I ran a Native Courts' Staff course for one week; so by then I must have gained a fair understanding of their work and of customary law. I also ran two one-week refresher courses for D/Ms and Kapasus, giving them talks on N/As and even taking them for drill. I supervised the payments of building loans to help local people construct their own houses in more permanent materials, and monitored their repayment schedules. The arbitration and administration of deceased estates, which involved interviewing families and determining members' shares from estates, rather like an executor, seems to have taken up quite a lot of my office time. The DC, early on, asked me to be 'transport officer', i.e. to coordinate and match staff needs with our available vehicles and to check the regular maintenance of vehicles; given my poor understanding of what went on under the bonnet of a vehicle, even though I could drive, I was an odd choice for this duty. There was a variety of small tasks such as: the issue of hunting licences, arms licences and ammunition permits to those deemed eligible: stores checks, arms checks and Boards of Survey (independent checks of other Departments' stores and authorising any 'write-off' of items); the registration of recovered ivory and the despatch of tusks to Government Stores in Livingstone; and a few times I ran local auctions, e.g. of elephant meat recovered, or of property seized by writ, etc. For my second year I was a member and the Secretary of the District Education Authority; this of course related to my work with N/A building plans. I kept the station's daily rainfall chart, too – though, apart from personal interest, I cannot recall to whom I relayed its vital information! From somewhere, my records show, I acquired details of the total inches of rainfall from 1914 to 1963: it averaged 50" (127cms) p.a., with 1962 having the highest at 75" (190cms).

It will be clear from what I have already described that the work involved a fair amount of travelling around the district, by landrover and/or bicycle, and sometimes camping for a night or two. But the real highlights for me were the village-to-village tours – very instructive and great fun. These had always been the main method by which colonial DCs/DOs got to know their Districts in detail, were seen, met the local people for whom they felt responsibility, and passed on to them any points of Government policy or instruction. Unlike many of my ex-Cambridge Course colleagues, I was not permitted by my DC to undertake such a tour until I had gained some experience and was reasonably proficient in ciBemba. We would go by bicycle with the senior N/A staff or the Chief himself, 3 D/Ms, 2 or 3 Kapasus, and about 10 porters; and I always took Black, my cook. Once the area to be toured had been decided, the N/A Administrative Assistant would plan the itinerary and night stops and would usually send letters to all the village headmen to give them advance notice of the visits. This notice, of course, alerted tax defaulters who would absent themselves in the bush during the visit, but would also lead to some merry gatherings of ululating women who would come to greet us on our way to their village.

I only had three full tours of this nature:
(a) Chief Mukupa Kaoma's area (half), with Second D/M Folo Lubushya, 37 villages over 13 days.
(b) Chief Mukupa Kaoma's area (other half), with S/D/M Andrew Ponde, 33 villages over 10 days.
(c) Chief Shibwalya Kapila's area, with the Chief himself and S/D/M Andrew Ponde, 27 villages over 6 days.

My diary's day-to-day record of what I found and did in each village on these tours makes fascinating re-reading for me today. My first full Tour Report may be of interest in indicating the reasons why we toured, what we were looking for, what messages we wished to get across, and how we supported the N/A in tax collection and public hygiene, etc. This is attached as **Appendix 1**.

Typically, we would visit four or five villages each day on our bicycles. Arriving in a village and being greeted, I would usually start by calling out names of householders from the N/A's tax register. Few men would be found in most villages; the headman or their wives would tell us in which

Copperbelt town they were working, and we had to accept this information for our statistics (though some might have run into the bush). Then I would give a speech in my best ciBemba, telling them for instance about the forthcoming census or elections, about the national political situation as we moved towards internal self-government, about development projects going on in the District which might be of relevance to them, and urging them to do more to help themselves in local initiatives. I'd ask about the state of their gardens and crops, their general health, schooling for the children, etc. Meanwhile a N/A Kapasu would inspect the *fimbusu* (latrines) behind all the houses and the state of their grain bins, and I would make a general observation of these too; occasionally this led to an immediate arrest for the contravention of a N/A rule on public health, and the Court Members who toured with me would try the case there and then and impose a fine. There were times when I had to lean heavily on the N/A staff to be more active in pursuing arrears of tax or court fines, as my report indicates. On my second tour five men were convicted by the Native Court for posting inflammatory and anti-N/A messages on trees as well as being tax defaulters, and, after keeping them under guard overnight, I had a D/M escort them to the Boma prison. But however poor or isolated a village was I almost always felt we had a friendly welcome. I recall in one village being offered a plateful of large hairy caterpillars, fried, which were clearly regarded as a delicacy: it would have been undiplomatic for me not to accept this treat, so I crunched and munched half-a-dozen of this (to me) strange food, with a fixed smile on my face, but politely declined a second helping.

One D/M with Black and the carriers would strike camp after we had left, and by the time we reached the end of the day's travelling we would find them at the next camp site with the tents up, latrines dug and the fires going for the evening meal; and I had the luxury of a canvas hip-bath behind a tarpaulin, for which Black would bring hot water. Carriers were recruited locally and some did not stay with us for a whole tour, so they were replaced by others as we proceeded. We paid them either in cash or in a mixture of cash and mealie-meal; sometimes they argued over the amounts paid, but we stuck to the standard rates which we'd told them when they started. Black was in his element on tour. One of his actions led to a family joke.

From Northern Rhodesia to Zambia

On the second evening he produced banana custard for my dessert, and I must have been excessive in my gratitude because he served me banana custard every night on tour thereafter – with such a great big smile I couldn't ask for an alternative. I should have liked to tour with Chief Mukupa Kaoma, but he was elsewhere (at the House of Chiefs) each time. My diary has this entry regarding my tour with Chief Shibwalya Kapila:

> *[In one village] I talked for a long time on development and probably made my best speech so far, the Chief expanding on my themes in forceful terms. He is a good speaker. He talks fast, excitedly and with conviction, playing his audience along with a great sense of humour and then crushing them with his climactic point.... The Chief came round to my tent for supper with me and we had a good long chat on all sorts of subjects.*

It was at the very end of my second tour that, when cycling back to the Boma, the D/M in front of me stopped suddenly and shouted loudly "*Cenjela!*" ("Look out!"). He had nearly cycled over what looked like an insignificant branch on the path, and I was about to follow him. It was actually a gaboon viper, over a metre long, motionless and difficult at first to see as the sunlight through the trees dappled the ground. This is one of Africa's most venomous snakes, and its bite was thought to cause death within some fifteen minutes if the correct antitoxin were not applied at once – and we were still much more than fifteen minutes from Mporokoso. It had been a near miss.

I actually managed to organize the building of two structures. It was on my second tour that I looked for a way of crossing the quite substantial Lupansa River in order to provide a short cut for vehicles and bicycles from Mporokoso to a relatively isolated area. A month later I had it built, under a S/D/M's supervision – another example of the indispensability of our Messengers. My second project was to build a small three-room dispensary at Nsama, the centre of an area that apart from some blindness also had quite a few cases of smallpox. I borrowed a standard design from the PMO, who of course supported this initiative. It was very basic and the plumbing was rudimentary, but it was in permanent materials, and I hope it continued in use for decades thereafter.

I should mention one amusing aspect of the fight against smallpox, a disease which was very prevalent when we first arrived. The serious-minded Herbert Nondo was the Medical Orderly working under Dryden Yikona, and was also the accepted referee of any local football matches. Before any game he would hold onto the ball and not release it for play until every player had submitted to his needle, inoculating them against the disease. Likewise he would board every Kasama-Kawambwa bus and not let it depart until he had inoculated every passenger. Thanks to the determination of characters like Herbert, smallpox was eventually eradicated throughout the country.

In the colonial service days every young DO was on probation for his first two years, with the official status of Cadet, and was only confirmed in his appointment when in that period he had passed the Civil Service examinations in the local language of the area in which he was posted, as well as in Law and in Financial Orders & Stores Regulations. I passed my FO & SR exam in early 1963. Three times I was booked in to take the Law exam in Kasama, and on each occasion "exigencies of the service" (i.e. some crisis) arose which forced me to forego the pleasure. As for ciBemba I was speaking in it constantly on tour and with as many people as possible, and was becoming quite fluent. I went to Kasama for the 'ordinary' level exam on 18th April 1963 – four written papers (two translations, syntax and a letter) and a twenty-minute oral with a White Father Missionary and a senior DO; I found it relatively easy and passed. There was no requirement to take the 'advanced' level for a couple more years, but I took it early, at the beginning of 1964; again it was with a White Father plus a local clerk from the PC's office. I recall that through nervousness I did most of the talking in the oral, but anyway I passed it with a commendation. This led to repercussions later in 1964, as I shall relate in Chapter 6.

4. MPOROKOSO, 1962-64: AROUND THE DISTRICT

If Mporokoso Boma was perhaps not the most attractive in its setting, for instance having no river beside it, the District at large was one of the most diverse in scenery and interest of any in the country. That was a major reason for us to love it. Let me describe its main features, and the places and people I was able to visit, travelling around the six chiefs' areas.

Mporokoso District, showing the three tribal areas.

As the above map shows, the southern half of the District was on the main Northern Province plateau. Running across it from west to east was the northern Muchinga Escarpment, connecting with the larger and better known escarpment of the same name which ran roughly north-south on the west of the Luangwa Valley (*muchinga* anyway means 'escarpment'). On this plateau above the escarpment lived branches of the Bemba and Lungu tribes; below it lived the Tabwa, in very different scenery.

In the south-east lived the Bemba Chief Shibwalya Kapila. I had a lot of dealings with him and I toured his whole area with him. To be honest, it was scenically the least interesting area: just lots of little villages at the headwaters of streams flowing south. As an exception, I do remember coming out of the endless bush onto the west-east short cut road to Mbala (then known as Abercorn) for magnificent long views over the land north of the escarpment, over the major Lungu area of their Senior Chief Tafuna. Chief Shibwalya Kapila's *musumba* lay five kilometres behind the White Fathers' Mission at Kapatu and, like most of his area, there was nothing special about it. His was one of only a few houses built in permanent materials. He was relatively well educated and had been a teacher. If I had to spend a night in the vicinity I would call on the hospitable Father Bedard at the Mission; this would combine work with pleasure, as he was the Manager of Schools for many of the local primary schools and he could also update me on any snippets of 'intelligence' on local political activities.

My first visit to Shibwalya Kapila was rather amusing. It was in September 1962, when I had only been at Mporokoso for seven weeks. I took Wendy with me. We also took the Chief himself and his wife who had recently given birth in the dispensary. The landrovers we used were of the 'soft-back' type – under the canvas roof behind the cab was just a metal floor and metal benches along the sides. Because of the Chief's wife and new baby, and because I did not want the Chief to have the indignity of having to climb out of the tail-gate of the vehicle when we reached his *musumba*, I put them in the cab beside the driver and with Wendy climbed into the back. The DC saw us leaving and was furious. To him my actions were the very opposite of how a PA officer should behave (we were the governing class!) and I was "not in control of the vehicle" either – I thought the driver was, and he knew the way. We heard when we returned that the DC had paced up and down all morning wondering what to do with this errant young Cadet. He even spoke to the PC in Kasama about it, over the Police Radio – so of course colleagues in all other districts heard of my apparent misdemeanour, with amusement! I wasn't bothered. We'd had a great day, with hospitality from the Chief who gave us eggs and tomatoes and a red hen when we left (this alerted me to the need always to take some gift when visiting a chief, and in the future I always did – usually of an alcoholic nature).

The Lungu area, due south of Mporokoso, was the poorest and least populated part of the District. But I visited Chief Mukupa Kaoma's *musumba* at least once a month and, after two village-to-village tours covering the whole of his area, felt I knew it very well. From the Boma one entered Lungu territory by crossing the northern, lesser, Luangwa River. The narrow road then followed the watershed southwards without crossing any streams for some 120 kilometres. This was a road originally built under the supervision of D/Ms. True, the soil in the Lungu area was different from that north of the Luangwa, but I always regarded this as the smoothest, straightest and fastest dirt road in the District, with rarely a pothole and needing very little maintenance. I was always conscious as I drove that the road, keeping to the watershed, passed very close to the sources of several major rivers in the District: the northern Luangwa, the Lupansa, the great Kalungwishi whose waterfalls I shall describe later, and the south-flowing Lukulu.

The first little turn off led three kilometres to Vincent Bulaya village which had a fine Primary School, only opened in 1961. I was fond of this school. It was the larger of only two in Chief Mukupa Kaoma's area, built and managed by Father Bedard of Kapatu Mission; the main classroom blocks had the distinctive arches of the Catholic design, and the offices had beautiful carved wooden doors. Apart from the times I went there to inspect further building progress or to sort out some alleged malpractice by the headteacher, it was also the starting point for my first village-to-village tour. And I took boys and girls from Mporokoso School to play sports against the pupils here.

Mukupa Kaoma was always my favourite *musumba* and I had reasons to visit it more than any other place in our first year, sometimes with Wendy. I could add that I always had a great working relationship with the Chief himself. Here is a quotation from my diary entry for 11th September 1962, my first visit there.

> Mukupa Kaoma is a really beautiful spot; a neat musumba with a fine office block, and the whole village very well irrigated. There's a lot of building going on, a dispensary and some individual voluntary building under the supervision of Duncan Banda from the Rural Development extension team. Having finished the accounts with Anthony Chipasha soon after lunch (the Lungu have almost no money!), I looked round all the building projects with the Chief. He is a most impressive person, only young middle-aged, intelligent, and well in command of what is going on in his area. He does a lot of work in the office too, and thus gets double respect from his people, from the older people just as a chief, from the younger and more educated ones as an administrator too. In the evening I went for a walk round the musumba with my camera. The little Rest House there (the size of my office at the Boma, but divided in two) is in a most perfect spot, perched on the crest of an escarpment with a magnificent view for miles south, and a bubbling waterfall within a stone's throw. It's a joy to go there, and I was only sorry Wendy couldn't come too this time.

Wendy was able to accompany me here two months later, and my diary entry for the 12th-13th November 1962 read as follows:

> I set off early for the Lungu area, taking Frank Sichangwa with me and Wendy, who had not yet been down that way.... We called in at Sambala first to warn them of the film unit's visit and the same again at Vincent Bulaya where we had a chat with Mr Ndakala and looked at the progress of the buildings. As soon as we arrived at Mukupa Kaoma I sat down to go through the latest trial balance.... Meanwhile Wendy was having the time of her life with the women's welfare, and later they gave her a patterned table mat made out of sisal, as a present. The Chief had just come back from the House of Chiefs. Wendy and I went for a walk along the escarpment in the evening and

she was thrilled with the place, as everybody is who goes there. After an early breakfast at the Rest House we went exploring at the base of the waterfall; great sport, but we were exhausted before the day started.

Wendy herself remembers a later visit she made here with a 5-week-old Alastair, on 3rd-4th May 1963, when apparently I left them with Black (our cook) while I set off myself with the N/A Administrative Assistant for Chitoshi where I spent the afternoon. She had a memorable encounter with an old lady who challenged her incorrect way of holding the baby as she stood outside the Rest House among the rocks. As translated by Black, the tirade amounted to: "If the baby falls, I shall bring a case against you in court!" Thereafter Wendy knew our child would always be safe in this country! Walking around the *musumba* she had to pause as each woman felt compelled to adjust the *impapa* to make sure all was well with the baby on her back.

Straight ahead at the end of the approach road to Mukupa Kaoma was the Lungu Native Authority administrative building. On the left was the large covered market building and the bottle store where I twice ran an election polling station.

On my visits I would often pop in to the Primary School, just down a slope from the N/A offices. It then consisted of just one double-classroom block, thatched and built of 'kimberley brick' – i.e. sun-dried large bricks of earth mixed with straw, rather than the more permanent burnt bricks and corrugated iron roofs; this was typical of most school buildings. The few teachers' houses had recently been rebuilt in permanent materials. This school was managed by the White Fathers at Lubushi Mission to the south, just off the main Kasama-Luwingu road. Its pupils only went up to Standard 2, and then the lucky ones went on to Standards 3-6 at the larger Chitoshi Primary School. I must have taken quite an interest in this and Vincent Bulaya schools, judging by the details I recorded in my tour report (see **Appendix 1**).

Further south was the *musumba* of Chief Chitoshi, himself a cousin of Chief Mukupa Kaoma. I used not to come here so often, as most of my work with the Lungu N/A was done at Mukupa Kaoma. But there were some N/A building projects going on and I would come to inspect their progress.

They also used to have a hydram here, which always interested me: the water power from the little river pumped water up the hill to the village (why didn't we have more of these clever and cheap little machines?). And it had the large Primary School, also managed from Lubushi. Chief Chitoshi died in July 1963; it was believed he had been poisoned by his brother, the ex-Chief, who thus regained his position – the tribal elders seemed content.

The Bemba area of Chief Mporokoso was quite large and well populated. His *musumba* lay three kilometres north of the Boma at Chishamwamba, just beyond Kashinda Mission. It was said to be the largest rural village in the country, but I don't know whether it truthfully justified that reputation. Certainly its innumerable houses and huts were all laid out in a neat grid pattern, just like those of an urban township. But I didn't particularly enjoy my monthly visits there. Discussions with the Chiefs were almost impossible: the first was old and fairly senile, and when he died his successor was often the worse for drink. The N/A was in practice run by a not very efficient couple, the Administrative Assistant and the Treasurer. But the two elderly Native Court Members were more competent and reliable, and our friend Eleazar Namweleu as 'traditional adviser' was the elder statesman who helped to keep things straight.

Kalabwe Mission of the White Fathers lay thirty kilometres west of the Boma, along the road to Kawambwa. The merry Father Ladouceur was based here. I recall that as a middle-aged French-Canadian he had little time for younger Dutch priests – "They try to preach against sin. What do they know about sin? But I, *moi*, I have known!" he would say with a wicked chuckle. The Mission was unfortunately struck by lightning on 3rd November 1962; much property and all the Fathers' personal possessions were lost in the blaze. It took them many months to rebuild it.

Further westwards, some seventy kilometres from the Boma, one came to a notable fork in the road at Mukunsa. I often camped here, especially during the census and registration of voters campaigns. The major road, and the bus route, continued west to the Chimpembe pontoon across the wide Kalungwishi River and so into Luapula Province and on to Kawambwa. Just before the pontoon a small track led through dense woodland for ten kilometres to the magnificent Lumangwe Falls.

We visited these Falls at least half-a-dozen times during our two years in Mporokoso, usually with colleagues as we had no transport. One arrived at the top of the right-hand cascade, at the very edge of the sheer rocks where the water plunged over at its highest volume. The lip of the falls gave one a most impressive view sideways, across their whole width of maybe two hundred metres, and a tree grew out of cracks in the rocks right at the lip.

I remember being at the bottom of the Falls in 1963 by their narrow exit gorge, with Leslie Allen and John Cochrane, but I'm not sure how we got down through the thick tropical rainforest – or up again. Spray rose all around and palm trees grew on the sides, continuously soaked in water. Looking up from there we could appreciate the whole width of the Falls as the water came over in one solid wall of white and green, and it was probably the width plus the proportions which gave these the reputation of being "second only to the Victoria Falls." The drop was said to be >30m (cf. Victoria Falls 100m). We fished, a first time for me, and I was the only one who caught anything. Leslie pretended to be furious: "Beginner's luck!"

Overlooking the Falls was a small Rest House, built by a previous DC. I do remember sleeping here with a D/M on camp beds on some later visit in 1963. That was the first occasion on which I had seen scorpions, walking over the concrete floor, and I insisted on sweeping them out before we retired for the night.

From Mukunsa the minor road veered off north-westwards and led down the western end of the escarpment into Tabwa country. Here one came to the Kundabwika Falls, also on the Kalungwishi River. I first visited these in early October 1962 with S/D/M Moses Lubansa in connection with the "Your Vote is Secret" film shows. Let me again quote from my diary:

We were up early from camp at Mukunsa village and left for Tabwa country, along the Chiengi road past Matobwe School where D/M John Chomba is building his house, and then called in at the Kundabwika Falls. As we drove down to the falls we passed the well-known rock paintings on the left, believed to be of Bushman origin; there's only one painting that we could see, and that is unrecognisable as anything in particular, but it's very interesting. Moses shot an ikanga (guinea fowl) as soon as we got out of the landrover. Then we climbed down to the water's edge and sat for half-an-hour just looking up at the falls and at the semi-jungle vegetation downstream. Apparently this is a place for crocodiles, but we didn't see any. The view from above is tremendous, looking at the falls and the Kalungwishi upstream; a most impressive spectacle. We then went on to Hollandi, where we had a couple of writs of summons to serve.

Moses confirmed the rumour I had heard that there had formerly been some annual Tabwa tribal ceremony involving the sacrificial throwing of two virgins over these Falls, either to placate the ancestral spirits or to ensure good harvests. Records were said to show that this practice continued (or was officially known about) until 1935; John Cochrane used to say virgins must have been in short supply after that date, but we had no evidence!

The Kalungwishi River, rising near Mukupa Kaoma, went over no fewer than four sets of falls in this area: the Chimpembe near the pontoon, the Lumangwe, the Kabwelume, and lastly the Kundabwika. We didn't hear of the Kabwelume in our days, for some strange reason; they were probably inaccessible (Wendy and I visited them in 2012 and found them the most spectacular of all). We counted ourselves lucky to have so many wonderful waterfalls in the District; the Lumangwe and Kundabwika were our favourites, but there were innumerable smaller ones too.

Soon after Kundabwika a minor District road turned off northwards and passed through a succession of villages in a heavily populated area to the *musumba* of Chief Mukupa Katandula, the junior Tabwa chief. Although there were no Native Treasury or N/A offices here, we had cause to visit the village quite often as there were several periods of unrest. It lay just to the south of the large Mweru Wantipa lake and alongside the long and wide Mofwe Dambo. A back road, or rough track, connected it eastwards with Senior Chief Nsama's *musumba*, passing one of Leslie's Game Guards' camps at Kikoma. The Chief was fairly old and uneducated, and struggled to do his best in maintaining order; we felt a little sorry for him. He was always so pleased to see one of us from the Boma, and much appreciated any support or advice (and bottles of beer!) we could give him.

Continuing on the major road from Kundabwika, which eventually led to Chiengi on Lake Mweru, one came to a series of wobbly little wooden bridges across the end of the Mofwe Dambo at Nkoshya village. This was an area with a high prevalence of blindness and smallpox. There were usually some men in canoes fishing with nets here, while women on the roadside would offer us fish to buy.

This was always an odd area geographically. The Mofwe Dambo connected Lake Mweru Wantipa with the Kalungwishi River, here running slowly at right-angles to the Mofwe through a flat landscape after its long descent down gorges and over waterfalls. Usually the lake drained out into the river, but sometimes the river overflowed into the lake, either way passing through the long dambo. I remember my confusion when on 16th May 1963 I visited the Mofwe crossing where S/D/M Andrew Ponde and a gang were rebuilding the bridges. This was just after the end of the rains, and the Kalungwishi's waters were high. Water seemed to be flowing the wrong way through the Mofwe Dambo – "uphill", as it were, towards Mukupa Katandula – and Andrew confirmed it had strangely been doing that all week. I found more evidence for this phenomenon later in a 1958 article by a pilot, published in the *Northern Rhodesia Journal*:

> In 1958 our flight area ended on the western shore of the Mofwe Dambo and Mweru Marsh flood plain, and we had to fly over the flood plain itself. I was struck by the fact that the fish traps on the Mofwe seemed to be the wrong way round, which indicated that the water flowed uphill; it was only later on that I found that the water from the flooded Kalungwishi ran into the Mofwe and thence into the Mweru Marsh. (G.D.B.Williams: 'Aerial Surveys in Northern Rhodesia')

But the dambo with its fertile surrounds was capable of supporting a large population, and its west side had as many villages as the eastern Mukupa Katandula road I have mentioned. Beyond these villages the minor road, heading north from Nkoshya to Kaputa, went through a tsetse control barrier and then through the Mweru Wantipa Game Reserve which included the lake of that name in its eastern portion. Yes, in those days (but, I fear, not any longer) there was plenty of game in the Reserve and tsetse flies were very prevalent; every vehicle leaving the Reserve was dusted and sprayed so as not to carry the flies to villages and further afield – nowadays, no game means no tsetse, and the barrier no longer exists. I went this way three or four times during 1962-64, twice in this direction: once by landrover when we nearly got stuck on the rickety bridge near its entrance and had to close the windows for a while because of the numerous tsetse flies, and once by bicycle (!) with two D/Ms when we were confronted by some elephants and then by a large herd of buffalo – Leslie had warned me in advance that there was a wounded and dangerous elephant somewhere up that road and of course we met it!

Mweru Wantipa is a lake and swamp system that has always been something of a mystery as its water level and salinity fluctuates so much. This could not be entirely explained by variation in rainfall levels. In fact it had been known to dry out almost completely. Its water was muddy in appearance, at times appearing reddish and slightly oily. In the local dialect *wa Ntipa* means "with mud" and this distinguished it from its larger neighbour Lake Mweru with its clearer water. The lake edges and swamps were dominated by dense papyrus. The lake itself supported a large population of hippos and crocodiles, and the number and variety of waterfowl and other birds inhabiting the surrounding marshes were fascinating.

Almost immediately on entering the Park the vegetation and scenery changed, and woodland was replaced by dense and impenetrable thickets of lower bush. This was the result of a geological fault at this point. I so well remember cycling past these endless thickets and looking out for irate buffalo. Botanical experts refer to this as the "Itigi-Sumbu thicket vegetation", dense bush which is simply impossible to penetrate. Typically it consisted of over 100 plant species woven together so tightly that a person was unable to walk through them. Even elephants forcing their way through these thickets barely left tracks as the shrubs sprang back to their original position. This interesting vegetation variety was endemic to this region and to a section of the Sumbu Game Reserve, and the only other region with similar vegetation was in central Tanzania. But this patch of Itigi-Sumbu vegetation, along the west shore of Lake Mweru Wantipa, was the largest. It represented a unique but poorly understood ecosystem, once a vital habitat for the black rhino before they were eradicated from the region, and it is now predicted that these important thickets too will soon disappear if conservation action is not urgently taken.

Soon after leaving the northern barrier and Game Guards' camp of the Reserve one came to Kaputa. When I first visited here in October 1962 I thought it seemed like the last outpost of the Protectorate, hundreds of miles from any centre, with little or no means of contact, and with the hills of the Congolese border only six miles away – an incredible place to live. A couple of Chief Mukupa Katandula's Kapasus were stationed here, mainly for the purpose of collecting fishing levies. There was also a small unofficial dispensary, manned by a lone Dispensary Assistant. It was 'unofficial' in that it had been built by a former DC of Mporokoso out of his 'roads budget', to help our good friend the PMO, who then had to juggle his accounts to provide drugs and medical aids for this 'non-existent' dispensary, and he used to fly there in his own little plane (he was the country's only 'flying doctor' and found his plane cheaper as well as easier to use than a landrover). Because of its proximity to the border, Kaputa (and especially its little dispensary) used to be a haven of assistance for many Congolese who had no such facilities, so they would come here in quite large numbers. On my first visit I had to arrange for two blind children to get collected, ready to go to the Blind School at Mporokoso, and I dealt with the Dispensary Assistant's request for a postal vote. I inspected the dispensary, where they were having bouts of dysentery and malaria as well as some cases of smallpox, and signed the visitors' book. At the small Primary School there I collected the headmaster who had applied for a postal vote, to bring him back with me to the Boma as otherwise he would never get his vote in in time.

Kaputa, because of its position, had some interesting history from the early colonial times, being a place where an old Boma used to be situated beside the Choma river. I think it is worth recording this.

> ### Chiengi and Choma Old Bomas.
>
> In the 1880s scramble for Central Africa both the British and the Belgians sought treaties with Mushidi, the powerful Paramount Chief of the Luba peoples who occupied most of Katanga. Alfred Sharpe was sent from the British Chartered Company's headquarters at Zomba

in what is now Malawi to meet Mushidi in Katanga, but his attempts to get a treaty signed were forestalled by Stairs, a renegade English agent of the Belgian King Leopold. By the next year, 1891, the King's 'Congo Free State' effectively included all of Katanga.

Sharpe, returning to Nyasaland [now Malawi], stopped to recuperate and to revive the strength of his ailing companions at the spot where the Chiengi stream enters the north-east corner of Lake Mweru, in an area that had for many years been independent of Mushidi. Impressed by the powerful personality and friendly attitude of the local Chief Puta, he hoisted the Union Jack and set up a station there. Chiengi was thus probably the first Government station to be established in what was to become North-East Rhodesia.

In 1892 Sharpe returned to the Mweru/Luapula region to make treaties of friendship with the local chiefs and to establish a civil administration to be controlled from Zomba. In doing so he set up a sub-station at Choma [Kaputa], at the north end of the great Mweru Marsh, which was a suitable staging point on the carrier route between Lakes Tanganyika and Mweru. This spot for a boma had the added advantage of being close to the 'town' of the retired slave-trader Abdullah Semiwe, the genuineness of whose retirement from business was the object of grave suspicion.

Semiwe himself was one of the last of the Swahili slave-traders who ravaged Central Africa in the 19th century. A tall, distinguished-looking man with a touch of Arab blood and much more than a touch of Arab courtesy, he openly regretted the passing of the good old days when "black ivory" and white formed together such a profitable commerce. He was certainly still involved in elephant poaching, but was very plausible in putting the suspicion on Greek traders from across the border. His town up on the Congo border was a pleasant place and very different from a normal African village. The residents still professed to adhere to the tenets of Islam; they called themselves Swahili, though there was clearly much admixture of local blood. What invited suspicion of Semiwe's activities was that there always seemed to be a great deal of money about. Taxes were paid in exemplary fashion, people were

Mporokoso, 1962-64: around the District

> always well dressed, and there was a considerable consumption of tea and sugar and other foodstuffs only available from shops – in an area where no crops were grown for sale; this all led to speculation that poaching for the white ivory trade continued, if not its old ally "black ivory" too.
>
> (Extracts from Mr Justice J.B.Thomson's article on 'Chiengi' in 'Memories of Abandoned Bomas' series, in *Northern Rhodesia Journal*)

As a postscript to that account, I should add that Choma only operated as a Boma from 1892 until 1902 when it was closed.

In January 1963 we had warnings that large numbers of Congolese refugees might come across the border to Kaputa. The Central Congolese Army had just captured Baudouinville after heavy fighting, and remnants of the Katangan forces and PA in those parts were fleeing southwards. Since their route from Pweto to Elizabethville (now Lubumbashi) was blocked, it seemed likely they might try to come through our District via Kaputa. The DC and Jeremy went up to the border to investigate, and Harry (our Police Inspector) set up a road-block at the tsetse barrier in the optimistic hope of disarming any military forces driving through the Mweru Wantipa Game Reserve, while I and the wives at the Boma prepared soup kitchens and medical supplies for any Katangan refugees. In the end the Pweto route became passable and they went that way; the scare passed. There was a second rumour of a likely Congolese Army invasion in September 1963, but that also came to nothing after our investigations.

Leaving Kaputa and travelling east (north of Lake Mweru Wantipa) the next place of interest, to me, was the Kangiri Red Locust Centre. The areas surrounding this lake and Lake Rukwa in southern Tanzania had for centuries been breeding grounds for red locusts. Records show there were widespread plagues in the years 1892-1910 and 1928-33, with swarms migrating from these lakes to the Congo and elsewhere. The vegetation on the west and north sides of Mweru Wantipa was especially favourable for locust breeding; this normally occurs some seven weeks after the first rains, and hoppers become adults capable of swarming by January-

February. Systematic investigation of locusts really began in 1938 from a headquarters in Abercorn (now called Mbala), to cover Rukwa to its north and Mweru Wantipa to its west, and a camp for fieldwork was established at Kangiri. The International Red Locust Control Service (IRLCS) was formally established in 1949, and all countries south of the equator were subscribers to its treaty and contributed to its services.

To begin with, control of red locusts in their breeding areas was confined to an arsenic-cassava bait used to destroy the hoppers; later a 6% gamma BHC spray was applied. The evidence was incontrovertible: low water levels in the lakes led to the formations of numerous strong swarms, and a single season's very successful breeding could be enough to start a plague, i.e. swarms migrating from outbreak areas to new areas (a "good" breeding season could increase the locust population by anything from 30-fold to 100-fold). Maintained flooding of the lake would reduce the significance of an outbreak area, while a permanent enlargement of the lake would abolish the bordering locust infested plains. Interestingly, David Livingstone visited Mweru Wantipa in 1867, crossing the Chishela Dambo, but he does not mention red locusts in his journals; either he had become used to them on his travels, or water levels were high enough at the time of his visit to cover up all but a few small strips of grassland beside the lake.

On the opposite side of the road from the Kangiri Centre was an airstrip at Chocha, where Derek Braithwaite (the PMO), used to land; I think he must have had an ongoing arrangement with the IRLCS to meet him there and drive him to his unofficial dispensary, as there was certainly no Government vehicle stationed in Kaputa in those days. I would hope the airstrip is still there and maintained, for emergency or even regular contacts with the present Boma.

Passing Kalaba School, the small road then crossed the Chishela Dambo, over a long and rickety wooden bridge, to reach Bulaya at the north-east inlet to Lake Mweru Wantipa. This was the normal and quicker route to reach Kaputa, but that bridge over the Chishela Dambo frequently caused problems. On one journey that way I recorded that the bridge was under eighteen inches of water. When checking the progress of the Census team in the Kaputa area on 8th June 1963 with S/D/M Andrew Ponde we had to get a boat to take us and our cycles from Bulaya across the dambo because the water was still about four feet above the bridges, let alone above the road which was invisible. I recall that, after spending an hour with the Census team, and paying them, Andrew and I absolutely raced back to get to the Chishela ferry before dark. We failed, but managed to make the ferryman hear us and got across. We spent the night at Bulaya, in Paddy McCormack's road camp and he gave us good hospitality. I also noted that we saw a lot of hippo in the dambo and these made a continuous noise all evening.

At Bulaya the Kaputa road joined the major Mporokoso-Sumbu dirt road and passed through the Sumbu Game Reserve. The first time Wendy and I came here was on 2nd September 1962, brought by John Cochrane. The scenery in the Reserve was new to us and different – bushes in thick clumps, and candelabra trees growing out of anthills, which we didn't see around Mporokoso, and occasionally clear signs of destruction by elephants; we looked hard for game all the way, but saw nothing. After nearly forty kilometres the road started to descend and, as we can vividly recall, brought us round a sharp bend for a most dramatic view. We had come out onto the edge of the last escarpment, to overlook Lake Tanganyika, here at its widest point, a real paradise of a view, with quite high hills on either side coming down to the shore. And so we drove down the escarpment to Sumbu.

At Sumbu there were three little thatched chalets comprising the Government Rest House, a little jetty for boats, a fish shed and a petrol pump. Beyond this was just a small fishing village. On that first visit we had a picnic on the lovely strand of sandy beach and lay in the sun – Wendy even got some sunburn, not realising how much hotter it was there at only 770 metres above sea level. Then we had a quick swim in the warm water, after which we saw water snakes swimming where we had been – but no crocodiles. John went off on security business and we just idled away the time in sheer bliss. At night all the little canoes and fishing boats put out into the Lake, and we saw their lights which they use to attract the fish. At 6.00 the next morning we walked along the beach, looking for any animals which might have come down at dawn to drink. We saw a waterbuck with her calf, and several smaller buck, but nothing large; however, there were scores of large footprints heading to and from the water and quite recent droppings. Then we had a look at the old Boma, and wandered round the pier.

Yes, like Chiengi and Choma, Sumbu had once had a small Boma, opened in 1895 to stop the slave traffic. Dhows would use the harbour to collect slaves and take them across the lake to Tanganyika and so on to the East Coast. Its first official, Captain Charles Livingston, late of the Black Watch, died there in 1896, eighteen months after being posted to Sumbu, and was buried there: his nickname was Chitimukulu on account of his great height (6'6"). Another official, C.Stevens also died there in 1903 and was buried alongside Livingston. We looked at their graves, and a few days later I wrote to the Editor of the *Red Hackle*, my regimental magazine, to inform him of the grave of an ex-Black Watch officer, Livingston. Stephens had died of blackwater fever, which was evidently a common disease in the 'pioneer days': of the 232 deaths of European officials in the territory prior to 1908, the *Northern Rhodesia Journal* could only give the cause of death for 56, but of these as many as 28 were reported to have died of blackwater fever.

In 1904 the area became the responsibility of the Native Commissioner at Mporokoso. In 1907 sleeping sickness was discovered there, and in June 1908 A.C.R.Miller was posted to Sumbu to arrange for the evacuation of villages from the lake shore. Having completed this operation by September 1908, Miller then closed down Sumbu Boma, moving his headquarters to Katwe on the Abercorn-Kambole road; Katwe Boma was itself closed in 1910. In 1914 there were Belgian troops for a time at Sumbu. They dug trenches below the Boma near the lake and also on the island in the Bay. A German gunboat shelled the place, but caused little damage – the First World War had even touched this remote corner of the British Empire!

We visited Sumbu several times during 1962-64. With its Rest House by the beach it was virtually an exclusive retreat for Mporokoso's Government officers and their families. One night in 1964 a Kapasu came to us at the Rest House with a woman who had been axed in her head by her husband. The blow was not fatal, but the nasty wound seemed to my inexperienced eye to be oozing brain. We applied first-aid and I then dashed back by landrover the 180 kilometres to Mporokoso dispensary with her, hoping she would not die on me on the journey. I handed her over to Dryden Yikona who passed her on to Kasama where she made a complete recovery. The husband was brought in later for his prison sentence.

Mporokoso, 1962-64: around the District

I also recall a long conversation I had down at Sumbu jetty with Paul Mathis. He had been a White Father, but had married a local African girl so had had to leave holy orders and was now a fish trader on the Lake. He was very concerned about the future of the fishing industry at Sumbu, which he maintained was being killed by the greed of the N/A which demanded too much levy from the fishermen; the traders who came through with lorries were also expected to pay levy and hence were not coming so frequently (he said Kopanakis, a Greek trader, came at night and thus evaded the levy). There were more fish at Sumbu than at Mpulungu, he maintained, but trade was definitely going to the latter. Paul also complained about the plan to build an ice plant at Kampinda instead of Sumbu; Kampinda's fishing was bound to fluctuate with the level of Mweru Wantipa, which in some years virtually dried up and took a few seasons to re-stock. Altogether, he felt strongly that Sumbu was being neglected.

Sumbu was not a tourist venue: that was at Kasaba Bay, further along the coast eastwards and actually in Abercorn (later called Mbala) District and only accessible by boat or a light aircraft. I once went by boat from Sumbu to Kasaba Bay with Harry Schneeman in July 1963, to do a Board of Survey there. We found it a real paradise. It lay on the isthmus joining the Nyika peninsula, some eighteen kilometres from Sumbu. The camp was in fact in Chinyika Bay, but over the sand dunes was Kasaba Bay itself where we could swim. Jack Curtis, the superintendent, had built the camp himself (four chalets and the dining/lounge block) out of stone and thatch, and they were very well constructed with all mod.cons. including electricity! The elephants, of whom I'd heard so much, came around in the evening and had a feed just outside the dining room. Fabulous! We went with a Game Guard for a walk over the isthmus to Kasaba Bay itself: no crocodiles, but it was a gorgeous long beach for swimming. Then we came back and got down to work on the Board of Survey – which didn't take us long! After lunch we went off in a boat, trolling for fish. In the evening one old elephant, 'Broken Tusk', came so close to our window that Harry jumped out of bed in a fright; one yard closer and his tusks would have been through the window.

Returning from Sumbu to the Boma, south of its Game Reserve and Bulaya and their many attractive candelabra trees, the road ran to the east of Mweru Wantipa but at some distance from the lake. I used to visit Mikose fishing camp and the large and lively fishing village of Kampinda on the lake. As I have said earlier, Mweru Wantipa suffered from irregular cyclical decreases in water level and this affected the fortunes of the fishing industry there. Kampinda was the main source of fish exports from the lake, having the best dirt road access from the south and so attracting the most traders – this in turn encouraged more activity by the fishermen themselves. My old files recorded activity at Kampinda increasing spectacularly from 1960 to 1961: with the same number of fishermen (191) the weights of fresh fish it exported rose in one year from c.744,000 lbs to 1,006,036 lbs and that of dried fish from c.200,000 lbs to 311,472 lbs, and these figures accounted for 85% of the total fish exports from the lake.

South of Kampinda one came to Nsama, the Tabwa N/A headquarters and the Senior Chief's *musumba*. I must have come here almost as many times as to Mukupa Kaoma – certainly once a month. It was a village of some size and had the advantage of a decent store – one of the few two-storey buildings in the District. The owner, Memmish, was a Turkish trader and was always very friendly and hospitable to visiting Boma officers; I stayed in his 'guest wing' on two occasions but had to be wary of his African wife who, I thought, was trying to seduce me. His own bed was in an enormous meat-safe, where we sometimes caught him taking a siesta, and he always wore a long blue Muslim nightshirt.

One visit we made as a family to Nsama, in January 1964, I had totally forgotten until I recently read Wendy's description of it in a letter to her mother. It was election time. Our Main (African) Roll candidate was unopposed so only the Reserved (European) Constituency was contested. We only had eighteen Europeans registered in the whole District: the Nsama ward had one voter (the redoubtable Memmish) and the Sumbu ward also had only one (Paul Mathis)! This entailed dozens of forms to complete for two pieces of paper in a box. The idea was that we would get Memmish's vote and then go on to Sumbu to get Paul Mathis's and have a nice time, by the lake – mixing business with pleasure. But to Wendy's mild annoyance we met Paul while we were on the way to Nsama, so we had no excuse to use Government petrol and go any further. However we had a gorgeous time, unexpectedly, at Nsama.

Mporokoso, 1962-64: around the District

Wendy's letter reads:

Old Memmish is impossible to draw – he's enormously fat and gross, in a sort of nightshirt only, with big stary eyes and a shock of grizzled hair. Bursting with hospitality towards his "brother Europeans", his Bemba infinitely better than his English, he was well in with the local UNIP officials but secretly a devoted supporter of the NPP (European party); and full of large incomprehensible whispers behind his hand in a great conspiratorial fashion.

We made a courtesy call on Senior Chief Nsama and, when he heard we were not going on to Sumbu, he invited us to stay with him! His lovely house was on top of a hill with fabulous views everywhere, and we had a wonderful time there, with royal treatment and boundless hospitality. Wendy's description continues:

There were the usual photographs in sepia, and embroidery and crochet work everywhere, plus a very nice suite of furniture and a mosquito net over the bed. We put Alastair on a camp bed. Chicken and rice for supper (plied with cokes and tea all afternoon) and then toasted mealies for a nightcap. Alastair and I joined the women and children in the large kitchen over the charcoal brazier idly chatting and playing while Mick and the Chief drank beer and yarned and talked politics all evening. Altogether it was very very pleasant.

Why I have recounted this story is that I believe no other European officer from our Boma had ever stayed in a chief's house, nor do I think any of our ex-Cambridge Course colleagues had enjoyed that kind of privilege with any chiefs in their Districts. We felt very honoured. And we must have been doing something right in terms both of easy interracial relationships and of burying any vestiges of colonialism.

Just eight kilometres west of Nsama was an interesting village called, variously, Semiwe or Abdullah bin Selemani, I first went there in October 1962 with S/D/M Moses Lubansa, principally to see what signs there still were of

Arab or Swahili influences. This was one of only three recognised Swahili enclaves in the country – a legacy of Tippu Tib and the slave traders. They had a mosque, although I didn't go in it, but I noticed an abundance of palms and a certain atmosphere like an oasis settlement. The villagers all understood kiSwahili but now they mostly spoke ciBemba and called themselves Tabwa.

The point about Arab or Swahili influence was this. All maps of the 1950-60s which described the country's different tribal areas showed the three Swahili enclaves: one at or near Ndola, the others at Sumbu and here near Nsama. All were associated with the slave trade. But it was never clear to me whether the kiSwahili speakers and current residents of these enclaves were descendants of ex-slaves or of ex-slave-traffickers who'd originally come from Tanganyika. Near Ndola's museum is still the 'Slave Tree', a national monument: the Swahili slave traders frequented that locality in the 1880s, built a stockade and used the shade of the enormous mahogany tree as a meeting place for buying and selling slaves. Sumbu would also have had kiSwahili speaking traders, being the harbour from which so many slaves were taken by dhow to Tanganyika (see p.64 above). I thought I had read somewhere that the Semiwe near Nsama had once been the headquarters of Tippu Tib (1837-1905), one of the most famous of the slave traders, but that could not have been correct as he had operated in Tanganyika and the Congo. But what I had not read in the 1960s was the *N.Rhodesia Journal* article on Chiengi and Choma old Bomas (see pp.59-61 above), and therefore I was unaware of the Abdullah Semiwe quoted there. I doubt whether that Semiwe had subsequently moved his village from the Kaputa/Choma vicinity to Nsama's. It would seem more likely that the Abdullah bin Selemani Semiwe was always here and the common name of Abdullah made any connection with Choma illusory. Anyway, villages normally took the name of the current headman, so their names often change – and maps are rarely up-to-date!

It was just eighty kilometres south from Nsama to return to the Boma, climbing the dramatic northern Muchinga Escarpment the lip of which lay only fifteen kilometres short of Mporokoso.

Yes, this was a District of great diversity and beauty, with its two lakes and two Game Reserves and many waterfalls, and there were so many places of interest, especially in Tabwa country. It is no wonder that we loved it and were intensely happy there. Our PC, Peter Clarke, visited Mporokoso on at least six occasions during our stay. During one occasion, in September 1963, he gave me 'first refusal' on an option to transfer to Mpika. Without needing to consult Wendy, I immediately declined his kind offer since "We are very happy here, thank you." Had I accepted we might never have had the excitements of a later transfer to Chinsali!

And how was I adjusting to the job of a Cadet, from any expectations I may have had in Cambridge? One entry in my diary in November 1962 is interesting in this respect. Wendy and I had been having a long conversation, mostly on politics, with a teacher who had called at the house one evening. I wrote:

> *I continued with Wendy, after he'd gone, on an assessment of my principles and how far I am putting them into practice in my work. I am beginning to realise the difficulty of seeing the wood for the trees. We agreed that personal relations do matter most in this job. But if we are aiming at a smooth handover of responsible government, even at a Native-Authority to District-Council level, the natural reaction of wishing to help and of assuming responsibility must be suppressed and the firm line must now and then be followed that it is they, our friends, who must decide for themselves; i.e. a reconciliation between sending them away satisfied with your answer (and seemingly on good terms with you) and telling them to pull their finger out and take the initiative, and thereby expecting a less satisfied reaction to you personally. It is a matter of character to do the latter without losing mutual respect or personal good relations.*

5. CHINSALI, 1953-64: LUMPA CHURCH BACKGROUND

On 14th July 1964 we moved, at twelve hours notice, to our second station, Chinsali. I must first set the background to the exciting and, at times, stressful year we spent there. The year was dominated by the 1964 disturbances involving the Lumpa Church headed by Alice Lenshina, and its conflict with Government. This was sometimes described as a 'religious war', but only one side was inspired by a religion. Very important factors were ones of embarrassment. The disturbances took place in July-August 1964, merely three months before Independence, thus being an embarrassment to both the outgoing colonial Government and to the incoming Zambian leadership during their interim period of internal self-government. Additionally, Chinsali, the centre of the Lumpa movement, was the home district of the then Prime Minister, Dr Kenneth Kaunda.

Many books have been written about the Lenshina Affair, most trying to be as objective as possible but still appearing to justify the Government's actions. Kampamba Mulenga's book *Blood on Their Hands* tries to describe the conflict from the Lumpas' point of view. John Hudson's book *A Time to Mourn* has a most useful summary on the early history of the Lumpa Church, and is very revealing on his personal experiences as DC of next-door Isoka District. I am aiming here, in respect of Chinsali District, to achieve a similar balance between objective facts and my own personal experiences. Over the years former colleagues have tried to persuade me to write and publish my own account, but I had excuses for declining: for the first ten years afterwards I was restricted by the Official Secrets Act, for the next ten I was conscious that this was still an embarrassing episode in Zambia's early history for Kaunda and his team, and thereafter I became too busy and anyway was conscious of the tricks that memory plays.

However, in 2011 I discovered some old personal files, the existence of which, like my diary on early days in Mporokoso, I had totally forgotten. These included:
- my diary of activities as a DO for the four days, 16th –19th July, 1964;
- my Annual Report as DC (later DS) Chinsali for 1964, submitted to the Resident Secretary (former PC), Kasama;

- my submission to the Commission of Inquiry into the Lenshina Affair, dated July 1965.

All these were marked 'Strictly Confidential'. In addition I found a 135-page A4 notebook containing intelligence reports submitted by former DCs to their PCs over the years 1955 to 1963, all marked 'Secret'; the contents of these reports are, for the most part, too lengthy for my present purposes, but the predictions they record are such that by late 1964 their authors could justifiably have said "Well, we told you so."

I therefore feel some confidence that the accounts in the following three chapters are reasonably accurate, in that they are based on records written at the time and are not the product of distorted memories harboured for fifty years since the events. However, we always have to be cautious about the truth: the Police say that two eye-witnesses of a crime will tell different stories; and two army commanders are likely to have very different views on how a battle is going.

* * * * * * *

Firstly, who was Alice Lenshina? John Hudson in his book *A Time to Mourn* gives this useful introduction.

> *The [Lumpa] church originated in 1953, at a time when political ferment had started but was still comparatively muted. As in the case of other messianic religious sects, the original impetus came from a real or imagined spiritual experience. It happened to a most unlikely person. Alice Mulenga Lubusha was a very ordinary village woman in her early thirties. Later she became known as "Lenshina", a vernacular version of "regina" [= queen]. Both she and her husband Petros were uneducated. Her father was the grandson of a Bemba Paramount Chief. She was born at her father's village, Kasomo, in April 1919. She had five children by Petros; otherwise her life had been completely uneventful. Kasomo was close to Chinsali, and within the Lubwa sphere of religious influence.*

Chinsali, 1953-64: Lumpa Church Background

The Rev. Fergus Macpherson gave a detailed first-hand account of how Lenshina described to him her spiritual experience, involving apparent death and rebirth, and how he responded. This account was, presumably with his permission, documented in an intelligence report of a former DC at Chinsali, which I inherited.

On 18th September 1953, when I was the ordained missionary of the Church of Scotland at Lubwa, Chinsali, a message was delivered to me to the effect that a woman from Kasomo had come to the Mission specially to see me. I was at the time in a Mission committee, so I asked that she should wait to see me at the mid-week service that afternoon. I also asked the session-clerk who had brought the message if he knew what special reason the woman had for this urgent call, and was told, "She says that she has risen from the dead."

At 4.30 a huge congregation had packed the church. I looked around to find the woman, and saw her sitting against the wall on one of the pews, looking very ill and weak. After the service I greeted her and asked her to meet me in the church buildings along with the local elders. While this meeting began the building was surrounded by a curious crowd.

Alice Lenshina Mulenga, a Bemba of Kasomo village, stated that she had been taken ill and died not once but four times, each time 'rising again' when mourning had begun. At her last rising, which seemed to have taken place on Monday 16th September, she stated that she had been called by Jesus to go and meet him 'at the river'. She had had to forbid the anxious crowd in the house from following her. She had then, she said, gone to the river, where Jesus had said to his people in ciBemba 'Mubwesheni, inshita yakwe tailafika' which means 'Send her back, her time has not yet come'. Then Jesus had come across to her and shown her 'a sign' and told her to go and visit the 'Abena kubuta' at Lubwa, who would have a message for her. 'Abena kubuta' literally means 'they of the whiteness' and it was apparent that

Lenshina was convinced that she must talk privately with the missionary Minister. It was therefore agreed that she should come again to church the next Sunday and see me after the service. She came again on the Sunday and I asked a senior retired catechist to be on call while Lenshina and I went to the Mission office. This course of action was approved by the elders as it was felt that she was sincerely anxious to meet me privately.

In the interview that followed in the office, she recounted her 'rising from the dead' and then said that when she had met Jesus he had taught her some 'inyimbo' (songs, hymns) and shown her 'Ibuka lya Mweo' (the book of life). She showed me a yellow mark on the white cloth which she wore around her shoulders and said that Jesus had lain the 'book of life' on her cloth and that the yellow mark was the 'icibe' (stain, moisture). He had not given her the book, however. With regard to the 'inyimbo' I asked her whether she had known them before, to which she replied 'of course not, it was He who taught them to me at the river'. I then asked her if she remembered them and she began to sing, softly, songs of a very simple evangelical theme. Unfortunately I did not write them down but one of them, typical of their sentiments, said 'tatwabuke mumana kano imitima yasambwa' meaning 'we shall not cross the river unless our hearts are washed'. It was then that Lenshina told me that Jesus had sent her to me (the 'abena kubuta') and that I would have a message for her.

I answered that I could not pass any verdict on her record of her strange experience but 'inasmuch as you were given life and health again when you were, as it were, at the gate of death (incipata ca i-mfwa) you should give thanks to God and serve Him from now on with your whole heart'. She gladly assented to this. The senior catechist was then called in and he offered prayers for Lenshina. He promised to resume her instruction as a catechumen with a view to baptism, which she had discontinued some time before through negligence. She promised not only to attend worship regularly but also to gather people for prayers at her village.

Chinsali, 1953-64: Lumpa Church Background

In the weeks and months that followed this meeting, as the news of Lenshina's "resurrection" circulated, small crowds began to gather at Kasomo village to hear her. From the beginning she claimed to be in direct communication with Jesus, who spoke regularly to her, and passing on these messages became a form of preaching, often accompanied by the songs she said Jesus had taught her. The Church leaders at Lubwa felt it was important to keep the group within the church; she was re-baptised into the Church of Scotland by the Rev. Paul Mushindo, and for a time joint prayer meetings were held. Initially the relationship between the Mission and Lenshina was friendly, but it gradually deteriorated when it became obvious that she was moving towards the formation of a separatist church with its own teachings, some of which were inconsistent with those of the Mission. Of particular concern were the reports that she was baptising her followers – people who had already been baptised by the Mission or the Catholics, or had been suspended by them.

Alongside Lenshina's claim to be in touch with the supernatural (or Jesus) was her promise to rid her followers of the fear of witchcraft. She began to insist that those wishing to be baptised should surrender to her any witchcraft materials they had, in a form of purification. It became clear that this cleansing ritual was highly attractive to the local people and was probably the main reason for the astonishingly fast growth of the support for Lenshina and her embryo church. Piles of surrendered materials soon accumulated at Kasomo. Most commentators from the 1950s thought that the missionaries had ignored, or grossly underestimated, the fear of witchcraft in rural African society. As John Hudson has written:

> *Widespread belief in the reality of witchcraft as the cause of many misfortunes, illness and deaths cast a shadow over the lives of rural people in those days. Even the local intelligentsia and committed Christians were not immune from this belief. Lenshina's recognition of the reality of witchcraft, coupled with her offer of forgiveness through a purifying baptism thus gave her a decisive advantage over the other churches.*

Of course, in the eyes of those who still innately had some belief in witchcraft the piles of surrendered materials, such as bones and charms, gave Lenshina tremendous potential power: **she** now held all the instruments of witchcraft and could, if she wished, use them to affect the lives of others. I, for one, never imagined that she did abuse the trust which came with the surrender of the charms, but from his reported behaviour in the late 1950s I suspected that her husband Petros was corrupt enough to have done so when it suited him.

There were several other factors, apart from Lenshina's spiritual connections and her campaigns against witchcraft, in the success of the new church-like movement. In Chinsali and elsewhere the presence of many foreign-run churches (Catholic, Church of Scotland, LMS, Watchtower, Baptist, Jehovah's Witnesses, etc.) showed that no single church had a monopoly over the path to salvation; so a new church could be just as effective. At a time when resentment against colonial rule was increasing, a church indigenous in origin and management offered some religious independence, more closely attuned to local feelings and needs. Allied to this was an argument, or belief, of many indigenous churches in Africa that God and Jesus were black, not white as the Europeans would teach, and it was the whites who had crucified Jesus.

Another factor in the early growth of the movement, mentioned in several intelligence reports of the time, was an element of compulsion or a mixture of promises and threats. Anybody who was disinclined to go to Kasomo for baptism, and cleansing from the powers of witchcraft, was open to the charge that they did not wish to give up witchcraft. The Missions' local evangelists thereby suffered hostility and, on entering villages, there was a total absence of greeting and hospitality – quite the opposite of the normal African virtues. The Catholic White Fathers were often accused of witchcraft because they wore rosaries. Lenshina and her close adherents would say: "Those who come to Kasomo will have rain on their crops this year, the others won't." It did not matter how hollow such a promise was if it was believed at the time. Particularly severe threats were used against those who attended communion in the Catholic or Church of Scotland churches; communion was one aspect of Christian ritual for which Lenshina had no equivalent, and she preached that anyone taking communion would soon die.

Lenshina's separatist tendencies might have been effectively discouraged and her movement contained within the Church of Scotland, to its great benefit, if Fergus Macpherson had remained at Lubwa during this formative period. But he went on overseas leave in November 1954. Effective control of Mission policy passed to the Rev. Paul Mushindo who was much influenced by his old-fashioned and narrow-minded mentor the Rev. Robert McMinn (Missionary at Lubwa, 1913-1940). Mushindo and Lenshina fell out; maybe there was male resentment at the emergence of an illiterate woman as a rival (and far more successful) church leader. During 1955 there was a final schism when Lenshina defied attempts by Lubwa to correct her unacceptable practices. She and her husband were suspended from membership of the United Church of Central Africa, to which Lubwa now belonged.

Later, in 1955, Lubwa tried to regain its former adherents through an evangelical campaign, but at Kasomo and elsewhere the evangelists were rebuffed. At the same time Lenshina and Petros were declared heretics by the Catholics who were also affected by defections. From the start, many people had taken to travelling long distances from other districts such as Lundazi, Mpika and Isoka to seek baptism from Lenshina. By the end of 1955 Kasomo had been visited by c.60,000 people, and they were still arriving at the rate of 1,000 per week. Churches had been set up over a wide area of Northern Province and Lundazi, and even on the Copperbelt. The church now became known as the 'Lumpa' church from the Bemba word for 'excel' or 'surpass'.

Fergus Macpherson always felt that Lenshina's 'resurrection' was "not a hoax" and wrote sadly, with hindsight, in 1958:

> *I was satisfied that, as a simple village woman, she was sincere in her desire to give thanks to God for her restoration to health, and that she did not start as a heretic or a schismatic.......What might have been a revival movement found the Church of Scotland so tied to its set practice and so wanting in zeal and vision that it had not the strength to contain Alice.*

Well, if history is full of lost opportunities this was certainly one. If the Church had sent Fergus back to Lubwa in 1954 (he was posted to a different Mission station) to guide future policy and events, a great tragedy of later years might have been averted. In 1970 we lived for eighteen months a few doors away from Fergus in a house in Handsworth Park, Lusaka, and I often talked to him about the 'Lenshina Affair' of course. He would, obviously, cast no overt criticisms against Paul Mushindo or the local Lubwa elders but, with humility, he seemed to carry a burden of guilt at not having persuaded the Church authorities to post him back to Lubwa after his leave.

We met Paul Mushindo several times in Chinsali during 1964-65. He was a charming, quiet man, always dressed in a suit and always going barefoot. We used to find it amusing, as much as revealing that Paul, brought up in a Church of Scotland school, spoke English with a pronounced Scottish accent, rolling his R's, while other Zambians spoke with a French-Canadian accent learnt in a White Fathers' school. I did regard Paul as somewhat unsympathetic to the Lumpa adherents and carrying some baggage from the early days of the Lumpa Church, so I was cautious in my dealings with him.

My book of *Intelligence Reports* contains examples of the inyimbo (hymns) mentioned by Fergus, together with 'Rules of the Lumpa Church' and many pages describing how the Church was organised, its dogma and rituals, and its effect on other religious organisations; some extracts are given in **Appendix 2**.

To begin with, daily services were held in a pole-and-dagga thatched hut at Kasomo; baptisms and confessions were held in two similar huts, and all the surrendered charms and fetishes were stored in another. All these huts were in a reed-fenced enclosure known as *Itempele* (temple), which also contained a separate hut where Lenshina was said to have her mystic communion with God and pronounce His words to her flock; only those who were baptised could enter this inner sanctum. In 1958 an enormous church, or cathedral, was built in burnt brick at Kasomo and thereafter the village was called *Sione* (Zion). A crowd of 5,000 attended the opening. The building's dimensions were 140' x 42', significantly a foot longer and wider than the largest local church at Ilondola Catholic Mission – 'Lumpa' meaning 'surpass'. By 1959 the Church's estimated membership was at least 100,000;

in Chinsali District alone it had sixty churches and a membership of over 35,000 – about 80-90% of the adult population.

By any standards the Lumpa Church was, from 1955, proving to be an extremely lucrative business for its founder and organisers. With around 300 attending church services at Kasomo, even a modest collection of one penny per head mounted up; more was charged for the thousands who came for baptisms and confessions. In addition, Lenshina received gifts in kind, which were placed in two storerooms. She had no expenses, since all labour was given freely. Lenshina and Petros toured the country, fund-raising, baptising and preaching. In August 1957 they were able to buy a Bedford 5-ton truck and, in February 1958, she bought a second truck on hire-purchase terms.

The influence of Petros over Lenshina was undoubtedly considerable. Since 1953 he was the real power behind the scenes, controlling the movement's finances and directing its ritual policy while she remained the spiritual figurehead. Despite having misappropriated Lumpa church funds in 1956 and being jailed for proposing violence in a public assembly, he was back as a deacon and main organiser in 1958.

I have hinted that there appeared to be an anti-European element to Lenshina's teaching, although this was mostly directed at the missionaries who, of course, were the Europeans most frequently seen travelling through the villages. The African National Congress was quick to take advantage of the nationalist aspect of the movement, and in 1955 its Chairman, Harry Nkumbula gave it his blessing, describing Lenshina as an "African spiritual leader of an African National Church." From 1955 until early 1957 there remained strong links between the movement and Congress, largely through two of Lenshina's closest adherents: Sandy Rain Mulenga, who was known to hold (and express) strongly anti-European views; and Robert Kaunda, an ardent Congress supporter and (a matter of later embarrassment) Kenneth Kaunda's brother. By late 1956 Congress propaganda was being put across in the Lumpa churches. Lenshina herself declared that the Government was attempting to destroy two African organisations – her church, and ANC which was "trying to deliver the country from the hands of the Europeans."

Later, as I have already said, Kaunda and the more active nationalists broke away from Nkumbula's ANC and formed their own Zambia ANC which later became UNIP, and boycotted the 1959 elections. Virtually all adults in Chinsali District joined ZANC which, like Nkumbula's ANC before it, strongly supported the Lumpa Church. Sadly too, children were now being discouraged from going to school, since most schools were obviously run by the "wicked" missionaries. But, in the following year, the nationalists by more overt acts of arson and disturbance overstepped the mark with Lenshina, and this must have been about the time when she tried to move her Church away from extremist politics.

What about Lenshina's relations with the Chiefs and N/As? Initially most of them welcomed the formation of the movement and several joined themselves in the early years. To withhold support would have been difficult in the face of its wide popularity. Although Paramount Chief Chitimukulu once summoned Lenshina to his *musumba* and told her to be careful, little control over her activities was considered necessary at that stage. But as the movement reached its height, it became evident to the Chinsali Chiefs that Lenshina could command more support and respect than they could. This fact was then exploited by her and her deacons, who began to show increasingly less respect to the Chiefs' traditional authority.

Another brush with authority was Lenshina's refusal in 1959 to register the Church under the provisions of the Societies Act. There was much correspondence between DCs of neighbouring Districts, the Registrar of Societies and even a solicitor in Broken Hill (now Kabwe) to persuade her to do so; apart from the legal obligation, they all recognised that the organisation of the Lumpa Church was a shambles, and that some control over its most extreme elements was not only necessary, but would protect Lenshina herself

In 1961 there was the period of *cha-cha-cha* and widespread disturbances across the Northern Province. It would appear that Lenshina now tried to distance the Lumpa Church from the nationalists' campaign, and that she herself preached against involvement by her followers in politics. But, as the 1962 elections came nearer and UNIP increased its pressure to gain as many adherents as possible, many people, either from genuine political

Chinsali, 1953-64: Lumpa Church Background

motives or from UNIP intimidation, left the Church to join the party. With the elections resulting in a UNIP-ANC coalition, the Lumpa Church followers felt increasingly isolated; they thought they could no longer trust the Government to be impartial as it was now being run by the Church's political enemies. Soon there were instances in Chinsali District of aggression and retaliation: Lumpa followers ostentatiously burnt their UNIP party cards, and in return some UNIP militants burnt down a few Lumpa churches.

In Mporokoso during the 1962-64 years we heard nothing about the Lumpa movement. My own assessment of this period, made with hindsight in 1965, included the view that, while I was quite satisfied in my mind that the Lumpa Church had started as a sincere sect under Lenshina, it had deteriorated (as the late Paramount Chief Chitimukulu had forecast) because of infiltration by political groups in 1957-59. In 1961 these political elements left the Church when Alice made some attempt to purge it, and as they joined UNIP reaction against the Church set in. This antagonism by converts to UNIP was very strong (just as nobody condemns smoking so strongly as an ex-smoker!). I could point out that if at one time 90% of the population of Chinsali belonged to the Lumpa Church, that figure must have included many if not most of the local politicians active in Chinsali in 1964-65. In 1963 UNIP followers throughout the Province were demanding party cards and intimidating those who did not possess them. While Lenshina probably encouraged her followers to burn their UNIP cards, this was obviously intended as an insult to UNIP, but in 1965 I did not regard it as having been a misdemeanour in law.

In spite of an agreement signed by the UNIP Regional Secretary and Alice Lenshina in August 1963 as a result of discussions to find means for peaceful relationships between the two organisations, Lumpa followers continued to complain of intimidation by UNIP followers, and towards the end of that year gathered themselves into seventeen new settlements in Chinsali District alone, where they intended to live on their own in isolation from Government activities and the rest of the community. While the Lumpas claimed these moves were for their own greater safety, so that they could practise their religion without interference, among UNIP followers this separatism itself created suspicion and fear as to the Lumpas' motives. These new settlements were founded without the approval of the Chiefs and were at once termed illegal. The legal position was, however, by no means any longer clear, since the orders regarding village movement, which were passed by the Chiefs in 1959, could have been invalidated when the recognition of Chiefs as N/As was revoked in November 1963, and the new Rural District Council had not as yet re-enacted orders of this nature. Be that as it may, the new settlements existed and were considered threats to security.

Following various minor incidents which occurred over Christmas 1963, Dr Kaunda (then Minister of Local Government) attended discussions between UNIP and Lumpa local leaders, at which it was agreed that the Lumpa followers should be persuaded to return to their old registered villages. Eleven 'peace teams', consisting of Lumpa Church deacons and UNIP Rural Councillors, toured the District in January 1964, and twenty two public meetings were addressed jointly by Mr Robert Makasa (the newly elected UNIP Member of the Legislative Assembly), the then DC and representatives of both sides. These tours undoubtedly contributed to the restoration of peace after the Christmas incidents, but the basic antipathy between the two groups remained. There were no signs of the Lumpa followers returning to their old villages; instead they consolidated their huts and gardens in the new settlements and were clearly determined to stay. At this stage, significantly, there was found to be no decrease in school attendance as had been expected; this suggested that, with the split between UNIP and the Lumpa Church, the latter's discouragement of sending children to school was no longer effective.

For the first five months of 1964 there was a period of uneasy truce, of mutual suspicion and fear, and of grotesque rumours. The Lumpa followers stockaded their villages to prevent further interference. The degree of tension that existed was exemplified in the causes of the first serious incident which occurred on 26th June 1964. A young Lumpa boy was cuffed by his UNIP uncle for not attending school and alleged he had been beaten up. His village of Kameko in Chief Mubanga's area promptly descended on the UNIP man's village and ransacked it. The Police arrived and arrested fifteen men, but for lack of transport had to leave five under guard at Chief Mubanga's village. These five were then forcibly released by the Kameko villagers. On returning to Kameko the Police were attacked by 150 men armed with spears and had to open fire in order to effect their withdrawal.

This unfortunate clash brought to a head all the suspicions and tensions which had been simmering beneath the surface since the beginning of the year. Dr Kaunda, now Prime Minister, flew to Chinsali on 13th July and informed Alice Lenshina and her deacons of Government's decision that all Lumpa 'illegal' settlements were to be vacated within one week and the inhabitants were to return to their original villages.

6. CHINSALI, 1964-65: THE LUMPA CONFLICT

This was the point at which I came onto the scene. The Prime Minister had given the Lumpa followers a deadline of just **one week**, from **13th July!** Later that same day I was told to transfer with immediate effect to Chinsali, to help ensure that his instructions were implemented. Just twelve hours notice! Why me? Having been in Mporokoso for two years I knew I was due for a move but my DC, Angus Macdonald, hinted that the PC's choice of me for the task was more because of my supposed fluency in ciBemba – that would be the medium in which I should be expected to use whatever persuasive powers I had to get the Lumpa villagers to move; my comment at the end of Chapter 3 anticipates this.

In fact we had some local leave arranged: dental appointments on the Copperbelt, and visits to old friends in Lusaka (the Musakanyas and Lavenders) lined up; these would all have to wait. And I was due to take my obligatory Law exam the next week; that, too, was put aside for these exigencies of the service, and in the end I never sat the exam.

As with the 1914 predictions for World War 1 of "all over by Christmas", I was told this would merely be a short secondment for perhaps a fortnight, three weeks at the most! We should just be prepared to camp in an empty house. So, on the morning of 14th July we set off from Mporokoso in a landrover – just Wendy, Alastair and James – for the six hour, 400 kilometres, drive to Chinsali. I knew nothing of the past events in Chinsali and had barely heard of the Lumpa Church, so I could be said to have arrived with an open mind, or just a blank one.

Shortly before my arrival, at least six of the total sixteen platoons of the country's Mobile Police had been sent to Chinsali and were camped in tents on what had until then been the Boma's golf-course. They had been regularly patrolling the District and especially visiting the many Lumpa villages.

Arriving in Chinsali on 14th July, I reported to the DC, and that evening he put me in the picture. We were at that stage the only two PA officers, an LDA having just gone on leave – never to return. I spent most of the following day, apart from a brief visit to Sione, hearing the Police views. I was told that the Prime Minister had given instructions on 13th July to the Lenshina elders that their followers must return by Sunday 19th July to the old villages where they had been registered, and that Government would assist them with transport and food (where necessary) to effect this move. My task was to implement this move, by persuading the Lenshina followers to accept the Prime Minister's orders, by arranging with them when and where they wanted transport or food, by liaising with their old villages to which they were to go, by opening up and running as a transit camp the emergency prison at Chinsali, and by liaising with the Police and Special Branch on the reactions of all sections of the community. It seemed an enormous task to accomplish in a week, but I had no questions to ask and immediately started organising the logistics pertinent to the operations.

My first week was certainly busy, as I was out on tour every day by landrover and then walking to the villages. It was a good way to get to know the geography of the District in a short time. I visited nearly all the Lenshina villages that week, accompanied by one or two D/Ms and on some occasions by two sections of a Police Mobile Unit platoon. A Police Officer was always present when his forces were represented.

I spent an average of two-and-a-half hours in each village, trying every argument I could think of to persuade the people to move, and arguing with their objections. Before proceeding to villages I always checked recent police patrol reports regarding the attitude they had encountered there. In most of these reports the villagers' attitude had been recorded as "hostile, truculent, uncooperative, etc." I suspected that if these were true reflections of the villagers' attitudes, it merely indicated that the Police were regarded with suspicion and quite natural dislike, as they always went armed, or that they had not won the villagers' confidence by speaking in their language. In my written report of 20th July to the DC on my visits over that first week, I recorded such phrases as "reception friendly and fairly interested", "reaction friendly but adamant", "reception very friendly." At no time did I feel the slightest uneasiness, nor could I perceive any tension on the part of the villagers. They were willing to argue with me, and they appeared to have all the arguments on their side except the main one – that this was a Prime Minister's order they were being told to obey. There was obviously a genuine fear of reprisals from UNIP if they returned to their villages, and most of them wanted some show of good faith by UNIP before they would indicate any willingness to move.

The main objections to a move I gathered from these first visits to the villages were: "We are all being classed as troublesome, when it was Kameko that started it." "Our freedom to live where we want to is being abused." "We cannot live with people who drink and smoke and who will persecute us for not doing the same." "We are to be moved like cattle, when it was UNIP or Government" (the two were seldom differentiated) "who moved us originally and burnt our houses and churches." "What guarantee have we of freedom of worship when living side by side with UNIP?" "It is UNIP's or Government's responsibility to rebuild our houses first, then we'll move." "The harvesting of our gardens will be very difficult – it is not the right time of year to move." "It is the cold weather. We cannot move in one day. We'll need somewhere to stay while rebuilding houses in the place we're to go to."

In my report to the DC I also said that the Lenshina followers were definitely playing a waiting game from which, as the law stood, they had little or nothing to lose. My conclusions, at that stage, were as follows:

It must be accepted that the P.M.'s policy (right or wrong) is to be followed by us. We have so far failed to implement it. The alternatives now stand:
(a) Strong Arm. To remove by force, not necessarily by bullets. We have no legal backing for this at all, and the Attorney General's views must be borne in mind.
(b) Compromise. Build houses for them first, thus removing their main objection. Government thereby loses face, as it is bound to do anyway. Government may however stipulate exactly where it wants to build the new houses which (if it thinks fit) need not be at the old sites but e.g. on the roads or easily accessible for constant patrol.
(c) Surrender. Leave them where they are. Contrary to P.M.'s instructions, and therefore a complete reversal of policy and dangerous.
(d) Give them more time.

At the time I could see no sense in what we were doing, but I had my orders and had to carry on.

It was fairly clear from my first week that my views differed from those of the DC. True, I was completely new to the situation, but he had only been in Chinsali for four months. He always wore long grey flannels with braces, whereas all the rest of us on bush stations normally wore shorts except on formal occasions; he looked as if he should be in a city office, and I couldn't imagine him on a bicycle. I thought he was more sympathetic towards the UNIP viewpoint than impartial. In discussions with me he would walk up and down his office, theorising and philosophising and throwing out rhetorical questions to me. In his eyes, it seemed, I was the one to do the running around, the daily tours to villages, and liaison with Police Officers who weren't quite his 'class'. I used to report to him most evenings on the results of my almost daily tours around parts of the District – strangely, I do not recall more than once being invited into his house for a beer or cup of tea on those occasions, so I had to give my stories at the doorstep. However, he was later in the firing line (literally) at Sione and acquitted himself there better than I had expected.

As I have indicated above, I had visited most of the Lumpa villages without a Police presence, and I was anxious to do so regularly in future, unarmed and just with a messenger. This very soon became my practice. I had a splendid S/D/M, Julius (I cannot remember his surname now), who not only was an ex-askari with a good row of medal ribbons but could also drive; so I could send him off on a short errand while I carried on talking in a village until he collected me. He came with me (poor chap) almost every day; if it was not a good policy to monopolise him in this way, at least we built up a great relationship of mutual trust – which at times was essential to get us through unharmed.

I thought the Lumpa villages were all **very** impressive (at least, those in Chinsali District; John Hudson was not as impressed by many in Isoka District, but they might not have been so well-established). Their appearance was exemplary; just what we in the PA had thought, on tour, every village should aspire to. All the houses were built in neat rows, their grain bins likewise, and their *fimbusu* (pit latrines) were also in rows behind their houses

Chinsali, 1964-65: The Lumpa Conflict

and nicely thatched. Most of them had defensive stockades, which were off-putting, but they, too, were neatly built. It made me sad that we were forcing them to leave such excellent places to return to old villages where the rest of the inhabitants did not show such domestic pride.

It was a mentally, as well as physically exhausting time. After the usual greetings in a village, I would sit on the *cipuna* (stool) offered, identify a deacon or headman, and then start trying to persuade them. It was as well that I knew my Bible, as they would so often throw out biblical quotations to justify their stance and I had to think of another biblical sentence (in ciBemba) for a counter-argument. But if I couldn't persuade them to agree to a move, at least the arguing was friendly and done with humour; I was enjoying myself at this stage.

The deadline of 19th July came and went. The tension rose. The Prime Minister, Kaunda, was away in Cairo when the deadline passed, and nobody in Lusaka knew what the next stage should be. The Permanent Secretary, Len Bean, directed that patrolling and constant visits should continue during the next week as before, and in the circumstances this was the only possible decision. If we had stopped patrolling suddenly, this would have created tension. However, local politicians began spreading the word: "the Prime Minister has said you must move by the 19th **or else!**", and that dire retribution would befall the Lenshina villages after the deadline. Soon it was being said: "the next time our UNIP Mobile Police come to visit your village they will come to kill you." I myself experienced the reaction to these threats on 22nd and 23rd July when visiting villages. There was no sense of aggressiveness towards **me**, but an atmosphere of uncertainty. Entering one village I was immediately asked: "Where are the Police? Are they hiding behind the trees preparing to kill us?" and in another village: "We know you are all right, but if we see the Police we know they will be coming to kill us." Fear was now leading to stubbornness, and they were now less willing to consider moving. On later reflection I realised that, in response to UNIP's propagandist threats, they were preparing themselves mentally for a fight which they had every reason to consider inevitable. Others suggested that the villagers had orders from Lenshina herself at this stage to remain where they were; I did not support this view, although I could not disprove it; rather, my impression was that any orders from Sione were obeyed or disregarded according to the feelings of each individual village and its deacon.

There then followed, as night follows day, the first two conflicts. On 24th July, a routine Mobile Unit patrol was ambushed as its leaders entered the Lumpa village of Chapaula – Inspector Smith and Constable Chanda were speared to death and the platoon withdrew under cover of fire. The next day the DC, supported by Police reinforcements led by John Bird (Assistant Commissioner of Police), attempted to reason with the villagers and to persuade them to lay down their arms. They started firing, the Police fired back, and the village had to be taken by force and destroyed; fourteen Lenshina supporters were killed and fifteen wounded in this incident – including women, who seemed to have a complete disregard for the effectiveness of bullets and urged their men to resist throughout the operation.

While the Police patrol went to Chapaula on 24th July, I went to two large Lumpa villages in the south, accompanied by just the faithful S/D/M Julius. In my absence, news of the Chapaula deaths flew back to the Boma in the form of *"Bwana mutali* has been killed" (the tall officer). James, our cook heard this - and, at first naturally assumed it referred to me! Fortunately, he used his common sense and made some more enquiries before giving the news to Wendy, who was now six months pregnant. Inspector Smith, whom I'd met a few times, was the same height as me (6'5") and also blond, and apart from his uniform we could have been mistaken for each other. All the same, it was a relief to Wendy when I returned home that evening, unscathed.

I had no hesitation in saying that the Police action on 25th July in dealing with Chapaula village was essential and justified, and seemed to have been carried out with the minimum of force required. It is necessary in a civilised society to take direct action when officers of the legitimate forces of law and order have been killed. On the other hand, I was surprised after the event that Inspector Smith had not anticipated the possibility of an ambush and taken appropriate precautions, in view of the UNIP propaganda. Mr Chapoloko, UNIP's Regional Secretary, later told me: "We did tell these people that if they disobeyed the Prime Minister we should have to deal with them." In my mind I held him primarily responsible for spreading the UNIP propaganda of "our Police will come to kill you."

Chinsali, 1964-65: The Lumpa Conflict

Events then moved swiftly. Word of this incident spread at once and many Lumpa followers took to the bush and made reprisal raids on neighbouring villages, burning and killing. When they heard about Chapaula – that the "UNIP" Police had, as promised, attacked a village – it was a natural psychological reaction for them to assume that "Government" had declared war on them. In a state of war both sides may be expected to attack; in this case the Police had, in their eyes, attacked first. Three Lumpa villages (and only three to my knowledge) therefore made counter-attacks with midnight raids on neighbouring villages and isolated farms. It should be pointed out that, had these attacks been properly organised, the death toll of UNIP followers would have been tremendous. But, from the evidence I received at Musanya, Mundu and elsewhere, the form of the attacks was to shout a warning from a distance and to waste time burning the huts as they entered a village, thereby (in most cases) giving the villagers time to escape.

It was on a journey to investigate such attacks that on 28th July another Mobile Unit patrol was ambushed twelve kilometres east of Mulanga Mission in the far south-east of the District; Inspector Jordan was killed and Inspector Hopwood wounded. I well remember Inspector Jordan, with his large droopy moustache; in fact, I had been having drinks with him and other Police officers in their camp the evening before his ambush. I also knew well the little rickety bridge across a dambo where the ambush had taken place, as it was on the way to the large Lumpa village of Chilanga which I visited often. The villagers had attacked the patrol with spears as it was crossing the bridge; Jordan got out of his landrover to fire at them, but his Sten gun jammed (as they sometimes did) and he was overrun; the rest of his patrol fled. The spot was immediately given the name of 'Jordan's Drift'.

The week following the deaths of the two Police Officers was a period particularly fraught with tension and danger. Police patrols continued to visit all the Lumpa villages, and I did also. But, as should be clear from preceding pages, I was keen to go without an armed escort and with a semblance of peace. My main aims in that week were to persuade the Lumpa followers to calm down and refrain from further reprisals, to dispel their belief that the police were "UNIP police" (as the local UNIP leaders continued to claim), to assure them that the door was still open for them to get assistance in moving from their present villages if they would do so in accordance with the P.M.'s orders, and to gather intelligence.

Accompanied only by the ever-trusting and trustworthy S/D/M Julius, I managed to get around most of the District in four days, though concentrating on the especially troublesome areas of the north-east, and beyond Mulanga Mission in the extreme south-east. On paths leading to Lumpa villages we would often find their sentries, looking for early signs of any police patrol. Our first shouts to them would usually be: "Awe mukwai, lekeni mafumo, poneni mfuti panshi, tuleisa mu mutende" ("No, drop your spears, put your guns down, we come in peace"), and usually we could then move into discussions with them. They certainly felt it was a war situation and in any future conflict they must strike first; moving from their villages was quite out of the question, and all my attempts at persuasion were now useless.

Chilanga was a very large and well laid-out Lenshina village, east of Mulanga Mission and near the Muchinga Escarpment. On my first visit, I remember, the reception was quite friendly and we had the longest argument based on biblical texts. I now chose to visit it a couple more times, since its inhabitants were almost certainly those responsible for both Inspector Jordan's ambush and some of the reprisal raids in the surrounding area. In two small villages beyond 'Jordan's Drift', places he had been on his way to investigate, we came across the grisly evidence of these raids: houses burnt, some with the residents trapped inside; corpses, now bloated and smelling, lying nearby where they had been overtaken in their flight and speared (we saw similar sights in the north-east too). We experienced other incidents and sights around Chilanga which remain vivid in my memory, sometimes haunting me to this day. Julius agreed with my decision that because of their nature they should remain *fya munkama fyesu* (our secrets) forever and unreported; if they were known by any higher authority this would lead to questions or formal inquiries and certainly to a ban on my movements without police escort – preventing my future peaceful contact with the Lumpas. They remain our secret, for which I feel no shame. We knew we were taking **calculated** risks, but we survived.

On 27th July, a couple of days after the Chapaula incidents, the DC and A/Com. Bird flew to Lusaka where they made first-hand reports to the

Chinsali, 1964-65: The Lumpa Conflict

Governor and the Central Security Council, attended by Prime Minister Kaunda. The decisions were quickly taken to employ the Army and, if possible, to capture and detain Alice Lenshina. Almost overnight the security forces in Chinsali were increased to two regular battalions of the Northern Rhodesia Regiment (NRR) and to no less than ten platoons of the Police Mobile Unit, and a Provincial Operations Committee (ProvOps) was set up. Security responsibilities were effectively handed over from the Police to the Army, but the DC rightly insisted that the Army should always be accompanied by a DO. It was at this stage that Peter Moss, one of my Cambridge Course colleagues, was seconded at very short notice from Mkushi to serve as an additional DO. Here, with his permission (indeed, at his request) I am able to quote some of his comments on events, on later pages.

In my subsequent Submission to the Commission of Inquiry I recall that I was scathingly critical of the Police.

> The Mobile Police did not come out of the disturbances with a very good record. Their first engagement at Chapaula completely shattered their morale. Thereafter they could only be used for safe road patrols and as a supporting arm to the Army, until conditions were safe for the latter's withdrawal. It is easy to criticize after the event, but I would make the following comments:
> (a) In the two serious Police engagements, the incidents of Insp. Smith and Insp. Jordan, the Mobile Unit chose a formation and method of advance which no soldier would have contemplated. I would not say they deserved what they got, but they failed to adapt themselves to the warlike nature of the situation. I was all for taking calculated risks, but one cannot do things in half measure: either you go with more than adequate numbers of armed policemen in uniform, ready for anything that might happen, or you go (as I did) unarmed, in very small numbers and plain clothes, and your approach is clearly one of peace. They fell between the two stools badly.
> (b) Training in the Mobile Unit since 1961 appears to have been directed to making the MU constable an ordinary policeman, rather than

leaving him as just a tough baton-swinger. The Unit is still very competent at dealing with Copperbelt riots, where little more than stones are thrown and the crowd is expected to disperse at a baton-charge. Here we were dealing with spears and guns, and with people who were in great fear. The MU dressed and acted in a para-military fashion without having the para-military training to deal with a situation of this nature. These remarks are not levelled at any individual, and it is to the credit of the officers in charge that the mistakes were seen and acted upon early and the MU given a secondary role.

With the Army's two infantry battalions now camped beside Chinsali airstrip, the decision was taken on high that all the Lenshina villages must be taken by a show of force, and that Alice must be arrested. The critical stage had been reached. It was planned that the two worst obstacles, Sione and Chilanga villages, should be cleared on 30th July. While the DC and Peter Moss went with 1 NRR (1st Battalion, Northern Rhodesia Regiment) to Sione, I went with 2 NRR to Chilanga.

At Sione the DC and the Army used the same procedure as at Chapaula when recovering Inspector Smith's body. As soon as the troops were in position in front of the village, the DC spoke through a megaphone saying if the villagers wanted peace they had to obey Government instructions, and those named in a list he read out should first come forward to surrender. He repeated this message four times. The reaction was an attack on the security forces, who were compelled to open fire. After some thirty minutes the firing stopped and the DC again appealed to the Lenshina supporters to surrender and lay down their arms, but this was ignored. According to all reports, the Lumpas' attacked the Army again with "frenzied fanaticism." Bows and arrows, spears and firearms were used, the villagers (men, women and children) fighting with complete disregard for their lives in the face of automatic weapons. The Battalion Commander then gave the order to advance into the village. The greatest resistance was met in and around the cathedral and, sadly, shooting had to take place even in its interior. Official reports said 59 men and 7 women were killed; 110 were wounded, given first aid and then transported to Chinsali Hospital. Alice herself managed to escape.

All accounts I heard of the Sione operations praised 1 NRR for their control of fire. The Commanding Officer, standing next to the DC, would observe Lenshina supporters taking aim with their weapons and just direct the fire of a sergeant or marksman by saying, e.g. "Man on the left anthill, take him out; man aiming, right-hand group, take him out." But when several men, and women, just charged there was no alternative but to stop them in their tracks. We had heard stories that Alice had promised her followers that their faith made them immune to bullets, that she had handed out "passports to heaven," and that some villagers were seen to be standing on top of anthills and "waving their arms in order to fly to heaven;" such stories about fanatics might not be implausible, but exaggerations did abound.

Peter Moss was personally present at Sione, and his comments are as follows.

*For the record I helped out the DC in Chinsali in three episodes over a period of four weeks: the first included being close to him throughout the Sione assault, when I actively participated not only as a learner/spectator but also in some of the operation itself. I was present when the army rocketed a house near the "cathedral" where they thought Lenshina was hiding. I walked down a line of **at least** 100 corpses which the Police had laid out in the sun that were loaded onto trucks and buried in mass graves near Chinsali Boma; I think the number usually mentioned may refer to the single mass rush of about 100 villagers straight onto the first burst of machine guns when the words "...be careful, they are using bows and arrows..." were recorded and not to the other shootings that took place elsewhere in the village.*

I left Chinsali on 29th July with 2 NRR and we camped overnight at Mulanga Mission, ready to move to Chilanga early on the 30th. Chilanga was the largest Lenshina village in the District, having over 300 huts. It was responsible for the deaths which Insp. Jordan's patrol had gone to investigate and the subsequent ambush. As a result, locally morale was low and over

From Northern Rhodesia to Zambia

300 UNIP villagers were gathered at Mulanga Mission for protection when we arrived; over the next week this number increased until, at its maximum, I estimated it to be 3,200 or so.

I then led 2 NRR to Chilanga. The village seemed deserted, the residents having fled into the bush at our approach, but I was convinced until we actually entered it that a trap was prepared. I therefore spoke at some length through a megaphone outside the stockade to the imagined crowd inside. We burned the village, as directed, and took all food and cooking utensils which we could carry (two lorry-loads) back to Mulanga for the refugees there – and to deny these means of sustenance to the Lumpas in the bush.

I was, of course, relieved that we had not needed to fire at Chilanga, but frustrated that we had not first surrounded the whole village, and had therefore allowed all the villagers to escape into the bush. The Commanding Officer, understandably, would not risk sending his men far into the bush in very extended lines for such a manoeuvre. While I spoke through my megaphone, he stood beside me with his pistol at the ready. Carrying out the orders we had been given to burn the village left me numb and angry – to be party to the total destruction of the finest African village I had ever seen, or would see! In useless consolation I took the enormous village drum as a personal memento, and we still have it.

As a footnote to the Chilanga operation I should add that, a few weeks later, I saw an article about it in *Drum Magazine*, published in South Africa, with a photograph of me chatting with some Company Commander at our Mulanga camp the previous evening about the welfare needs of the refugees there. I hadn't noticed any photographer or journalist there! I wish I'd kept that photo. It was only in this year (2014) that I managed to get a copy of the article and its photographs sent to me from Johannesburg. The text of the article in the September 1964 issue of *Drum*, entitled 'High Priestess of Death', seems to me clearly to have been written at second-hand by somebody who was not present; the exaggerations and the collation of every rumoured story about the Lumpas are examples of sensational journalism at its worst. But the action pictures are all of the Chilanga scene; those of Sione were probably taken the following day, after the attack on it. I suspect they were taken by an army officer and subsequently passed on to *Drum*.

Chinsali, 1964-65: The Lumpa Conflict

Some might regard the method of these operations as bizarre. The Army was, quite correctly, "acting in support of the civil authorities"; so, at Chilanga, I was the lone civil authority (plus Julius) with a whole battalion supporting us!

Returning from Chilanga to Chinsali on that fateful 30th July, I immediately had to check how effective my preparations were for handling the 411 Sione survivors in 'the cage', the emergency prison. Food and blankets were distributed at once, and we had on hand hospital staff who inspected individuals for injuries and checked the hygiene issues (toilets). The abiding memory is of the ghostly silence: faith in their immunity from bullets had been shattered, perhaps their faith in Alice Lenshina had been dented, certainly they found it incredible to be in their present plight. This silence continued for days and was especially eerie as the majority of those in 'the cage' were women and children; they were in a severe state of shock.

For the next week both Peter Moss and I, alternately, led 2 NRR to all the other fourteen Lenshina villages and systematically destroyed them. As I was by this time the only officer who knew all these villages, having visited fifteen in my first fortnight, I also spent some time on reconnaissance flights with Army officers to indicate their targets. On these occasions I found no village occupied and there was no fight.

But Peter had a very different experience at one village, on 4th August, leaving him feeling very sore if not traumatized, as he recounted.

> *I was dealing with a huge massively stockaded settlement somewhere not far from Shimwaule. I was with Col. Courtney Welch's 2 NRR battalion and 10 or 12 platoons of the Mobile Police. I had only spoken a few words in ciBemba through the blue regulation loudhailer when the occupants opened fire with muzzle-loaders and bows and arrows, at which point I made the announcement that the Civil Authority had to hand over its responsibility to the military. All military hell then broke loose! Many villagers, old and young, were killed and wounded.*

> *After Sione and this action, in which I thought the Army and its new recruits had behaved badly, I recall having a long discussion with the DC in which I said that we did not seem to be approaching the problem in the humanitarian PA way which we all understood. I felt by then that we were probably going too far and had lost our way by carrying out these military coercions. He sent me to see my own PC, Mark Heathcote in Broken Hill, who told me bluntly either to resign or to go back and follow orders.... I followed orders and, working as far as I could within the system, managed to save some lives.... I took a few days' break in Mkushi where I was DO at that time. This led to my return to Chinsali where I was with the Army again, firstly to handle an operation against a Lumpa stockaded village on the Luangwa escarpment which turned out to be deserted (all except for a scared cow elephant!).*

The next phase was the hunt for Alice Lenshina herself. On 1st August, two days after Sione and Chilanga, Senior Chief Nkula reported that two Lumpa deacons had come to tell him that Alice wished to surrender and was at Mwanachanda village. On 2nd August I therefore set out with two companies of 2 NRR for Mwanachanda in the marsh area near the Chambeshi river, well west of Lubwa and Sione. I repeatedly asked ProvOps if I might go alone on this mission, but my request was refused. My view was, and still is, that if Alice wished to surrender she would want to do so to the Chief or to the administration who knew her, not to armed forces who had just fought at Sione; she would be lacking confidence, and would need to be approached openly and with no semblance of trickery. This exercise failed, as I knew it would, because she took fright on hearing the approach of 300 soldiers through the trees, and much time was wasted in trying to get clear information as to her whereabouts from the villagers there. In fact, she left the village not five minutes before we entered it, dropping her handbag on the path. (An earlier exercise had taken us to search for her at Shiachepa in the west of Chief Nkweto's area, but the rumour prompting it had probably been false.) A third exercise was mounted a few days later when it was rumoured that she was in hiding in caves north of Mbesuma Ranch, and once again I walked miles with the Army to no effect. However,

Chinsali, 1964-65: The Lumpa Conflict

she did surrender in Kasama District on 11th August, to special Government envoys sent to contact her. She was given a guarantee regarding her own safety but warned that she might have to face criminal charges; she was flown to Ndola, and two days later she and her family were placed in detention in Mumbwa. If she had surrendered, to me or the Chief or the Army, on 2nd August it would probably have made little difference to ProvOps's plans for the destruction of Lumpa villages.

Meanwhile, the scenes of fighting and massacres had shifted to Lundazi District, on the other side of the great Luangwa Valley. Here horrific atrocities were committed. But, as I was not there, that episode is not relevant to my main story other than in the immediate transfer of 1 NRR from Chinsali to Lundazi and in the recognition that there must be no more retaliation. Again, John Hudson has summarised it concisely in his *A Time to Mourn*, as follows:

> As soon as news of the attack on Sione reached the Lumpas in Lundazi District, they decided to retaliate. At 02.00 on 3rd August a large group from the Chipoma settlement attacked Lundazi township, rampaging through it for several hours. About a dozen people were killed.... The Police Station and its armoury of weapons were captured. Unusually, both the DC and the DO were away from Lundazi that night.... Two companies of 1 NRR were airlifted from Chinsali, arriving at 10.30. Two other attacks by Lumpas were made, in the north of the District, and Chief Chikwa was killed.... On 4th August an operation was mounted against Chipoma.... The action lasted 40 minutes. 81 Lumpas were killed, 43 were wounded and 11 captured....

> On 5th August the Prime Minister, Kaunda, visited Lundazi and instructed UNIP officials not to retaliate against the Lumpas around Chief Chikwa's.... here was concern about possible UNIP reprisals against isolated Lumpa settlements, of which the most vulnerable was Paishuko.... ProvOps had planned to send a 1 NRR patrol on 6th August to disband Paishuko and to take the people into protective custody pending resettlement. The mission was postponed*. On the next day Paishuko was overrun by UNIP supporters; every man,

woman and child was massacred. When the Army reached it on 9th August it was a smouldering ruin. Examining the corpses littered around the soldiers were horrified to find that most of the victims had been subjected to the most appalling tortures and methods of killing.... Experienced Army officers, used to the sights of battle casualties, were deeply shocked and angered by what they saw, and the horrors had a disastrous effect on their morale later.

Why, the rest of us asked, was the mission to disband Paishuko postponed and on whose orders? Rightly or wrongly, we could only assume that it was a political decision taken at a high level, to allow the local UNIP factions to get in first with their own methods of retaliation and revenge. It certainly produced the most horrific and shameful atrocities of the whole Lumpa conflict.

From 14th July to at least 11th August I had been travelling around Chinsali District virtually every day. It was still winter and very cold, and I often got up at 03.00 a.m. for dawn patrols. Apart from my frequent visits to the fifteen Lenshina settlements which I have mentioned, I, of, course called on the Chiefs and on the Mission stations, as much for intelligence gathering as for checking on their feelings of safety and giving them assurances.

There were six Chiefs. The four Bemba Chiefs' areas, from north to south, were: Mubanga, Nkweto, Senior Chief Nkula, Mukwikile; the two Bisa Chiefs lived on either side of Mukwikile's area, Kabanda in the south-west of the District and Chibesakunda in the south-east between the Great North Road and the Muchinga Escarpment. Before and during the conflicts the Chiefs had faced dilemmas. As I have said, at one time some 90% of their people were Lenshina supporters; then their traditional authority had been flouted by the establishment of the separate Lumpa villages; and UNIP's nationalist campaign had left them unsure how much that authority would be further eroded after Independence. In theory they might wish to be paternally fair to all their people, even to 'errant children', but impartiality became impossible. The most troublesome areas for me and the ones I most frequently toured were those of Chiefs Nkweto and Chibesakunda (where lay Chilanga), and perhaps it was no coincidence that I found the attitude of those two Chiefs most actively pro-UNIP. Looking back now, I cannot recall the faces of any of those Chiefs; my relationships with them were superficial, and totally different from the close personal dealings I had had with the Mporokoso Chiefs.

There were four Missions. Lubwa, where Fergus Macpherson had listened to Alice's story, was just eight kilometres down the road from Chinsali. Rev. Bill McKenzie was now Minister in charge here, assisted by Rev. Paul Mushindo. Bill was perceived by some in the hierarchies of the United Church and the PA as having strong pro-UNIP rather than impartial views; I did not share that opinion. I wish we had had the time to visit Bill and his wife Margaret and their young family more often, even if (at this stage) I was far too busy to go to church at Lubwa on a Sunday. In the north, close to Chief Mubanga's, was the White Fathers' Catholic Mission of Mulilansolo. It had a beautiful church building, approached along a lovely avenue of trees. I remember having breakfast here, so on at least one occasion I stayed the night. The Fathers were certainly most kind and hospitable, and once gave me a pot of home-made honey to take back to Wendy. In the opposite direction, beyond Senior Chief Nkula's, was Ilondola Mission; I did not get to know the White Fathers here so well. Ilondola's church building was one of the largest in Northern Province, and had been used by Alice Lenshina as the template for her great church at Sione (see p.78). The third White Fathers' Mission was at Mulanga, where I often called on my way to Chilanga and other places near the Escarpment; I well remember the Dutch Father Hugo Hinfelaar in charge there. Likewise I used to call on Sir Stewart Gore-Browne at his Shiwa Ngandu estate in Chief Mukwikile's area, to check on his safety and to hear his appraisal of the situation. I shall return to him in the next chapter.

I must also mention conversations I had with Robert Kaunda, the Prime Minister's elder brother, who lived with their aged mother, Helen on the family farm just outside Chinsali. Robert had been a prominent member of the Lumpa Church and one of Alice's closest lieutenants, until he fell from grace for alleged misappropriation of funds. Clearly his Lumpa connections were now an added embarrassment for the Prime Minister. He seemed an intelligent man. I remember him telling me in 1953: "I was there when she died; I felt her body, and it was quite cold and stiff like any other corpse, and she wasn't breathing; but the next day she opened her eyes and woke up." Just as Fergus must have done with Alice herself eleven years previously, I listened to Robert's story without making a judgement but fully convinced of the sincerity of his beliefs. Whatever medical/scientific explanation there might be for Alice's 'death' seemed irrelevant in the face of the human capacity for belief.

The Lumpa Church had been banned. Various problems remained over the whole of August and September after the obvious military actions had been finished. On the administrative side there was the problem of rehabilitation, both of ex-Lumpa followers and UNIP followers who had lost their homes. On the security side it was necessary to account for all ex-Lumpas who had deserted their villages at the time of the Army attacks and had taken to the bush. Obviously both problems went hand-in-hand.

I was glad when, in early August, a Social Welfare Officer arrived to take over from me the day-to-day responsibility for 'the cage', as that released me for my daily tours of the District. And in mid-August a Rehabilitation Committee was set up. This was composed of the DC, myself, the Social Welfare Officer, the Manager of Schools, an Agricultural Assistant, and several local politicians; some Chiefs and Missionaries were invited to attend from time to time. The Committee's task was to co-ordinate the various aspects of rehabilitation: deciding who should, or should not, be allowed to return from 'the cage' to their villages; the issue of clothing, food and blankets to those in 'the cage' or others in the District who had suffered; the building of new and larger villages where ex-Lumpas and UNIP followers were to live side by side in harmony; persuading UNIP refugees at Chinsali and Mulanga to go back to their own villages or join these new settlements; starting agricultural projects such as tobacco, as well as subsistence farming, at the new settlements and elsewhere; re-integrating children into the schools; checking on medical supplies and outbreaks of diseases, as well as public health in 'the cage' and in the new settlements; and informing the security forces of any ex-Lumpa gangs known to be still at large. I was not keen on how this Committee operated, as it allowed the government side to be dominated by local politicians, who were not exactly impartial in their opinions or activities. But the DC thought that by bringing them in "we would give them a job to do and they would feel important." As a rule, meetings lasted three hours, with only half-an-hour devoted to the important administrative points, while the rest of the time was spent in criticisms of the security forces for their alleged inactivity, and in bitter accusations against ex-Lumpa followers.

Meanwhile, the next stage for me in early August involved combing the bush and trying to get people back into their villages to resume normal life. Peter Moss came back to Chinsali for a spell to help me with this; but I do not recall the DC doing much touring around the District in these exercises, after the traumatic events he had personally experienced at Sione.

Peter and I, separately, went on several flights in small aircraft in early August to drop leaflets over most of the bush areas where we suspected ex-Lumpas to be hiding, urging them to return at once to their old registered villages. They were asked to put white circles on the ground to indicate to the next air patrols that they were willing to surrender. Sometimes I was flown in a helicopter from which, leaning precariously out of the side, I would shout through my loudhailer to a group we had spotted. I estimated that over 4,000 ex-Lumpas returned to their villages during August, largely as a result of our leaflet airdrop. During tours around villages in that period I certainly came across many who had returned, somehow, at some time without having passed through 'the cage'. My problem was to see that they integrated well into their old society. They were still afraid at this stage, and not warmly received by UNIP followers. When I visited a village they remained in two distinct groups, both to greet and to listen to me. This I half expected and it did not unduly worry me; I felt time would heal this antipathy.

The area around Mulanga Mission was a special problem. I estimated that we had to account for some 850 ex-Lumpas, all from Chilanga, and these were still at large on the borders of Chinsali and Lundazi Districts. I spent eleven days, from 16th to 26th August, combing the bush in that region with the Army, trying to locate the groups who were in hiding, and dealing with the 3,200 UNIP refugees at the Mission. With the help of the Red Cross we were able to give generous medical and welfare assistance to these refugees, but the greatest problems there were the control of disease and the fact that the refugee camp was a hotbed of rumour. In the vast no-man's-land which had been created by the exodus of both sections of the community it was impossible for the Army to operate effectively without local guides and villagers' reports. At the same time we could not allow UNIP villagers to return to their homes unless, and until, we were satisfied that the surrounding areas were clear. Above all I had to make sure that no revenge was taken and that the Mulanga refugees did not take the law into their own hands. It was clear to me that the stage had been reached when, theoretically, neither side was on the offensive but both sides were in fear of each other. A delicate and gradual process of 'forgive and forget' had to be started, although its success could not be immediate; hatred would only prolong the tension. The atmosphere in the bush and in Mulanga was not easy to describe, but I felt we would succeed better if we could play it our way and were not being constantly thwarted by directives from ProvOps Kasama or MainOps Lusaka, who were not on the spot.

Peter Moss recalls one episode of this time as follows.

That period was followed by a long stint by land and air hunting down the large Lumpa group that had been responsible for the murders of Inspectors Smith and Jordan. You and I, Mick, were present when some Lumpas finally gave themselves up to Chief Chibesakunda. I actually was at the Chief's house (covered by a single machine gun manned by a Lieutenant whose name I have forgotten, that had been placed with a line of fire over our heads!) and helped Chibesakunda speak to the assembled crowd when his voice totally failed him! I think that John Wyatt, the DO from Mpika, also helped you and me with the prisoners.

Confidence was just being built up nicely and the crowd at Mulanga were well under control when Simon Kapwepwe, then Minister of Home Affairs, visited Mulanga by helicopter on 14th August and made a speech, the substance of which was written down by Father Hugo Hinfelaar who was present.

That he has come himself to hear and see for himself all the sufferings of the people. Now you are together, driven by a common enemy. The food is bad, sleeping is bad, there are many diseases. Who has inflicted all this on you? Lenshina and her adherents. You should not take these people any longer as real men. People who eat their dung, washed their bodies with urine, fill themselves with germs, change into a devil, even five times worse than a devil, they actually would be wild beasts. When you find a wild beast eating in your gardens or trying to kill you, what would you do? You would come together and start to follow it till it is dead. And even after its death you would break its legs, spit on it and roast it above the fire till nothing is left anymore. Our Government is determined to destroy this wild beast. We should follow it to the end, and everybody is called to collaborate with the army and police till the country is all right again.

When Kapwepwe made his speech at Mulanga I was in the area but not close. He had just finished speaking when I arrived, and I was grateful to Father Hinfelaar for his written record of the gist. I still have the original of this, signed by him. The spirit and manner of Mr Kapwepwe's speech destroyed all the work we, and the Missionaries, had so far accomplished, renewed the hatred and encouraged violence. Various headmen, with whom I spoke immediately afterwards, said Mr Kapwepwe had told them to go and hunt the Lumpas and to kill any that they saw. The situation was clearly explosive, and I went straight back to Chinsali where I handed a copy of the above with my comments to my Permanent Secretary, Len Bean (whom I had met only once before on our arrival in Northern Rhodesia: see Chapter 1). It was a lucky coincidence that I found him at Chinsali on a surprise visit by air from Lusaka, and was able to update him in person. I was, however, embarrassed when Col. Welsh of 2 NRR, who was there too, told Mr Bean that "Mick is the only person around here who knows what's going on." I was told that Len Bean, on his return to Lusaka, handed a copy of Father Hinfelaar's note on Kapwepwe's speech directly to the Prime Minister. Kaunda visited Mulanga himself four days later and gave the people the exact opposite message, and thus brought the situation back to where we wanted it.

I was led to believe that Kaunda and Kapwepwe had a great row when the former heard about the latter's speech; this may not have been true, since John Hudson's account (below) of a security meeting on 17th August which he attended as DC Isoka makes it clear that Kapwepwe on that date was still pressing for a 'final solution'.

It is quite clear that Kaunda himself did everything possible to persuade the opposing sides to resolve their differences peacefully. He travelled to Chinsali personally on two occasions for negotiations. He returned a third time on 17th August to preside over a meeting attended by top Provincial security and administrative officers plus Chiefs and party officials. The agenda was mainly on what should be done with ex-Lumpas who had surrendered or been captured. Many of the party officials and Chiefs had lost relatives. Led by Simon Kapwepwe, whose aunt had been killed, they made impassioned demands that the army should be ordered to exterminate all the Lumpas as dangerous vermin. Kapwepwe was almost hysterical with rage and grief.

Kaunda listened to these tirades for some time, saying little. As the denunciations continued, the security and administrative officers became more and more uneasy, fearing the P.M. would feel obliged for political reasons to accept the demands for a 'final solution' on Nazi lines. Kaunda rose to sum up. He acknowledged that many wanted revenge and to see the culprits eliminated. He paused, and the meeting waited for his order to this effect. Instead he ruled that the Lumpas were "to be forgiven and accepted back into their villages." There was an amazed silence; the security and administrative officers sighed with relief.

This was a humane solution and the right decision. But it took great courage for Kaunda to make this decision in the face of extreme pressure from his own party to do otherwise. A deeply religious man, he may have felt that as he had sown the wind of political agitation he must now, through the restoration of harmony, quell the whirlwind of violence he had reaped. He might also have realized that the security forces, after their Paishuko experiences, might have refused to obey orders to exterminate all Lumpas.

Chinsali, 1964-65: The Lumpa Conflict

Throughout this period I had an excellent and jolly collaboration with the 2nd NRR of the Army. The Commanding Officer, Lt Col. Courtney Welsh, with a bristling moustache, had been seconded from 3rd Bn The Parachute Regiment, with which (by strange coincidence) I had done my parachute training at the end of National Service. We got on extremely well, both seeing the funny side of his battalion being in support of this young DO who was the sole civil authority. We had already destroyed Chilanga and some six other Lumpa villages; we'd had three expeditions together chasing Alice Lenshina. Once, when Julius brought in a woman who said she'd seen Alice, the Colonel said, "Tell her, if she can really take us to Alice, I shall personally give her all the satisfaction she could desire"; his meaning was tactfully lost in the translation! Again, after our fruitless tramp around the Mbesuma hills he said with some asperity: "So what do we do now, Mick? Wait for your next hot tip?" But in fact he forgave me for asking him to act on reports I'd received which turned out to be idle rumours.

After the hunt for Alice, we were both under orders from Lusaka and ProvOps Kasama to comb the bush for ex-Lumpas, and both knew this was crazy. The loyal Julius came with me for this mad march north from Mulanga along the Muchinga Escarpment, the battalion spread out in extended line and inevitably broadcasting its position to any ex-Lumpas who might have been there. We camped en route for ten nights; I was fed and accommodated with the officers and Julius in the sergeants' mess. I used to wear my Black Watch balmoral bonnet, so that I could return the salutes of soldiers without their embarrassment. One day we had a visitor (how on earth did he find us?); he was in army uniform and he too was wearing a Black Watch balmoral! "Good heavens, what are **you** doing here?" we both said at the same time. It was Colonel Bruce Hamilton, who was now the British Army Liaison Officer with the Northern Rhodesia forces. He reminded me that the last time we had met was in Berlin when I had rugby-tackled him (then a Major) into the rose bushes after a Mess Night; what an incident to remember! He didn't stay long and I never met him again.

I felt strongly that, by now, our use of the Army in support of our immediate tasks was misguided. In late August I therefore asked, through the DC, for the immediate withdrawal of troops from the area east of Mulanga Mission, so that I could continue alone to scour the bush for ex-Lumpa groups.

Col. Welsh and 2 NRR left Chinsali, according to my records, on 31st August. At the time, many criticisms were made against the Army by other PA officers, and by local politicians who seemed to expect more dramatic and decisive military actions. In my later submission to the Commission of Inquiry I wrote:

I have the following comments to make regarding the Army.
a) The Army had to be called in, on 28th July. For reasons given elsewhere, the Police were no longer able to deal with the changed situation. Everybody thought there was a state of war, and some might have taken the law into their own hands if the proper tools had not been used.
b) Once committed, the Army was acting in support of the civil authorities, and I would stress most strongly that in my experience the individual officers cooperated with the administration perfectly and respected the fluid code of "support of civil powers" in a remarkable way. There was never the feeling that the Army was in charge and therefore that things might get out of hand or that local assessments might get overlooked.
c) It has been said that the Army used too powerful weapons. In the engagements at Sione and elsewhere, where I was not present, the control over the troops was reportedly superb. When every opportunity has been given to allow the situation to be handled as a civil power action, then the military takes over, and one does not do things in half measure in a battle. Innocent people were killed (to my mind they were all basically innocent anyway, if misguided), but an army commander would be justified in using automatic weapons if otherwise his own troops would be killed unnecessarily. In brief, one's philosophy must change as soon as one is committed to battle. There was never any unnecessary slaughter that I know of.
d) The Army cannot be used effectively unless it has clear objectives and clear tasks to perform. It was therefore greatly frustrated at times by being asked to do tasks for which it was not suited – tasks which by its nature it could not do by compromise or diplomacy. For instance, searching hundreds of square miles of bush for gangs in hiding was all very well, but the commander knew

he was not expected to kill anybody he found unless they attacked him first. It therefore developed into the farcical situation of a battalion guarding a DO on his travels and embarrassing him by their presence.

e) 2 NRR was comprised of virtually untrained troops, many having served for only four months before the troubles started. The soldiers were thus not confident in themselves at first, and the operations were taken very slowly and carefully to build up their morale. Control was excellent and they were soon a very competent fighting force.

f) The Territorial Army units were useless, and even in their role of guarding Missions their lack of discipline and unruly behaviour was embarrassing.

g) The Army was withdrawn at the right time – perhaps a little late, certainly not earlier than was safe. Units returned on request when a specific role offered itself.

Some time in late August Peter Moss also left, returning to Mkushi. Recently he has made the following comments on his Chinsali experiences, agreeing with me that it was difficult to approve of what went on in dealing with the situation.

It was a deeply traumatic experience for me. I had become a proficient Bemba/Lala speaker and like the rest of us was working at grassroots level – so much so that I believed strongly that we were getting it VERY wrong. I had gone to see Mark Heathcote because I thought that there should be a high level change in approach to the problem. I was profoundly shocked by the whole thing. But I do not think the DC could have handled the situation any better than he did. Soon after those tiring events I returned disillusioned to Mkushi. After the Lumpa campaign I vowed never to have anything to do with the Provincial Administration again, and thus began my move in 1965 to the Department of Game and Tsetse Control.

That broadly concludes my account of the period of conflict itself, based mainly on the record of my written submission to the Commission of Inquiry. What views did I have in those days of the fundamental causes, and could it all have been avoided?

a) Could the Lenshina movement have been contained within the Mission's influence if Fergus Macpherson had returned to Lubwa after his leave? The possibility is a nice thought, but probably over-optimistic.
b) Political infiltration and pressure on Lenshina followers from those of the nationalist movement, from 1961 onwards, was clearly the major factor. It was this which persuaded the Lumpas to move off and establish their own villages, thus causing suspicion and perhaps fear among the rest of the population and leading to the tit-for-tat of burning churches and UNIP cards. I felt that the local politicians bore the greatest share of blame, since they encouraged or even advocated the campaign of hatred from the start.
c) Although the Lumpa villages were arguably illegal and flouted the Chiefs' authority, would tension and conflict have been avoided if they had been allowed to exist – if, for example, they had thereafter been segregated, ignored and ostracized, with no access to local markets or other normal amenities? With Independence gained, might thousands not then have left the Lumpa Church and sought a return to normal Zambian villages?
d) Was Kaunda's ultimatum of only a week's deadline to move the correct and realistic way forward in July? I did not blame him, but thought he was wrongly advised. Should not the political leaders have done much more to prohibit the local propaganda of "the next time our Police come, they'll come to kill you"?
e) Were the Mobile Police and, later, the Army used in the best way? And did the Police themselves increase the likelihood of the initial conflicts by their methods of patrolling?

The DC admitted that he had only accepted his posting to Chinsali with reluctance after some officers senior to him had refused it. While I was critical of his attitude, I agree entirely with Peter Moss's recent statement that he probably "did the best that could be done under very trying circumstances." One of the biggest problems that we all faced, and the DC more than anyone, was the lamentable means of **communication** with which we had to cope and which led to insuperable coordination difficulties – especially in contrast with the speed and efficacy of the bush telegraph which was working all too well!

7. CHINSALI: THE AFTERMATH, INDEPENDENCE AND FAMILY LIFE

While I was out and about so much during those first months in Chinsali, from late July to September 1964, I confess that I saw little of Wendy and young Alastair. I am sure I told her only the barest minimum of what I was up to, to reduce as far as possible any worries on her part; I'm also sure that I had full confidence in her being able to make the most of her situation 'back at the ranch'. So what was she doing? How had she been coping?

It was a strange time as there was no longer any rhythm to the days. Wendy never knew when, or if, I would be at home or requiring a meal, but had always to be ready with a packet of sandwiches or other sustenance for me to take on trips – or with breakfast in the dark before dawn. In his turn, James had to put into practice skills like bread making that he had learnt by watching Black at work. Supplies in the store in Chinsali, across the stream in those days and quite a walk away, eventually dwindled to a choice of 'tinned corned beef' or 'corned beef in tins', and with James Wendy had to devise as many ways as they could of making it seem palatable. The shelves in the store didn't really fill up again during our whole time there. The one advantage Chinsali had over Mporokoso was a Boma herd, which meant fresh milk was always available.

At the same time, Wendy had to create and maintain a pattern for young Alastair's life in an unfamiliar place, and to keep calm and cheerful. Without toys, they found plenty of bugs and seeds as they pottered about to keep themselves amused. From the ridge on which we lived she could look out over the endless bush only knowing that I was out there somewhere. She remembers the number of people who greeted her as she walked around the township, and this made her glad that we were still in Bemba-land. Above all, she always remained immensely grateful to James for his quick actions to find out which *Bwana Mutali* was the one in the news buzzing round the Boma when Inspector Smith was killed; this made her realise that he was looking after her.

Soon after the battle at Sione, there was a general alarm arising from a report that some fifty Lumpas armed with spears were approaching the

Boma offices; these were on the top of the ridge, and by now were surrounded by barbed wire. As the only two European women, the DC's wife and Wendy with Alastair on her back were "rounded up by Police bristling with ferocious weapons" and escorted from their houses to the Boma for their safety. In the event, there was no danger: the approaching group were just a dozen Lumpa women coming to surrender.

From the start of the conflicts Chinsali was visited by numerous officials. Reading John Hudson's *A Time to Mourn* now, we discover that one visitor was Dr Hope Trant, who had delivered Alastair in Kasama Hospital. Her Isoka and Chinsali episodes are vividly described in her autobiography, *Not Merrion Square*, and add much to one's appreciation of what the medical and surgical teams were quietly dealing with at that period – and it is amazing to read what, at her advanced age, she was able to contribute in medical help. Dr Trant, once based in Mwenzo Hospital near the Tanzania border, was now living and working in Isoka. On 24th July she came from Isoka to Chinsali on a routine trip, and was immediately involved in dealing with the injured from the Chapaula incident of that day (the murder of Insp. Smith) and its aftermath; many of those wounded in the police action there on 25th July were taken to Isoka where she dealt with them, along with a surgical team which had been flown up from Lusaka. She came to Chinsali Hospital a few more times to help Dr Derek Braithwaite, the PMO, after the Sione battle. The DC's wife was most hospitable to them and to other visitors at this time, but what a pity that she didn't tell Wendy of such visitors and involve her in entertaining them – especially Hope Trant!

We were often able to entertain to lunch the crews of NRAF (Air Force) planes on their visits, although we could not put them up overnight. Wendy got to know most of them and they became good friends. On 12th August they flew her and Alastair to Lusaka where she stayed for two nights with Jim and Margaret Lavender, colleagues from the Cambridge Course, a necessary trip to purchase supplies for our second baby expected in October.

Wendy still remembers vividly passing the Lumpa women and children who were sitting in 'the cage', unnaturally silent and looking hopeless, as she walked down the side of the wire on her way to the bottom of the hill. She was conscious that a strong feeling of fear still existed in the District, as well as desperate poverty; hundreds of people had lost their homes and possessions, their crops and their work. One day, in the early months, a man came to her door with a leopard skin to sell. She knew all the reasons why one should never buy such things as this would encourage poaching, but this was his prized possession. He didn't want to sell it, but was desperate for money. Normal rules could not be applied in Chinsali then, and she bought it for £2; it still reminds her today of the straits to which people can be brought so quickly.

It was in late August that the Rev. Colin Morris from Lusaka had led a team of Missionaries around the District, in the hope of bringing about reconciliation in the villages and perhaps bringing back to the United Church some of its former members. In my opinion this move by the Church, though laudable, was a failure because it came too early and because the Missionaries were not known personally to the local people they approached (Colin Morris, I later heard, did not even speak ciBemba). Much more success, and real lasting success, was achieved by the local Lubwa Minister, Paul Mushindo, who tackled the problem slowly and patiently.

By the end of August it was all too clear that we were required in Chinsali for the long haul. The optimistic secondment for "two weeks, three at the most" had now lasted for at least seven. My feelings at this stage, recorded in a letter to Wendy's parents, were: "We've been mucked about a lot – nobody's fault exactly – but we don't want to move again, so we'll make a go of Chinsali until the end of the tour." So in the first days of September we returned briefly to Mporokoso to pack and move on a permanent basis to Chinsali. We stayed with our last DC there, Angus McDonald, who arranged a superb farewell party for us. This included roast suckling pig, a fitting way of dealing with the last of the piglets we had inherited from Harry Schneeman. My own memory is blank on that; I must have been too mentally exhausted. The only thing I do remember is that, on leaving our familiar and beloved Mporokoso for this last time, we had not driven more than ten kilometres before I burst into uncontrollable tears – and I am not ashamed to admit it even today. Stopping overnight in Kasama, we were flown on the last stage to Chinsali. Arriving there, we recall with some regret that the DC's wife did not even offer us a cup of coffee, let alone lunch – how very different from the normal PA hospitality we had been used to!

At this stage we moved into a larger house next door, as there was little chance of a more senior DO being posted here; painters had started to re-decorate it while we were away, but didn't complete the job until the end of September. But at least we could unpack and have all our personal belongings around us. Black Mpundu's family would not allow him to come, but Daviness and her children were reunited with James. We took on Wilson, as a cook replacement for Black.

Meanwhile, I was very busy for much of September trying to locate ex-Lumpas in the bush and visiting many villages to monitor progress on 'reconciliation.' I was still determined to get the surrender of those ex-Lumpas still at large, but the only way was to win their confidence. They had been afraid of the security forces and they might be afraid of me too. Accordingly I walked through the bush day after day, usually unarmed and accompanied only by my good S/D/M Julius and a couple of guides chosen from those ex-Lumpas who had already surrendered to me (there was just one occasion, when I was again near Chilanga, that I took the precaution of having a pistol hidden in my shorts in case I had to defend Julius and myself). I was still strongly of the opinion that things would not be normal in the villages unless they were made to look normal. The security forces had done their job of clearing areas of gangs as best they could; it was now up to the villagers to lead a normal life, moving freely to their gardens in the bush and visiting other villages. There were several instances, particularly in the neighbouring area of Chief Chibale in Lundazi District, where ex-Lumpas had returned to their proper villages in peace, but lived in a state of starvation through fear of approaching the authorities, while UNIP villagers feared them only because they didn't know what they were doing. The Police, on the reports they had received, were not keen to visit the villages in case there was a fight, and it was necessary for me to go myself with a Kapasu to show everybody that all fears and suspicions were groundless. If the local people would not make the effort to make normal contact, fear and tension would remain.

The DC was due to go on leave in mid-September, and we could barely wait with patience for him to go. The PC, Peter Clarke, and many of the older colonial civil servants were leaving at or before Independence. Who would succeed as DC Chinsali? We were told that the position had been offered to several officers of some seniority and experience and they had all declined this poisoned chalice. I found myself left in charge, as the man on the spot – or in the wrong place at the wrong time – and, after 'acting' for a couple of weeks, was eventually confirmed as District Commissioner as from 14th October 1964, at the tender age of 27. I did then comment, in a letter to my parents-in-law:

Meanwhile, I have no 2 i/c, am completely on my own in the administration, with only a couple of inexperienced clerical staff and of course D/Ms. All other executive officers have resigned or demanded transfers except two who are to be dismissed soon anyway. What a laugh! I'm certainly not bitter, but I'm physically and mentally completely exhausted, and feel I've done enough solid work and put my own life in danger enough to warrant a square deal. After all, it affects our family life which at this particular time should be so important, but that just has to take second place. What we need is some local leave, which is clearly impossible until somebody comes to join me, either senior or junior.

But as a letter confirming the telephoned news of my promotion did not reach me until early November we did not make the final move into the DC's house until then.

In September Wendy used to take Alastair every afternoon to the swimming pool, as it was so hot. This was a bright blue concrete pool, far superior to the earth pit at Mporokoso, across the other side of the golf course where the Mobile Police were still encamped, and it had a shallow section for small children where Alastair could cool down blissfully. It was obviously used by off-duty Police officers too.

The next major event on the family side was the birth of our second child, Ruth, in the Kasama Cottage Hospital on 6th October. Only ten days before that I had been hoping that Wendy could give birth in Chinsali Hospital so that I could be on hand; the change of plan may have been as much to avoid any possible complications (there being no qualified midwife in Chinsali) as a visit in September from Dr Trant, who would be in Kasama in October and "reserved" Wendy for her personal attention again. So I drove her and

From Northern Rhodesia to Zambia

Alastair in there on 1st October. Ruth was born at 06.05, weighing in at 7lbs 7 oz, coming with a face presentation but none the worse for it. Wendy required one and a half pints of blood so the Kasama option was justified.

I came back to Chinsali the next day, 7th October, with Alastair and somehow must have coped – presumably I was not so constantly out on tour that week. A later letter of mine to my mother-in-law said: "I had a glorious ten days with Alastair to myself, except that while I was at the office I had to hire a young lady to keep him amused. Wendy thought he had grown up a lot when she got back, but it was only that in her absence we had invented a few new tomboyish games to play. He's fun." After staying in Kasama for those ten days she was given a lift back home, with Ruth in her arms, in Derek Braithwaite's (PMO's) Cessna aircraft, which was a treat.

Scarcely had we adjusted our domestic life to this new and beautiful arrival than Independence was upon us, on 23rd/24th October. I arranged the main ceremony for midnight on 23rd in front of the Boma, with the D/Ms lined up on parade beside the flagpole. The D/M I'd instructed to play his bugle was fairly drunk by midnight, and his rendering of the Last Post as the Union Jack was hauled down was scarcely recognisable. The new Zambian flag was hoisted, and I had to lead the assembled spectators in singing the new National Anthem; I was surprised and disappointed that so few of the leading local politicians present seemed to know all the words, but Wendy and I sang with gusto. The fireworks display was rather a disaster; the man in charge of it dropped a lighted cigarette or match into the box of fireworks and most of them went off at once, with squibs darting all over the place. It could have been merely amusing; but 150 metres below our Boma terrace was 'the cage', and panic seized the ex-Lumpa inmates who thought the shooting had started again!

After the midnight flag raising ceremony, Independence Day itself was celebrated with school sports, tribal singing and dancing, a cinema show, and speeches by the Chiefs and the Rural Council Chairman. At ten smaller centres in the District celebrations also took place. There was a noticeable lack of overt enthusiasm during the celebrations and few signs that the real meaning of the country's Independence was understood by the majority of villagers. Several subsequent tours by party officials were needed to make the picture clearer.

Zambia's first Cabinet, 24 October 1964.

Ministers of State

Lewis Changufu
Defence

Aaron Milner
Cabinet & Civil Service

I should mention that all DCs had received secret instructions earlier in October to make sure that before Independence they burned all files held which were marked 'Secret' or 'Strictly Confidential', so that there were no later recriminations against the old colonial regime. This was exceedingly repugnant for me with my views on the value of historical evidence, and Wendy was absolutely furious, but orders were orders and I complied. But before burning them I painstakingly copied by hand all the main contents of the secret intelligence reports, and these made up the file I have now been able to draw on (see the beginning of Chapter 5)! I was, later, nervous at carrying these through a Customs inspection when we went on leave to the UK.

On the organisational side of my life a lot changed, either at once or over the next few months. The PA was now to be called the Provincial & District Government (P&DG); DCs were renamed District Secretaries; we already had a Magistrate, to my relief, but he soon had also to take over the supervision of the local customary courts; the Police were now, in theory, entirely responsible for law and order, and two of my D/Ms were transferred to them; the Prisons Department took over responsibility for the normal prison from me (but not 'the cage') and another seven D/Ms transferred to this, to carry on what they had been doing under me; the Ministry of Finance became responsible for the Boma accounts and my accounts clerk. But the largest burden taken off my shoulders in all these reorganisations was the supervisory responsibility for the new Rural Council, when a Local Government Officer was posted to Chinsali at the end of the year.

If some people were confused about the meaning of Independence because they still saw me, a European, in the Boma office, I went out of my way to let it be known that I was now an officer of the **Zambian** Civil Service

Mporokoso, 1962: Saturday afternoon tennis tea, with the Collingwoods and (right) DC Ian Macdonald

The Governor, Sir Evelyn Hone, inspects the D/Ms when opening Mporokoso's new Boma, May 1963

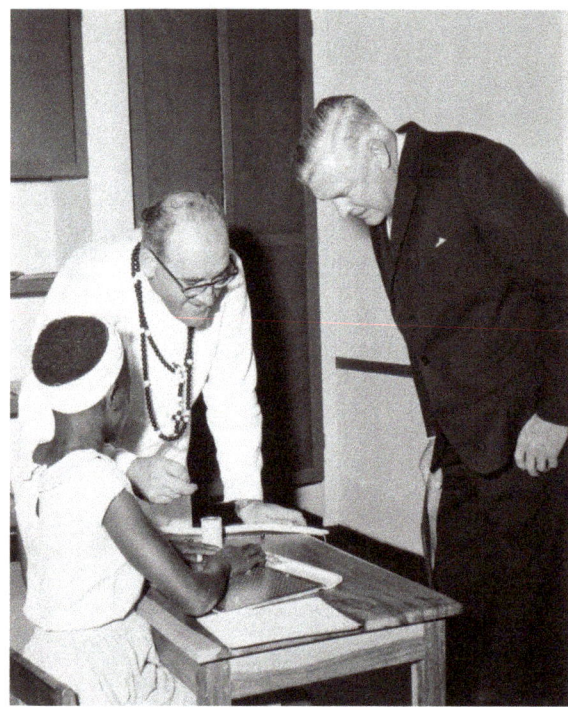

Father Carriere and the Governor with a girl reading braille, at the opening of Mporokoso Blind School, May 1963

Our last house in Mporokoso, built in 1904 and now a "national heritage building". (photo by Max Keyzar)

A typical village scene on tour, Mporokoso District 1963 (photo by Max Keyzar)

Mukupa Kaoma Women's Welfare

The Tabwa Native Court officials, 1962: Court Clerk, a Kapasu, Senior Chief Nsama, a Court member (Assessor)

Binnes Kaite and his scouts at their camp, Kapumo Falls, Mporokoso, 1963

Chiefs Mukupa Kaoma, Chitoshi and Shibwalya Kapila, 1962, on our way to the House of Chiefs' elections

Senior Chief Nsama and family outside their house, January 1964

Alan McGregor at the lip of the Lumangwe Falls, 1963.

Chishela Dambo, 1963; ferrying our bikes over the submerged road and bridges

A regular visitor to our chalet, Kasaba Bay

The interior of Sione "cathedral", 1.8.64; bloodstains still on the floor

Guarded by Col. Welsh as I issue an ultimatum outside Chilanga village, 30.7.64 (photo from NRR army archives)

Discussing the welfare of refugees with an army Company Commander at Mulanga Mission, 29.7.64. (photo from NRR army archives)

Some of the starving Lumpas I had brought into Chinsali hospital

With the Musakanyas in Lusaka, July 1965: Mubanga, Musonda, Flavia with Ruth, Valentine and Shula, Alastair and myself

The Kuomboka: the royal barges arriving at Namulunga, March 1967

Avid Orbit readers, Kitwe 1971 - and their teacher too!

Our children in the Kitwe garden, 1973: Eleanor, Ruth and Alastair

Wendy and myself in our Kitwe front garden, 1973

Kashiba pontoon on the Luapula, 2012: exporting ubwali for ubwalwa

The 2012 reunion at Lupungu village, Mporokoso: Wendy with James and Daviness and their family

Chinsali: The Aftermath, Independence and Family Life

working for the Government of Zambia. Yes, I found a DS's responsibilities were less than a former DC's. But because of the nature of Chinsali it was more difficult for me than other DSs to divorce myself entirely from responsibility for security matters, given the need for very close coordination between rehabilitation, famine relief, police activities and intelligence work. So I chaired the District Intelligence Group and sent off the weekly secret Intelligence Reports to the (now) Resident Secretary in Kasama (for lack of confidential staff Wendy had to type these for me). I may add that the new Resident Secretary, Bill Baker, seemed to have complete trust in me and never interfered with me – the old colonial adage of "trust the man on the spot"; I got on very well with him, never abused that trust, and reported to him regularly.

I have mentioned, above, the redeployment of many Messengers to the Prison Service and the Police. I now have little recollection of how this was achieved. But I hope that I interviewed each D/M individually and put the future options to him so that he had a choice. I do recall that, from the time I took over as DC/DS, I would often get the parade of D/Ms to 'stand easy' after the morning inspection, and would try to explain to them the strategy I was adopting with regard to 'reconciliation', so that they would understand how to behave when the Head Messenger or I sent them off to visit villages – usually on a fact-finding trip to assess the attitudes of villagers. They were very much my 'eyes and ears', supplementing any reports I received from the Police. I would also tell them where I was intending to go that day (or week) and why. These exchanges of information were of course meant to be confidential, and they usually remained so; but where we would be visiting did not need at this stage to be such a secret, to catch anyone by surprise, as it had previously been.

Then there was the office situation. I had just two clerical assistants. I don't remember anything about them, and obviously must have had much less of a personal relationship with them than I had had with those in Mporokoso. They were barely competent. But I was the only P&DG **officer** on the station for the next nine months. As will be clear from the following pages, I was still out on trips around the District most days, with the occasional night(s) away too. In retrospect, how on earth did I manage to cope with all the office paperwork, which would have continued to arise, when I was so infrequently at the Boma itself? I had not yet learnt to dictate and there was nobody who could take dictation. I certainly took a lot of incoming mail back with me to the house in the evenings and drafted longhand letters to be typed the next day. I must have managed, somehow.

In October I had been able to bring the Rehabilitation Committee to an end, parcelling the political responsibilities to the Rural Council and getting on myself with the administrative and security work with the officials concerned. These included (now) two Social Welfare Officers and three Community Development Assistants. We still had the 7-ton lorry donated to us by Oxfam in August, for the continuing distribution of food, blankets and second-hand clothing to those in most need as new homes were being built. Eight new settlements had by now been started in the District, taking advantage of the fresh desire to live in larger village units for development and a sense of security. Assistance in their construction and further development was given to most of these by boys of the Zambia Youth Service based at Mpandala near Shiwa Ngandu, by the Community Development Officers who established village committees and did so much to foster harmony and community spirit, and by Agricultural Assistants who planned and supervised the growing of Turkish tobacco. All these new settlements were composed of UNIP and ex-Lumpa followers, except in Chief Chibesakunda's area (around Mulanga Mission) where mutual antipathy was strongest. I estimated that altogether over 6,000 ex-Lumpas in the District and the nearby part of Lundazi District had been rendered homeless by the security operations, but that most of these returned to their old villages or these new settlements without trouble and indeed without the administration's knowledge. They represented the more moderate elements of the Lumpa Church and integrated themselves into their old community with relative ease. But over November and December I was constantly touring around the larger villages and particularly the new settlements to observe the progress in reconciliation – I knew it was an uphill battle, and could be lost if in a village some insults were carelessly thrown.

In early November a senior civil servant and ex-DC, Hugh Thompson, who had been appointed to a new post of Rehabilitation Officer, came up

Chinsali: The Aftermath, Independence and Family Life

from Lusaka and opened a camp at Kotito in Mbala District. He and I then liaised closely. Any ex-Lumpa in my 'cage' who, as agreed by the Chief's representative and a local UNIP official, was still unfit for a return to his/her home village or a new settlement, was transported off to Kotito. Here they were 'de-indoctrinated', I suppose along the lines of de-Nazification in British prisoner-of-war camps, until they were deemed to have become acceptable to a Chinsali community. It was a mammoth logistical task and one demanding detailed records of those sent, those returned, those left in my 'cage', those left in Kotito, etc. It took up a lot of my time, but it was necessary. My Annual Report for 1964 said: "1,700 ex-Lumpas passed through the cage between August and 20 November when it was closed; of these, 750 were transferred to Kotito."

In early December Hugh Thompson informed me that Kaunda, now President, would be coming to Chinsali with most of his family, partly to spend Christmas with his mother and partly to review the progress on rehabilitation. As the DC's house was the largest in Chinsali, Wendy and I "would have the honour" (as he kept emphasizing) of accommodating the Kaunda family! We had to rush around making lots of domestic arrangements. We could cope with the President, Mama Kaunda, their youngest four children and a nanny in our house; an ADC and the two older Kaunda boys were to sleep, I think, in Bill the Magistrate's house next door; and two empty houses were kitted out for Hugh Thompson and several Cabinet Ministers who would be coming too. State House cooks would travel up by car from Lusaka, to help Wendy and Wilson, our cook.

Come the day, all went very smoothly. As the President's plane landed at the airstrip, I had the amusing task of lining up the reception party; as DS and therefore the President's local representative, I took precedence; I asked the various Cabinet and other Ministers to sort themselves out into whatever order of precedence they mutually agreed, and they entered into the humour of the occasion. Back at the house, I had the Head Messenger ready to raise the Presidential Standard up the flag-pole as we arrived. We had James dressed immaculately in a white uniform, like the State House staff, to do the serving of pre-dinner drinks and the waiting at lunch. Kaunda was of course teetotal; I wondered whether others present took soft drinks from choice or out of sycophancy. The Presidential party then went off for the afternoon to visit his old mother, Helen, at her Shambalakale farm.

In the evening we somehow hosted a sundowner for at least seventy persons – all the civil servants and local politicians plus numerous visitors from Lusaka; I am not sure how we managed that. The evening meal was a great success, although I cannot recall all the details. There were eight present: the Kaundas, the Resident Minister from Kasama (Robert Makasa), Hugh Thompson, two Cabinet Ministers and ourselves. Wendy got Wilson to bake a loaf in the shape of a fish eagle, the national emblem, laid it on a mini-flag of Zambia, and invited Kaunda to cut off the eagle's head. The atmosphere was very relaxed: conversation flowed easily, even when it inevitably touched on the present problems of reconciliation and rehabilitation. I do remember being encouraged to tell the President exactly how I saw the situation – even if I displeased Robert Makasa with my criticisms of local UNIP officials. I described how long the process was in a village to build up mutual tolerance between UNIP and ex-Lumpa residents, and how one drunken insult from a UNIP member could destroy all the good work and bring us back to square one. He understood entirely and sympathised.

After the meal we all trooped off to Lubwa Mission where we watched, in a field and under rain, a film called "Zambia 1964" put on by the Information Department; a couple of hundred Lubwa folk were present too. At some stage, either that evening or in the morning, Wendy had a great time with Mama Kaunda. Her twin babies, one of whom (Cheswa) we should meet again in 2012, were about ten months old while Ruth was two months, and the two mothers merrily swopped babies to cuddle and quieten them. The President and his family went off in the morning to Lubwa, to visit the grave of his father David (one of the early Missionaries there, who had come from Livingstonia in Malawi), before flying off. Yes, it had been a great honour for us to entertain the Kaundas. Whenever we met again in my later career, the President used to greet me cheerily with, "Ah, Mr Bond, my tallest civil servant."

On Christmas Eve we had a tea-party for twelve local children, including two young McKenzies from Lubwa. The Christmas meal itself started in the evening at 21.30: avocado pear, turkey, chicken, sausages, roast potatoes, cabbage, peas, pudding, mince pies, wine, coffee, liqueurs and chocolates –

Chinsali: The Aftermath, Independence and Family Life

how Wendy got hold of all these items I cannot imagine. We had Bill and Margaret McKenzie, a Mission accountant, Bill our bachelor Magistrate, and the sole remaining Mobile Police Officer. We were amazed to hear the McKenzies say that this was the first time they had been invited to a meal at the Boma; whether that was because the previous DC had been a Catholic or because of Bill's assumed support for UNIP, we didn't know. It was also, he said, the first time they'd really had a Christmas feast with all the trimmings; he had been brought up under a strict Presbyterian regime, where Christmas was regarded as just an ordinary day, certainly without any material or culinary delights – his father had "religiously gone to work on Christmas day" – whereas Hogmanay was thoroughly celebrated in every way.

The year 1964 ended in relative peace. The rains helped to dampen any thoughts of mutual aggression, and 'reconciliation' was beginning to work, hesitantly, in the villages. The Rev. Paul Mushindo told me that by the year end he had re-baptised into his Church some 750 ex-Lumpas, through patient work, and the Catholic Churches at Ilondola and Mulilansolo had been getting similar successes.

I have previously mentioned Rural Councils. These were established in every District in November 1963. Because of all the tensions and conflicts, it is fair to say that the Chinsali Rural Council never really got off the ground during 1964 until about October in time for Independence. Although all its members apart from Chiefs were local UNIP officials, even towards the end of the year they found it hard to get 100% backing from their electorate to raise revenue from local sources or to accomplish much needed self-help schemes such as emergency school development. But on the brighter side, after I had handed over to them responsibility for the political aspects of rehabilitation they showed a notable ability to make sensible if unpopular decisions for what they saw as the general good of the community. Chiefs at first found it difficult to accept their position in a Rural Council dominated by local politicians, but very soon they were taking a genuine interest in the Council's activities, if not taking much active part in the debates. Chief Mukwikile, the best educated, was the exception. He was elected Vice-Chairman, and in the Council Chamber was able to identify himself with the views of other members, without losing the dignity of being a Chief – he was just referred to as "Councillor Mukwikile."

From Northern Rhodesia to Zambia

I felt very privileged to get to know Sir Stewart Gore-Browne at Shiwa Ngandu. As I have said earlier, I used to call on him during the period of the conflict, to check on his safety and to gather any intelligence reports he had. Shiwa was in Chief Mukwikile's area, but not far from Mulanga Mission. When I became DS I used to visit him about once a month for brief chats; I was only able to take Wendy with me on one such occasion, to meet the 'old man.' The background of this incredible person, his development of Shiwa Estate over the decades and his long contribution to the nationalist pre-Independence movement are essential parts of Zambia's history and have been recorded in so many books. I shall not repeat his story here.

The library was where I usually had an 'audience' with the great man. He too knew, of course, of his friend Kaunda's initial order that Lenshina's followers should move from their new villages in a week, and of his subsequent decision for a policy of reconciliation, of 'forgive and forget.' He was always interested to hear from me my accounts of the difficulties in effecting this policy; but all he could do was to sympathise and give me encouragement to continue my efforts. On one occasion, probably in December 1964, he summoned me in connection with his citizenship. He had of course opted for Zambian citizenship at Independence, but in those days this involved renouncing any other citizenship, in his case British. In that library I as a magistrate had to witness and countersign his renunciation and, when it came to it, he had an understandable struggle with his emotions. I believe the provision for dual citizenship is now to be included in the revised constitution. I remember too that the Grand Old Man showed me with great pride two old photographs hanging in a passageway: one was of King Edward VII, personally signed by King George V as a gift from him for Sir Stewart's part in the lying-in-state of his father; the other was of himself in full cavalry uniform on guard at one corner of the late King's catafalque.

There was a story, which Sir Stewart may have told me himself, that in the pre-Independence days when he was entertaining many of the nationalist leaders he had walked into his sitting-room to find Justin Chimba and Princess Nakatindi (two future Cabinet Ministers) "in flagrante delicto" on the settee; I could only imagine his monocle jumping out at this. The balcony which led off this room gave a glorious view not only of the beautiful gardens

Chinsali: The Aftermath, Independence and Family Life

and the avenues of blue gum trees but of the lake in the distance, too. And on the flagpole was the old man's personal standard – *a chipembele* (rhino) on a green background.

After the stresses of 1964, 1965 was a much quieter year. We socialised and went out as a family. Bill the Magistrate, the only other European on the station, kindly took us off to the nearby Chipoma Falls and on one occasion to the famous Kalambo Falls near Mbala (we had no car of our own, and I would certainly not use Government transport for family outings). There was a very pleasant District Education Officer and his wife, who lived in a house opposite the ex-golf course. Near them lived a new District Agricultural Officer, who had come from Lusaka and seemed quite worried by life on a bush station; joining him and his wife for a chat, we were amused as he tried to hit balls on what was left of the golf course while she followed, busily knitting as she walked.

Wendy has other recollections from late 1964 and 1965. There were usually a lot of children around our house who all played with Alastair and took him off with them to play; as we had observed with the Kaunda children, the older ones always looked after the smaller ones. She has very clear memories of seeing a D/M walking calmly towards her, far in the distance, with a golden blob round his knee level, bringing Alastair back home when he'd gone off to explore on his own. The little boys used to try their hardest to get the immature mangoes off the row of trees round the edge of the golf course by hurling sticks at them. Alastair could often be found down there under a tree, on his own, solemnly waving a tiny stick upwards – mimetic magic. Children would sit on the draining board in her kitchen area, singing in delightful harmony. And we had chickens and some muscovy ducks.

As the situation around the Boma became more settled, the ladies of the Chinsali Women's Welfare came to call on Wendy and invited her to join them. This delighted her: it was a big improvement, to see that they had got it going and were running it themselves. Esther Malama was the leading light, wife of my Mporokoso accounts clerk who had retired to Chinsali. To raise money they had a deal with a local man of means: they would go to one of his gardens in the bush and harvest his millet, for 1/- for each basket. They went off in a line with huge empty baskets and knives, teapots on heads, and babies on backs, including Alastair. It was a long way, and the work was hard: they would cut off the heads of the millet with a twist of the wrist and it took a lot to fill a basket. It was probably not just tea or water in the tea pot as everyone was very cheerful throughout. Thus were the Welfare's funds earned!

Wendy negotiated some lessons in pot-making with a wonderful old lady – and had to sit beside her with a small piece of clay, copying all her moves. "*Ndi kafundisha? Mwa!* (Am I really a teacher?)", the old lady would say. It was fascinating to learn, even though the result was a considerable disappointment to pupil and teacher! The tools included a piece of cardboard, an old, chewed corn cob well singed, bits of gourd cut with zigzag edges, a pebble, some special leaves, chippings from a special tree and sticks for the fire. We still have the teacher's pot. One of Wendy's many local activities in 1965, when the general situation in Chinsali itself had returned to normal, was to run adult education classes in the township. These became quite popular. She even persuaded me to give a series of lessons in Elementary Mathematics – so I must have had some spare time. I don't enjoy teaching, as she does, and I don't think I was at all successful in this enterprise.

For the last months of 1964 it was still necessary to supply food to some 3,500 persons in the District and part of Lundazi District. These included destitutes, refugees, those still detained in 'the cage', and all others whose grain-bins and foodstocks had been destroyed during the conflicts. The cost of this famine relief to the Government was c.£8,000 to the end of 1964. The famine position was aggravated by the fact that insufficient subsistence farming had been done in many areas owing to the general state of tension and villagers' fear of going to cultivate their gardens in the bush. I reckoned that in the early part of 1965 the situation would deteriorate further when the next harvest was due, as insufficient *citemene* (slash-and-burn) cutting had been done before the rains started, to provide everybody with crops.

The District was quiet and back to normal until 19th January 1965, when large numbers of ex-Lumpas decided to leave the District. Nearly all ex-Lumpas from the eastern border, including those in Chief Chibale's and some from Chief Nkweto's areas and totalling about 2,000, gathered into

Chinsali: The Aftermath, Independence and Family Life

one large group and migrated south-eastwards over the Muchinga Escarpment. For over a week they were not traced. Eventually many were found and came in to Chief Mukungule's Court in Mpika District, together with some from Chief Chikwa's area who had been living in the bush for six months since the Paishuko incident. We had located them by spotter aircraft and had dropped leaflets for four days running. Their condition was miserable, and many had to remain in hospital for some days to combat the effects of malnutrition and starvation. The Lundazi people were brought to Chinsali where I re-opened 'the cage'. The remainder went straight to Kotito Camp, and I fought hard to ensure that they did not return to Chinsali again for repatriation at that stage. Another 1,000 or so left the villages in Chief Mubanga's area in the north-west and were picked up near Malole in Kasama District; they also were sent to Kotito.

It was obvious that this migration was organised, and I had every reason to believe it was Alice Lenshina's sister, Nellie Mulenga, who started it. Why did they go, and where were they going? Some talked of going to the Copperbelt to seek work, some of going to the Congo or even Angola, others talked vaguely of seeking a "new Canaan". It was reasonable for us to guess they might try to go to Mumbwa, where Alice was in detention. We needed to stop them, since few seemed to have much idea of the distances involved and they would suffer from starvation on the journey. They were not in the least aggressive, but they might appear so to the inhabitants of Mpika and Serenje Districts as they passed through, and they might be tempted to steal food or clothing to maintain themselves. They made one thing clear to me: they did not wish to live in Chinsali District any longer where, they claimed, they still suffered insults and minor intimidation all the time from others who were supposed to be welcoming them. I could not blame them for this. They made no complaints against the administration or Government, which had been regularly supplying them with food and essential clothing and blankets; their complaints were against the more irresponsible elements of UNIP.

This was the time when I had to go off into the bush again for days on end, after doing several flights in a spotter aircraft and a few landings from a helicopter. These flights were fun. The small Cessna spotter aircraft, I recall, was regularly piloted by an elderly man of the Police Reserve. Sitting next to him I once noticed that he seemed to be having visual difficulties with his bifocals, moving his head up and down. "Have you got any problems with your glasses?" I asked. "Only when coming in to land" he replied – and we were doing precisely that at the time. On another occasion, with a moderate breeze, we landed virtually broadside on the Chinsali airstrip, and careered off onto the grass along the side; we survived, and the plane was undamaged. The helicopters had no doors, so I had to trust the seat-belt as I leaned right out to shout through my megaphone to any groups we spotted. And, landing in a clearing or *dambo* to refill with fuel from the jerry-cans, I was still aware of the possibilities for an ambush and was glad when we lifted off again.

On the ground my base was the isolated *musumba* of Chief Lundu, twenty kilometres beyond burnt-out Chilanga and on the edge of the Muchinga Escarpment. It seemed an odd place for a Chief to live, when most of his people lived down in the Luangwa Valley below. And it was in Lundazi District, not mine – though I had long since ceased to observe the niceties of boundaries. With S/D/M Julius again and local guides we walked all day for several days, trying to locate the migrants. That was the area in which we expected them to be, as further north we had come across a trail of possessions they had discarded (including a sewing-machine or two!) as they became exhausted and hungry. The berry season was over, there was no game on the slopes, they would be starving, wet (it was the rainy season), and in fear. We went down and across innumerable gullies, with memorable views over the North Luangwa Game Reserve in the distance, but with little success at first. At last we did come across a few small, frightened groups and they were encouraged to indicate where some larger groups were. In the end I managed to persuade about sixty to follow us back to Lundu where I had lorries waiting.

One thing I had noticed when I met the groups in the bush was the absence of children and older people; this made me suspect they had been reduced to some form of cannibalism. They were very weak; eight died on the lorries on our way back to Chinsali. Before breakfast the following morning my friend Derek Braithwaite, the PMO, invited me to attend while he performed eight post-mortems (I watched just the first three); this has been my only

Chinsali: The Aftermath, Independence and Family Life

experience of such a procedure. He too had his theories, and was particularly keen to see the contents of their stomachs. These turned out to be, in most cases, purely leaves and grasses and sand while two, he told me, did contain what might be elements of human flesh. Yes, it was sad to see such evidence, but also humbling to realise the depths to which humans in some crises feel they have to descend. But I had done my best to rescue the survivors from similar calamities further along their intended journey. Later I visited Mpika Boma for the first time, a delightful station, to liaise on these matters with the DS there.

After the major 1964 events Derek had, quite deservedly, been offered the award of an MBE, which he had declined on the grounds that "I was only doing my duty." He was proud of having been a graduate of Newcastle's Medical School, when it was part of King's College of Durham University. I later visited him in his retirement bungalow near Wisley Horticultural Gardens, and we stayed in contact through Christmas letters until his death in 2008 from Parkinson's Disease.

Because of its troubles, Chinsali certainly had more than its fair share of visitors. The Government Rest House, which was another of my responsibilities, was always full. And ever since we moved into the DC's house we had a constant stream of visiting civil servants, mostly from Kasama or Lusaka. Wendy began to refer to it as the "Chinsali Hotel." Counting up, she found that over the first seven weeks of 1965 we had put people up for thirty six nights. As they were almost all males on their own, they made considerable work in terms of washing and ironing. We did however get refunds from Government of 22/6 per night and 6/- for a lunch. And in February we had a DO living with us for a couple of months, plus his dog: he was working entirely with Hugh Thompson on the rehabilitation of the remaining Lumpas in 'the cage' I had had to re-open. By the time we left Chinsali, we had also entertained to meals no less than thirteen members of the Cabinet and almost as many Parliamentary Secretaries too, so we became known to them before meeting many of them again in our Lusaka days. Senior politicians and civil servants seemed keen to hear first-hand what was going on in the infamous Chinsali District, now that the troubles were over. At least it made me feel we were not entirely forgotten by the Government.

From Northern Rhodesia to Zambia

We had been granted a few days' leave from 17th March and had booked ourselves into Kasaba Bay on Lake Tanganyika. This was to entertain my old school friend, Mike Brearley, who was on the MCC cricket tour of South Africa – he did not become captain of the England cricket team until 1976. We had to cancel, due again to 'exigencies of the service.' I was summoned to Kasama for a briefing with the State Advocate about the forthcoming tribunal regarding Alice Lenshina's continued detention (or not). My advice was that, if she were released, all plump women in Chinsali who might resemble her would be in danger of being murdered. In the end, Alice opted to stay in prison for her own safety. The tribunal in Lusaka became a short paper exercise, and we could have gone to Kasaba Bay after all. So instead we took a week's local leave to visit Lusaka (Valentine and Flavia Musakanya), Choma (Malcolm and Judy Mitchell), and Livingstone (Richard and Ruth Pelly) – all Cambridge Course colleagues – and of course to see the magnificent Victoria Falls properly for the first time. We did, too, manage to catch Mike Brearley in Lusaka. It was a wonderful trip; we needed the break and certainly felt better for it. The young children did well to put up with 3,300 kilometres of driving. I have no record of who acted as DS in my absence, if anybody!

A second but smaller Lumpa migration took place in April 1965 from Senior Chief Nkula's area. It appeared to me that this was organised by one John Museba, and accordingly I had him arrested and detained for twenty eight days under Section 31 of the PPS Regulations (Preservation of Public Security). Some 330 ex-Lumpas were picked up near Mpika and, against my wishes, sent back to the Chinsali 'cage' for repatriation to their villages. For months they refused to go, and I did not intend to use force. They only wished to join their friends in Kotito Camp, or to go to the Copperbelt where it was clear they would aim for the Congo. They were not detained, and legally they could go where and when they liked; I saw it as my job to dissuade them from going anywhere except back to their villages. A later 'goodwill' tour by three Cabinet Ministers on 19-20th June failed to persuade them so to do. But that visit was largely nullified by the speech of the Resident Minister, Robert Makasa, who made accusations against the Watchtower Movement; if Watchtower adherents came under fire from politicians, the ex-Lumpas naturally felt there was little hope of goodwill towards them.

Chinsali: The Aftermath, Independence and Family Life

At the end of May we had an official visit by Valentine flying in in his new capacity as Secretary to the Cabinet, with his friend Dominic Mulaisho, my Permanent Secretary in the Office of the President (which embraced the P&DG), plus the new Rehabilitation Commissioner and two psychiatrists who'd been having a fresh look at those ex-Lumpas still held in Kotito. This was very brief but most enjoyable. Then in the first week of June we had a visit from the Vice-President, Reuben Kamanga, and four other Cabinet Ministers. As we didn't know for how long they'd stay, Wendy just prepared lots of roast chickens in advance plus salad ingredients. We gave them a sundowner of course, but this time for only about 30 people, not the 70 of the President's visit.

The next week we took a long weekend holiday trip to Mbeya in Tanzania, with Bill the Magistrate in his little car. It was only about 300 kilometres from Chinsali, but a completely different world and breathtakingly beautiful. We stopped on the way for a picnic lunch at Tunduma, the border post where Dr Trant had a sort of hotel (she, having broken her leg, was now working every day at Mwenzo Hospital, 15 kilometres away, so we didn't see her). The Tunduma customs unfortunately wouldn't give us any Tanzanian money as their banks were not accepting Zambian money until the change-over from Federal to Zambian currency was complete. (Back in Chinsali, we had just finished the mammoth exchange exercise, with old people coming in with vast sums of money to change, all in coins. They had buried their savings for safety, as there were no banks, and even the Post Office could involve them in a journey of 150 kilometres; and they didn't like to keep notes as these burn.) However, undeterred by this minor detail we carried on and found an Indian trader who let us have £5 on a Sunday morning, and a driver going southwards who changed some more on Sunday evening. After all, we weren't asked to pay hotel bills till we left! We were overcome by the scenery in southern Tanzania: very lush vegetation, bananas and bamboo and millions of conifers in plantations everywhere. One place of interest we visited, halfway between the border at Tunduma and Mbeya, was where a meteorite had landed centuries (or millennia?) ago. We crossed a minor rift valley in the sunset with the Mbeya range of mountains a magnificent backcloth, a blue silhouette against the darkening sky. We arrived back on the Monday to receive another five important visitors from Lusaka.

I had to fly across to Lundazi in early July, with Bill McKenzie and some others, to meet the Commission of Inquiry and to answer their questions on our submissions. We stayed and had our discussions in Lundazi Castle. This exotic edifice, turned into a hotel, was designed and built as a Rest House by an eccentric DC in the 1940s; it was in the style of a small Norman castle, with thick walls and narrow slits for archers, overlooking a lake; it had a dungeon, high turrets at each corner and battlements all around.

My old friend Angus McDonald was Secretary of the Commission which was chaired by Judge Pickles of the High Court. One member of the Commission, picking up my comment that right at the beginning I did not agree with what we had been asked to do, asked me why I hadn't resigned. For a few moments I was lost for words. Resign? What good would that have done? I was there, I had a job to do, I soon knew as much about the Lumpa villages and the situation as anybody (apart from Missionaries and Messengers perhaps), and if I'd left who else would step into the vacuum? As I struggled with my thoughts, Judge Pickles came to my rescue. "You felt like a soldier; you'd argued your objections, but now you just had to obey orders. Any other course would have been like **desertion**?" "Absolutely," I replied.

Re-reading my submission today (it was classified as "Strictly Confidential") I see that I did not pull my punches on various aspects. I argued that the local political leaders must bear the greatest blame for the disturbances, since they encouraged or even advocated the campaign of hatred from the start. It was clear even during the early weeks of the Rehabilitation Committee in late 1964 that they still thought along the same lines. I had heard the two most important of them say that if the ex-Lumpas caused any more trouble (e.g. non-cooperation, not violence), the Army would be sent to deal with them again and "they would have to be shot." The Rehabilitation Committee broke down mainly because the security forces were not hunting the "criminals" with enough aggressive intent to please the local politicians. The same spirit, I went on, still prevailed during 1965 in certain quarters despite the goodwill tour by Ministers. At recent public meetings the Political Assistant and the UNIP Regional Secretary, returning from a meeting with the Resident Minister (Robert Makasa), had told the crowds that nobody would have a loan or be allowed to join a cooperative unless he had a party

Chinsali: The Aftermath, Independence and Family Life

card; that youths were to start at once on door-to-door demanding for cards; that a secret anti-Government organisation existed in Chinsali, members of which would automatically be recognised by their unwillingness to burn bricks for school buildings. I argued that all this propaganda, whomever it was aimed at, did not promote the good relations in the villages which was essential to rehabilitation, and ran counter to Kaunda's policy of reconciliation.

When I eventually read the Commission's Report I found it generally bland. In accordance with its terms of reference it dwelt at some length on "the origin and development of the former Lumpa Church" and on "the relations of the former Lumpa Church with the public, Government, native authorities and other religious organisations", but in no more than a watered-down version of the intelligence reports I had retained. As to the "causes and circumstances of the outbreaks of violence" it said no more than some pre-conflict passages I have described in previous chapters, but in an appendix gave a day-by-day diary of events. It ended by making recommendations for continuing the proscription of the Lumpa Church and Alice's detention. But it did pick up one of my pleas, regarding reconciliation and Robert Makasa's attitude, in this way:

> *We must cut down on party propaganda, on slogans such as "it pays to belong to UNIP", "UNIP is power" etc, since these will continue to divide the Chinsali society completely. Above all, we must have a new Resident Minister.*
> Conclusion of my "Submission to the Commission of Inquiry, 1965."

> *In conclusion, your Commissioners would repeat that no success can attend any venture unless there is sincere tolerance, patience and understanding on the part of the people. In this regard your Commissioners consider it a matter for regret that the Resident Minister of the Northern Province is not only adopting an intolerant attitude himself towards the former Lumpa followers but seems to be interfering unduly with the administration of the Kotito Rehabilitation Centre. They therefore consider it necessary to recommend that this Resident Minister be made aware of the need to adopt a genuinely tolerant attitude and to ensure that the*

regional party officials in his province follow suit.
Final recommendation in the Commission of Inquiry's Report, 1965.

Later in July, I handed over to a Zambian DS and we packed to go on a well-earned leave. We had a farewell party in our house; Robert and Mama Helen Kaunda attended among others. The new DS in a speech made a point of saying how glad everyone should be now that they were to have a Zambian in charge, but Helen Kaunda countered this (in ciBemba) with a gracious compliment to me for my work. What I cannot recall was how I made my farewells to all my loyal Messengers and Boma staff; I hope some of them, including S/D/M Julius, were also at the party.

We sent all our worldly possessions to Government Stores in Lusaka. At the time I was under the impression that my next posting might be to a middle-ranking job in one of the Ministry Headquarters. We stopped for a couple of nights in Lusaka, where we again saw Angus and had a delightful time with the Musakanyas. I felt very ill. This was diagnosed as a bad case of jaundice or hepatitis A from which I have since been declared immune. I was certainly a frightening colour of yellow when my parents met us in London.

So many images of the 'Chinsali episode' have remained indelibly imprinted in my mind, while the discovery of the documents has helped to jog the memory on the order of events in the foregoing account. It was certainly a year during which I worked very hard and must have become both mentally and physically exhausted. But second only to Mporokoso, Chinsali was "our home" and we had come to love many aspects of it. I would not have missed the experiences for the world.

What irked me, then and since, was the general perception by others who linked the name Chinsali with only the dramatic events of July-August 1964, totally overlooking the aftermath. For me, the next ten months had also been of great importance, if frustrating and less dramatic, as we relentlessly pursued the uphill task of trying to achieve reconciliation in the villages; our efforts in this seemed generally to have been undervalued, or at least misunderstood. Later in life I came to learn that this is the common fate of the aftermaths of conflicts, e.g. Rwanda, Bosnia, Sri Lanka, Dafur; in today's jargon, they just "fall off the radar."

8. BANCROFT AND CHINGOLA, 1965-66

Our three-month leave back in the UK was not a great success. We had no home there of our own, so we were mostly living out of suitcases at our respective parents' homes, alternately. My parents were no longer used to crawling infants and the inquisitive Ruth committed many sins in their eyes. Worse for us, while we were bursting to tell everybody all the details of our most exciting, if not exhausting, first three-year tour, they listened politely for only a short while and then moved on to tell us a lot of their local gossip or of the politico-economic situation in Britain which was of relatively little interest to us. It was a much needed break, but we were glad to get back to Zambia in mid-November 1965.

Departing on leave in the July, I had called in at the P&DG Ministry Headquarters in Lusaka where, contrary to my earlier assumptions, I was informed that my next posting would be as District Secretary of Bancroft. With Independence my own status had changed: I was no longer a member of the British Colonial Service on its "permanent and pensionable" terms but an expatriate officer of the Zambian Civil Service, on a renewable three-year contract basis. On our return to Lusaka I reported at P&DG Headquarters to seek confirmation of my posting and my Permanent Secretary, Dominic Mulaisho, kindly invited Wendy and me to have lunch with him; through our links with Valentine we could now count Dominic as a personal friend as well as my boss.

I then bought a car for the first time, a second-hand green VW; we collected our possessions from Government Stores and drove to Bancroft. James was happy to continue working for us and somehow, a week or so later, he came to join us there with his family. Young Lameck, our junior servant/gardener and no.3 at Chinsali, turned up soon after we arrived. He had come to try his luck on the mines, like thousands of others, and by chance saw me above the heads of a crowd. We were pleased to see him again, and very soon he was doing wonders in the garden.

Bancroft was a one-officer station in P&DG terms and the smallest and perhaps most insignificant Boma in the Western Province (later renamed the Copperbelt Province). In fact it had only a few years earlier been upgraded to full District status, having previously been a Sub-Boma of Chingola District, just as Kalulushi was and remained a Sub-Boma of Kitwe. As the town and District were not renamed Chililabombwe until 1968, after we had left it, I shall continue to refer to it here as Bancroft. We found I was taking over from another of our Cambridge Course colleagues, Jonathan Leach and his wife Jane, who went on leave a couple of days after our arrival (we have not seen them since).

After three happy and exciting years in the Northern Province, we found several shocks in adjusting to life and work in a Copperbelt town. There were tarred roads virtually everywhere. We had electricity and telephones. At dusk Lameck, who was used to lighting hurricane and pixie oil lamps for us in Chinsali and placing them in every room, would go round our Bancroft house switching on every single electric light until we explained this was unnecessary. Wendy had to get used to an electric cooker, instead of her familiar wood stove. Within 200 metres of our house was a row of two-storey buildings containing well-stocked shops selling almost everything one could need, plus a bank and post office, the Town Council and a commercial garage and filling station.

But the most significant change, for us, was to be surrounded almost entirely by Europeans in our 'low-density' residential area. All our neighbours seemed to be expatriate civil servants, including several teachers at the Primary School. Even in the United Church of Zambia (UCZ), whose church services we began to attend regularly, I do not recall more than a dozen Zambians in the congregation. This inevitably brought a great change in our social lives, after having been two of at most five European adults in the Chinsali setting. In terms of the Zambian post-Independence scene we frankly found this somewhat strange.

Bancroft, like the larger Copperbelt towns, consisted of two adjacent towns. The major part was the mine township, situated around the bottom of the prominent hill. Famously, the houses on the one road winding up this hill were occupied by senior mine staff in strict order of status, with the General Manager living at the top next to the mine's central offices. I think I only went up that hill about three times in my whole year there, to meet Mr Stevens, the General Manager. Again, all the 'low-density' residential

Bancroft and Chingola, 1965-66

houses at the bottom of the hill were occupied by so-called Europeans – in fact most were of Rhodesian or South African origin, and for the first time we had to become used to hearing their accents and even the ugly sound of the Afrikaans language. The mine had the reputation of being the wettest on the Copperbelt, which through constant pumping allowed all mine township residents to water their gardens for free. The other part was the smaller civic township, encompassing the Government offices, the Town Council, the Primary School and the shopping area as I have indicated.

At the Boma offices I had a very experienced secretary, Gwen, the elderly wife of the Primary School Headmaster. With her I had to learn to dictate for the first time. Another new experience for me was having to perform the not infrequent weddings as, ex-officio, the Registrar of Births Deaths & Marriages for the District. Together Gwen and I used to fill my office with vases of flowers for these occasions. No religious element was appropriate in these ceremonies, but I usually gave the marrying couple a solemn lecture about their act being "in the eyes of the Law" and therefore not to be undertaken lightly or wantonly. One man was marrying for the fourth time – this time to his first wife again – and this really seemed a triumph of hope over experience ("Are you both quite sure?" I asked them). Delays sometimes occurred when a divorced person only had a 'decree nisi' and was still waiting for the 'decree absolute' but I don't think I was guilty of allowing bigamy by carrying out the ceremony too soon. There was one young Japanese bride who was so eye-catching that I might well have muddled my words and asked her "Do you take me …?"

It was all so different from the work on rural stations where we had spent our first three years. For instance, what on earth did I do here with the smart District Messengers, when there were no chiefs to communicate with or roads and bridges to repair? Gwen used them a lot for just hand-delivering letters. For much of the time the main work was of an intelligence nature, watching the local political scene and ensuring that everywhere was peaceful. We had a Labour Officer there, one of the few African civil servants of any seniority, and of course he kept his ear close to the ground in the mining environment. With him and the European Police Inspector I used to have my weekly intelligence meeting, and then dictate to Gwen my two-page report, marked 'Secret', to the Resident Secretary in Ndola – the very military Colonel Middleton, previously of the Indian Army and the very epitome of a colonial officer in appearance and lifestyle.

A mere twenty kilometres north of Bancroft was the Congolese border at Kasumbalesa. I used to go there quite often to visit the Immigration Officer, red-haired Bill Hayes, and his wife; on the social side, I cannot think why I seemed never to have invited them to drop in on us when they were in Bancroft for shopping, as they must have had quite a lonely existence up there. But intelligence work was the main reason for my visits as we had to know what was going on over the border. Bill used to keep a very attentive ear to Congolese activities during my whole 1965-66 period there, and I gratefully used his tales to inform my weekly intelligence reports.

The Mines Secretary and I were the two ex-officio members of the Town Council. I much enjoyed the many dealings I had with its officers and indeed the Council debates. But this, too, at that stage seemed to be an almost entirely European organization.

As to family activities, our old home cine films remain the best reminders of the happy times we had in Bancroft, and of Alastair and Ruth playing in the large back garden with the children of our teacher friends, Alwyn and Eiddwyn Roberts. With other teacher friends, Declan and Heather Smith, we have continued to have contact to this day. Wendy, more than I, used to visit the high density African part of the civic township, as a member of the YWCA there (Young Women's Christian Association). This area, around the side of the central hill, was the original Chililabombwe which means "croaking frogs". Down there, also, was the Mine Farm; we used to get fresh pasteurised Jersey milk from it most days, and vegetables too at crack of dawn on Fridays – if Wendy arrived down there before the queue grew too long! Wendy also took the opportunity of going down a deep mine with a select group; this was almost certainly the Konkola mine, up near the Kasumbalesa border, reputed to be one of the deepest mines in the world.

As I have said, we regularly attended the UCZ church at the top of the main street. We really appreciated the fact that this represented a coming together of many Nonconformist church denominations: it made the UK seem decades behind in that respect. Three-year-old Alastair went to the

Bancroft and Chingola, 1965-66

Sunday School there. When the Minister was on leave I was one of those lay members who filled in and ran a few services, preaching on topics relevant to what I saw as the prevailing practice of adultery among of the Europeans of the time!

Christmas 1965 was quite a mixture for us. Two days before, we held a party for all our friends' children. On Christmas Eve we had a dinner party for eight adults, with a turkey. We were invited to spend Christmas Day itself at the Mine Farm, having at some stage made friends with its manager and his wife, whose infants were the same ages as ours. Alastair and Ruth of course loved their first experiences with farm animals. For Wendy and myself it was a great pleasure to be invited out, as we had been so used to doing all the entertaining ourselves over the previous year.

But I confess that for the first three months I found insufficient work to do in Bancroft and, after my previous years' experiences, I frankly felt a little bored. Maybe Colonel Middleton noticed this, for in February 1966 he told me to take over Chingola District too, i.e. to be DS in two places at the same time. From then on I used to commute on a daily basis between the two Bomas, usually spending the afternoons in Chingola. By coincidence or fate, it was again from the former DC Chinsali that I took over responsibility in Chingola and, as in Bancroft, I was the sole P&DG officer there. Then things changed.

On 11th November 1965 the British colony of Southern Rhodesia had declared UDI (Unilateral Declaration of Independence) under its Prime Minister, Ian Smith. The possibilities of this action had been foreseen and discussed in the international community over the summer. While we were on leave in the UK and ever since our return to Zambia, I had been convincing myself that Britain could not, would not, allow this to happen and would, despite colonialist arguments of 'kith and kin', send in an invasion force against the Rhodesian Europeans. I was therefore all the more shocked when Britain did nothing to retaliate against Smith and Rhodesia, and even afterwards I was not convinced by the excuses of military impracticality. I was so angry that I seriously contemplated renouncing British citizenship and becoming a true Zambian. I didn't; in the end I went back to my original principles of following a 'suicide career', willing to serve

From Northern Rhodesia to Zambia

Zambia as an expatriate until I was no longer required. And I doubt whether Zambian citizenship would have enhanced my career prospects at all. What I did do, when visiting Lusaka for a conference of DSs, was take part in an anti-UDI demonstration in front of the British High Commission: my name was taken, and I subsequently learnt it was placed on a list of 'prohibited immigrants' to Rhodesia – a status of which I was quite proud! Of course, in the European communities of Bancroft and Chingola there was much support for UDI. I was careful only to give the Government's views, without saying they were mine too – after all, I had to appear an impartial civil servant.

Landlocked Zambia had been almost completely dependent economically on transit routes to the south (Rhodesia, South Africa and the Mozambique port of Beira) both for its exports of copper and for its imports of oil, coal and many foods. In mid-1965 1,075,647 tonnes of imports and exports, representing practically the whole of Zambia's trade, was carried over Rhodesia Railways. Rhodesia itself supplied 33% of Zambia's imports and took 93% of its exports. The border between Zambia and Rhodesia was now closed, and sanctions operated in both directions. The economic and social effects on Zambia were enormous. Briefly, the emergency actions Zambia took, with some foreign help, included the following:

British and Canadian Air Forces' Hercules transport aircraft brought oil from Dar-es-Salaam. This operation was taken over by ZAC (Zambia Air Cargo) which over the next 3 years carried 150,000 tonnes of freight, half of it copper, between the Copperbelt and Dar-es-Salaam.

- Fleets of lorries also took copper to Dar-es-Salaam up the Great North Road; this gravel road became known as the 'Hell Run' because of the frequency of accidents on it. Later the Yugoslavians developed it to tarmac standard in order to increase traffic capacity between Zambia and Tanzania; over this 1,930 kilometres route went, in 1966, 7,154 tonnes of copper and 4,648 tonnes of inward cargo. Associated with this was the development of better port facilities at Mpulungu on the south of Lake Tanganyika in 1966 and a transit depot at Isoka.
- A Tanzania-Zambia Mafuta (TAZAMA) oil pipeline was then constructed, and an oil refinery built at Ndola.

- The Kariba North Bank and Kafue Gorge hydro-electric power stations were built.
- Later, other long-term projects were developed such as the Maamba Colliery, to replace the previous reliance on coal from Wankie. At the time of UDI, Zambia got 95% of its coal requirements (1 million tonnes) annually from Wankie.
- A start was made by the Chinese on constructing the Tanzania-Zambia Railway (TAZARA), although it was some years before this was completed.

The next eight months were, in my mind, dominated by three exercises. Firstly, I had to deal with petrol rationing, recently introduced as a direct result of Rhodesia's UDI. I had to open and run offices in both Districts. Chingola as the larger town with many more vehicle owners was the greater task, and there I had two ladies working full-time to receive and assess applications for fuel and to award ration coupons. The crisis was so great that to begin with the fuel ration for most private motorists was less than a gallon (say, 4 litres) per week. Every so often I had to arbitrate when the ladies were confronted by irate European locals who needed more fuel to keep their businesses afloat, especially those running transport companies with dozens of vehicles. It was a time-consuming exercise.

Secondly, there were mine strikes in both towns, mounted by both the Mineworkers Union of Zambia (MUZ, the African union) and the expatriate miners' union – the first demanding that the pay differential between Zambian and expatriate workers be reduced, the second objecting to the process of Zambianization in the mining industry (moving at a snail's pace compared with the civil service) which rendered some of its members redundant. The strikes involved me in a lot of hard work, in close collaboration with Special Branch and the local Labour Officers. I recall that at one stage we worked solidly for seventy two hours without sleep, checking and acting on lists of the miners. The loss of copper production at this critical stage of reaction to UDI would have been economically disastrous to the country if the strikes were not broken. The President had anyway introduced emergency regulations because of UDI, and under these we could (and did) arrest several strike leaders and activists. I cannot now recall all the details of our actions but I do remember, with the Police Officer and acting on a tip-off from my Special Branch colleague, calling one evening on the expatriate Union leader at his home in Bancroft, where he was having a get-together with other leaders. When he opened the door to me his jaw dropped in astonishment and he put his hands forward as if to be handcuffed: "How did you know of our meeting?" he asked, clearly concerned he had a mole in his midst. All I did on that occasion was go inside and warn his friends that they had better return to work in the morning (or else, what?). Finally we had a personal visit from the Minister, Mr Munukayumbwa Sipalo, who graciously congratulated us on what we had achieved – whatever that was.

Thirdly, there was the reality of a rush of Belgians and other Europeans fleeing across the border from Elizabethville. Sese Seko Mobutu had come to power in the Congo; in May 1966 he changed that large city's name to Lubumbashi and in December of that year he nationalised the highly profitable mining company of Union Minière du Haut Katanga. Of course all the refugees were well-to-do and reasonably self-sufficient and had their own cars. All I had to do, with advance warnings from Bill Hayes at the Kasumbalesa Immigration Post, was to ensure that they were able to change their money and buy petrol (giving them immunity from our rationing system) and see them on their way southwards.

The dominant feature of Chingola was of course the great Nchanga Copper Mine and its vast open pit, reputed to be one of the world's largest man-made holes. Coming from Bancroft one passed the pit and had views of all the large slag heaps, the mine's smelters, cooling towers, pit-heads for the underground mine, and other buildings behind. Memorable, too, were the gigantic dumper trucks which made their way down to the bottom of the pit, to be loaded with about 100 tonnes of copper-bearing earth from an excavating leviathan; each tyre on the truck was about four metres high. As in Bancroft, I obviously made courtesy calls on the Mine General Manager and his top staff but, apart from keeping them informed in relation to my activites on petrol rationing and the mine strike, I had few dealings with them.

Bancroft and Chingola, 1965-66

At the Solwezi turnoff on the road into Chingola was a prominent large tree, which we and our children dubbed the 'Christ tree' because it so resembled the crucifixion! Halfway between Bancroft and Chingola, beside the bridge over the young Kafue River, was the Hippo Pool, which was designated as a national monument. We often used to go there to swim, as a family or with friends. There was another place, also called the Hippo Pool. This was further down the Kafue and beside the Kalulushi-Mufulira road: it was a larger pool, with amenities which made it a popular picnic spot, and we used to visit that too. Neither pool had any signs of hippo or crocodile.

It was in the evening of 12th June, while we were playing monopoly with our teacher friends, that Wendy started to go into labour with our third child. With great reluctance (as she was winning the game!), she allowed me to dash her from Bancroft into Kitwe Hospital. I wanted to be present at this child's birth, having missed those of the first two. The nurses told me she should rest a little and nothing would happen for a couple of hours. So I went out of the hospital for a smoke. When I returned after an hour, Eleanor had already been born, just before midnight – ever keen and never late. So I had missed out again, and countless other instances have occurred over the years of me letting her down, she tells me!

We now had three children, and each with a different birth certificate because of their dates of birth: Alastair's (March 1963) was from the Federation of Rhodesia & Nyasaland, Ruth's (October 1964) from the Protectorate of Northern Rhodesia, and Eleanor's (June 1966) from the Republic of Zambia!

One evening in early 1966 the Massed Bands of the Zambian Army came to Bancroft and in the Chililabombwe football stadium gave a delightful display of marching and counter-marching to music, finishing with a 'beating retreat' ceremony. The stadium was full. As the senior Government representative, I had the privilege of taking their salute as the bands marched off; not having a hat of my own, I had to borrow one to return the salute properly. In April we were invited to another army ceremony, in Ndola, when new Colours were presented to 1NRR by the President. In the reception afterwards we were able to chat briefly with Mrs Kaunda, who remembered us from Chinsali (see pp.122), and also with Valentine and Flavia Musakanya who were there too. Then, on 29th August, we met the

Kaundas again when the President was given the Freedom of the Municipality of Chingola. As both the DS and a Municipal Councillor I was treated with some respect (including a chauffeur-driven Mercedes), but I had no particular duties to perform. Wendy was highly impressed by Mrs Kaunda who asked her whether she'd had a boy or a girl – she had actually remembered that Wendy was pregnant when they had met in Ndola. The President himself, when he greeted me ("My tallest civil servant!"), jovially commented that I must be "overworked and underpaid", perhaps referring to the period of the mine strikes. Most commentators at the time agreed that the President seemed to have aged significantly over the last year; all the negotiations to avoid UDI and the worries about how Zambia could continue to cope with it had taken their toll on him personally, even if he put on a brave face in public.

I have mentioned above that Wendy used to cycle down to Chililabombwe township to join in the YWCA activities. One day in February, while she was out of the room making tea, she was elected Branch President. There was a Women's Sewing Club, which she also enjoyed – it brought back happy memories for her of earlier days with the Mporokoso Women's Welfare. She and friends also started a local Consumers' Association, as food prices rose. But dominant among her various local voluntary activities was her involvement in ZSCHC, the Zambian Society for the Care of Handicapped Children. She and other ladies founded a Bancroft Branch in February 1966. On one occasion, when members were seeking charitable donations for this, she was horrified at some of the racist reactions they received; for example: "Oh, I'm not giving anything for **African** children; these people are **never** grateful, despite all we've done to civilise them!" Wendy's particular contributions to the ZSCHC Branch were to run a fund-raising competition, to organise a social in September and a Night Club in October, and to make preparations for the opening of a Day Centre. It was all time-consuming, but very worthwhile.

One of the most bizarre little affairs I involved myself in, of a typically old PA type, was a disagreement between two local Chiefs over the boundary between their traditional areas. I don't remember either Chief, but I must have met them both to hear their arguments. What I recall is writing a supportive letter on behalf of the Bancroft Chief to the DS Chingola (myself), and then from Chingola writing counter-arguments on behalf of the Chief there back to the DS Bancroft, copying both letters to the Resident Secretary at Ndola. Two further letters followed. Colonel Middleton must have thought young Bond was losing his wits and needed a break because, soon after this, I was instructed to move to Mongu in early October! No, in fact there were other reasons for the move. Wendy was annoyed at the timing of the move, primarily because, after only seven months from starting the ZSCHC Branch, her Day Centre was just about ready to be opened.

For some odd reason I was not immediately replaced by another DS (I would have expected a Zambian) in either Bancroft or Chingola; I merely had to hand over the keys to the safes to my secretaries in each place.

9. MONGU, 1966-67

This was, with hindsight, a strange year and not the happiest for either Wendy or myself, even though we liked being back in a rural District.

In early October 1966 I was transferred from Bancroft/Chingola to be DS in Mongu. At the same time I was told that I was to take over as Acting Resident Secretary of Barotse (now called Western) Province in November, for a temporary but unspecified period. We travelled as a family in the old green VW, for the first time encountering the long dirt road from Landless Corner through Mumbwa and Mankoya (now Kaoma), while James and his family followed with our worldly goods on the usual Bedford 5-ton flat.

The District's official title was Mongu-Lealui. This, like so much else, reflected the different way in which Barotse Province was regarded. In colonial times it had been definitely a separate Protectorate within the Protectorate of Northern Rhodesia. The Litunga, the Paramount Chief of the Lozi, lived at Lealui and under the old colonial indirect rule system had evidently enjoyed more prestige in the Government's eyes than other paramount or senior chiefs. Consistent with this concept that the Litunga's Barotseland was different, special (even superior?), the Government's chief officer there had always been called a Resident Commissioner, not a Provincial Commissioner as elsewhere in Northern Rhodesia.

The Province was also very different from others in that it was dominated by the Zambezi river which flooded dramatically across a huge area every year, rendering many roads impassable and river transport vital. The soil was white and very sandy, unlike the red soil of much of the rest of the country. Mongu was perched on a ridge overlooking the flood plain and was joined to the main river by a channel. Unlike in the Northern Province, the people kept large herds of cattle (out on the plain for half the year); meat was cheap and we could get plenty of fresh fish.

My DO, Mr Nyumbu, was an elderly and hard-working Lozi, not greatly endowed with imagination, who clearly resented my presence on the scene as a young non-Lozi expatriate. I was more than content to leave to him the more mundane and time-consuming work of handling all the *milandu* (problems and issues) of individual people: e.g. taxes, trading and fishing licences, liaising with local chiefs and village headmen, deceased estates, etc. He had more dealings than I with the local politicians and particularly the recently formed local District Council. To give him his due, he also organised a very successful Annual Agricultural Show on the town's showground, with a band, craft stalls, children's sports, *makishi* dancing and many other forms of entertainment.

In my first month Mr Nyumbu took me to meet the Litunga at his palace in Lealui. The palace was set in a large grove of trees on a slight rise, with views in all directions across the flood plain. A high reed stockade enclosed an outer court which contained a dozen or so thatched houses of normal size, and from this one went through a lower stockade into an inner court where his closest family members had their various houses. His own house was very wide and had an enormous high thatched roof. I cannot recall much of our meeting. Mr Nyumbu in traditional manner lay down on his back, clapping in humble greeting to his monarch, while I just bowed and shook hands. The Litunga had a long sad face and droopy jowls and these features were replicated in other members of the royal family such as Princess Nakatindi, a high-ranking politician who became a Minister of State. I had no (need for) further dealings with the Litunga for the rest of our time in Mongu.

The Resident Secretary when I arrived was Mr Mwale, a delightful old-world Zambian from Eastern Province – in his fifties, pipe-smoking, very laid back and jovial, and if he hadn't been very sincere in all he did I might have thought he was trying to copy the caricature of an old colonial officer. He was to go off to the UK for some "refresher" course, and sadly I was never to hear of him again.

The Resident Minister of the Province, Mr Monga, was quiet, gentlemanly and dignified. He was a Tonga from Southern Province, and I suspected that he had been given the status of Minister because he was one of the few senior politicians from that Province who had not been supporters of Harry Nkumbula's rival ANC party. It was my first and only experience of working alongside, and in some senses for, a Minister and, looking back, I'm sure I failed to make the most of the situation. As the Province's most senior civil servant by position (but definitely not by age or length of service – I was only twenty nine), my role was in effect the equivalent of a Permanent Secretary but on a smaller scale. Yet I barely had discussions with him more than once a week. He'd ask me about specific events, and I must have given him reassuring responses as he seemed content just to let me get on with my normal duties of generally coordinating (rather than overseeing) the efforts of all Government departments in the Province. He was a charming man, and if I'd reported to him more often and made a point of getting to know him better I'm sure we could have had a more productive relationship.

My main preoccupation while Acting Resident Secretary and, I suspected, one of the reasons for my posting to Mongu at this time, was to organise the movement of a large group of refugees who had recently fled across the border into our western Kalabo District from the fighting in Angola. Fortunately for me the main responsibility lay with UNHCR (the United Nations High Commission for Refugees), and they had already set up a large temporary camp in the south of Balovale District, just north of the Barotse Province boundary. But I had to liaise with the UNHCR representatives and to give them guarantees that we could as a team move the refugees there. The team I assembled comprised the obvious: primarily the Provincial Public Works Officer for transport, the Provincial Marketing Officer for sacks of food, the Provincial Roads Engineer, the Provincial Medical Officer, the Provincial Commissioner of Police and the Special Branch Officer. But nature gave us a time limit. **We** had to transport them by road from Kalabo through Mongu and Lukulu into the corner of North-Western Province before the Zambezi's annual flood covered the roads. This was expected to be by early December in that year – it is always a couple of months later that the Paramount Chief decides to leave his summer palace at Lealui for Limulunga on the edge of the plain, in the colourful Kuomboka ceremony (see 151 below). I 'assumed' authority, as if it were a declared state of emergency, to commandeer every available Government vehicle in Mongu and Kalabo, and I don't recall any departmental officer being uncooperative in this. We made it in time, just.

In November I went by motorboat to Kalabo to see how the collection of refugees from its western border was going, what transit accommodation and food they had been given, and what logistical problems there were in loading them all onto vehicles for the bumpy ride across the floodplain to Mongu. Kalabo, incidentally, was where Alice Lenshina and her husband

Petros had been imprisoned since their transfer from Mumbwa prison in 1965 – it was surely the remotest place in the country from their former home. Had I known this I would certainly have wished to visit them out of curiosity, but I only learnt of this fact after that first trip to Kalabo. I also paid a visit, in early December, to the refugee camp in Balovale District to see how the inmates were settling down. The UNHCR staff had initially arranged tents plus camp kitchens and ablution blocks. By the time of my visit they were getting the refugees to build their own pole-and-dagga huts and to construct proper brick latrine blocks and a meeting hall. The latter was intended for some teaching – adult literacy classes to begin with, doubtless to be followed by the equivalent of primary school classes. Because of the numbers, a second camp was later established at Mayukwayukwa in Mankoya District, east of Lukulu.

When that refugee episode was over, a new permanent Resident Secretary arrived, a Mr Nyirenda. He didn't appear to have much of a civil service background or ethos, and he might have been a political appointee (perhaps a relation of Wesley Nyirenda, the first Speaker of the Parliament). He was very full of his own importance and, try as I might, I didn't get on well with him. I obviously reverted to my substantive position of DS.

I find it difficult to recall how I spent most of my next four months as DS. I certainly spent more time as a quasi-provincial officer, liaising with and co-ordinating the work of the provincial Heads of Departments, since Mr Nyirenda did not seem to establish a good working relationship with the expatriate officers (or vice versa). Many of my visits to villages were by landrover with the Special Branch Officer for intelligence gathering only, while others were to see the progress of various new agricultural or brick-making cooperatives. One aspect of the former life of a DC/DO had disappeared. We no longer went out for a fortnight's tour through the villages, inspecting them and meeting the people and seeing they were paying their taxes; tax collection was now a responsibility of the Rural Council, whose visits around villages were more political in nature and probably didn't, for example, pay much attention to public hygiene.

Wendy and I found it difficult to make friends among the Lozi. After our three happy years in the Northern Province and a year among Bemba

Mongu, 1966-67

speakers on the Copperbelt, it was hard not to make comparisons. The Bemba always seemed to be interested in you, as a welcome stranger, and pleased to see you. Meeting you on a path or in a village they'd always greet you (*Mwapoleni, mukwai*) and then ask you who you are, where you've come from, where you're going, what you're doing, etc; this was customary politeness and genuine interest. The Lozi, if they didn't recognise you, would just walk past. They even had a special word for strangers or newcomers to Barotseland which meant 'those who cannot walk in the sand.' True, we made little attempt to learn their language, but their general attitude did not encourage us to do so.

We did, however, attend the great Kuomboka ceremony. Mongu was almost overwhelmed by the number of visitors who arrived to see this colourful annual event, and we found ourselves putting up a Cabinet Minister and his wife in our guest wing and three pilots in the study.

My transport as DS consisted of two landrovers, a motorboat and four horses; I was not accustomed to the last items. Many of the other senior officers used their departmental boats for trips with their families at weekends, motoring along the canal from the little harbour to the Zambezi. I took the high moral stance that my boat was for business, not for leisure, although I knew that I was thereby depriving the family of some fun. In fact I rarely used it. I went along the canal half-a-dozen times, and once to Kalabo again. When the river was low, in October, the pontoon across the Zambezi to Kalabo travelled only about 100 metres, but at the height of the floods the pontoon would effectively start from Mongu harbour and take twelve hours – one had to book a passage days ahead. I certainly had three trips by boat up the Zambezi to Lukulu, which was a delightful spot on a bluff above the river and had a Mission, a small hospital and a Government Rest House where I stayed the night. But I always used the Boma's boatman/mechanic who was, after all, paid to maintain and operate the boat.

As for the horses, I never rode them. Their presence reflected the way the old colonial officers had had to get around the District, before the advent of 4x4s for tackling the Barotse sand. The Local Government Officer, and his lively partner who opened the one small hotel in the town (the 'Lyambai'), were keen to exercise the horses and I was happy that they should. There was one amusing incident. The oldest horse died. Shortly afterwards, Government auditors came to do a check on the Boma holdings and a week later I received a peremptory letter asking me to explain why I was "deficient in one vehicle" and how/why I had disposed of it "without it being properly written off by the authority of a Board of Survey." I replied that the said vehicle had been buried with full equestrian honours under a Veterinary Officer's supervision, and asked them how I should account for an unauthorised increase in my transport fleet – by the imminent birth of a foal. I heard no more.

Most of the Provincial Heads of Departments were still expatriates. Of the few senior Zambians the ones we got to know reasonably well were the charming Provincial Education Officer and the Provincial Information Officer and their wives. I recall the PEO, Mr Shonga, coming to me one day in great distress. He had come back from touring schools in western Senanga and Sesheke Districts with the Resident Secretary (Mr Nyirenda) who, he said, had expected him to line up some young female teachers for his nightly gratification. I could only advise him to take this up with the Minister (Mr Monga) or make a formal complaint to his Permanent Secretary in Lusaka. The PMO, an African-American, was another of Mr Nyirenda's ilk. When I was in Lukulu during a visit of the Minister of Health, I was made fully aware that all the small hospital's nurses were expected to "entertain" the Minister and PMO and their friends for the night – I stayed in my Rest House and declined their invitations to join them and "be sociable."

There was a large Secondary School. Its excellent Headmaster, Edward Robinson, was a brother of the Bishop of Woolwich who had written the controversial book, *Honest to God*. Wendy saw more of the Robinsons than I, but we both knew and socialised with several of the teachers. I can recall one incident with a teacher. While I was Acting Resident Secretary, the Minister asked me to help him reprimand an expatriate teacher for denigrating his ministerial status. The teacher, who regarded himself as a 'man of principle', took the line that he only respected a person and not the position a person held. I lost my patience with him and told him he was stupid and arrogant, and that in any decent society one respected authority whether it came in the role of Chief of Police, Paramount Chief, Minister, or

Mongu, 1966-67

in his case Headmaster – the alternative could lead to anarchy.

A teacher put on film shows every month in the Court House. There were a couple of cricket matches with teams of Teachers v. The Rest. We also had a tennis tournament, in which to my surprise I emerged the champion. But Mongu's main social life centred on the Club. If I went there of an evening perhaps more often than I should, the excuse to myself was that I needed to "keep my ear close to the ground", to "feel the pulse" in this enclave of Government activity. The Club was supposed to be open to all residents but was in effect still a 'Europeans Only' bar.

There was certainly an undercurrent of racist attitudes among many of the expatriates, even if not overtly expressed. I did try to encourage some Zambian officers to join the Club, but none was keen and they clearly considered it was for expatriates only. The situation reflected one of Mongu's problems, namely that its middle class consisted entirely of Government officers, posted far away from the bright lights of Lusaka or the Copperbelt, with no other Europeans of more permanent residence with whom to mix. Mr Nyirenda asked me to get him honorary membership of the Club, because he was the most senior civil servant; when I told him its constitution had no such provision but he'd be very welcome if he joined and paid the small membership fee like everybody else, I was in his bad books. Another incident with him concerned the funeral of 'Bobo' Jackson, the large Meteorological Officer who had died. All his expatriate friends wanted to drape his coffin with a Union Jack, but Mr Nyirenda told me this would be wrong in independent Zambia. In response I suggested that if he happened to die while serving at the Zambian High Commission in London would he not wish to be covered with the Zambian flag, not the Union Jack? I won the argument. Sadly, I was the only person who could lay their hands on a Union Jack – the one I had taken down in Chinsali at Independence; they used that, and I didn't get it back afterwards.

The area of Government offices and staff houses at Mongu was on a gently sloping promontory. According to a *Northern Rhodesia Journal* item on place names, Mongu "is a corruption of *Mwa Ngu* meaning on the nose – the bluff on which Mongu is situated sticks out into the plain like the nose on a face." Our first house was the second in the row looking onto the old grass airstrip.

The Minister's (formerly of course the Resident Commissioner's) was at the top end of the slope, with a gorgeous view over the whole of the Zambezi plain, the DS's was next, and then the Resident Secretary's.

Our children were all still of pre-school age during our stay in Mongu: Alastair 3½-4½, Ruth 2-3 and Eleanor 4-16 months. Our old home cine films have captured this interesting stage in their lives. They were a sufficient handful to keep Wendy occupied for most of the time, but she developed a little pre-school play-group by also entertaining the young children of neighbours. Both the nature of my work and the poor driving conditions on sandy tracks severely restricted our opportunities as a family for exploring the surrounding areas. We did sometimes visit the Local Government training centre at Namushakende (the Barotse equivalent of Mungwi) and the Catholic Mission at Sefula, both fifteen kilometres to the south, and Limulunga, a similar distance to the north. It was from some Swiss acquaintances in the Paris Mission at Limulunga that we acquired our Alsation puppy, Robbie, whose plate-like paws even at that age told us he would grow large. Robbie stayed with us until we eventually left the country in 1973. In the month before we left Mongu I was able to take the family on a tour for three nights in the north of the District, camping beside the Luena and Kabompo rivers and at delightful Lukulu; we wished I'd been able to show the family more of the region.

The most worrying incident for the family was Eleanor's sudden illness at 13 months old – uncontrollable shaking and turning blue. We rushed her down to the hospital, but the doctor and nurses were perplexed as to a diagnosis and it really looked as if she might die. They accordingly treated her for everything, including possible meningitis. Eventually the continual shaking did stop and she slept. The next day she had completely recovered and was cheerfully bouncing once more. What it had been we shall never know, but it had certainly given us a fright.

At the beginning of 1967 the First National Development Plan was published, after two years of preparation since Independence. The main architect of this 5-year plan was a Mr Heseltine, an expatriate who'd previously worked in Madagascar and who was now the Director of the Office of NDP. We all read the parts of the Plan affecting Barotse Province (the rest was in an extremely incomprehensible jargon of economics).

Mongu, 1966-67

Those who had been in Mongu for some years could recall visits of investigation by economists/planners, but little consultation as to what officers on the ground might consider feasible. In the time-honoured British way of facing the challenge of implementing the Plan, we formed committees. By April I had established an embryonic District Development Committee, as had my colleagues in other Districts. These involved some District Council members and local politicians plus representatives of every Government department operating in a District (as Mongu was a Provincial HQ, many departments had no separate District representative, and the role was covered by the Provincial Officer).

Then all DSs had to attend a conference in Kitwe to discuss Plan implementation. This was a nationwide conference with about 800 delegates: representatives of the mining, engineering and manufacturing industries, of all major commercial interests, of agriculture, education, health and transport, as well as of many branches of the civil service. When we split into cognate groups, in the DS group I boldly proposed that the Government should set up separate posts of PDO (Provincial Development Officers) since, from my brief experience as Acting Resident Secretary, a Provincial/Resident Secretary would be too busy on other duties to coordinate the work involved. Before the end of May 1967 I had been appointed as the new PDO for Barotse Province and handed over the DS position to Mr Nyumbu – who felt due recognition at last. This also meant that we, as a family, had to move from the designated DS's house on the old airstrip, to a smaller one way down on the road to the hospital; for me, this was an exchange of a fifty metre walk to my office to one of two kilometres. Once I had ceased to be the DS we had far fewer visitors to entertain, but this situation was also helped by the opening of the Lyambai Hotel.

The conference of DSs at Kitwe had been jointly chaired by the Cabinet Minister, Munukayumbwa Sipalo, who knew me from the mine strikes (see the previous chapter), and by Aaron Milner, Minister of State for the Civil Service. I was grateful that Mr Milner had taken on board my proviso at Kitwe that PDOs should be answerable through their Resident Secretaries to the Permanent Secretary, Office of the President, in Lusaka and **not** to the Director of the ONDP, Mr Heseltine, a very cold and remote character. What my budget, transport and secretarial assistance were in my new role I cannot recollect; I must have had some. I had a small office in the Boma, where I set up my own filing system and covered the walls with coloured magnetic dots and strips to indicate progress on each and every item of the development programme throughout the Province. I soon established a reporting system from every DS, with agendas and minutes of their District Development Committees to keep me up-to-date. Next, I established a Provincial Development Committee whose membership included all the Provincial Heads of Departments plus a select group of local UNIP politicians, and asked the Minister (Mr Monga) to chair it. We had our first monthly meeting of this committee in June, and I recall persuading Mr Monga that each meeting's agenda should concentrate on three departments for presentations and detailed scrutiny, while receiving briefer reports and discussions on all others.

For the September meeting of our Provincial Development Committee we had some heavyweight visitors from Lusaka: Simon Kapwepwe (now Vice-President) and Mr Heseltine. They were going to come by road from Livingstone via Sesheke and Senanga. I asked Mr Nyirenda whether I should go to meet them in Sesheke and escort them from there, given that I could more usefully employ myself in the practical details of setting up the meeting; he decided he would go to Sesheke (another chance for some nocturnal 'entertainment' for him?), leaving me as, in effect, his deputy, in charge at Mongu. The visitors arrived. Heseltine upbraided me for not personally meeting them at the Provincial boundary – "that was your big mistake" – and any mention of the agreement with Mr Nyirenda on this issue was swept aside and denied by the latter. Kapwepwe took the chair at the meeting, totally dismissed my agenda, and thereby took several officers completely by surprise by asking for detailed facts and figures for which they were not prepared. It was a deliberate political manoeuvre by Kapwepwe and Heseltine to blame expatriate officers for the relative lack of progress on the Plan in Barotse compared with other Provinces. I was not permitted to speak. I would have wished to point out that this Province suffered from communication and transport problems because of the flood plains and a sandy soil. I was also sure, but would not have said in public, that another reason was the undercurrent of apathy and hostility among local politicians towards central Government in Lusaka.

From my perspective, after all my preparations, the meeting was a disaster. The invitations to myself and several expatriate Heads of Departments to a sundowner at the Minister's that evening were revoked and, instead, four of us were told by Mr Heseltine to report at the airport the following morning to accompany the visitors back to Lusaka "for further talks." The Provincial PWD, Agriculture, and Water Affairs Officers and I duly presented ourselves at the airport in the morning. Here, to his intense embarrassment, my friend the Special Branch Officer was instructed to frisk us for any possible weapons before we boarded the plane with Kapwepwe and Heseltine (I never recovered my nice little penknife). At Lusaka we were taken to Special Branch HQ and effectively kept there under open arrest, with no explanations being given. SBOs took us under guard down to the Lusaka Hotel in Cairo Road for lunch where, by very good luck, I saw the national Director of Water Affairs who had also attended our meeting in Mongu, and quickly whispered to him what seemed to be going on. I heard later that within the hour four Permanent Secretaries including my own corpulent Michael Bwalya were thumping the table in the office of the Cabinet Secretary & Head of the Civil Service (our friend Valentine Musakanya) demanding chastisement of those who had treated their Provincial Officers so abominably.

The President was apparently woken from his siesta to be told by Valentine what had gone on, and this led to not the first argument involving myself between Kaunda and Kapwepwe. Michael Bwalya came personally to rescue the four of us from Special Branch HQ, and early the next morning he personally accompanied us by plane back to Mongu, where I imagine he had strong words to say to Mr Nyirenda. He told me he wanted to calm the probable apprehensions other expatriates there might have had after our sudden departure under escort. He also admitted that in Lusaka they had seen the likelihood of some trouble brewing for me and apologised for not moving me in time. Now, within a matter of days, he arranged a transfer for me, on promotion, to my next job as Senior Principal (Housing) in the Ministry of Local Government & Housing in the capital.

During our stay in Mongu Wendy had been predominantly occupied with bringing up three small children; and she ran the little pre-school play-group. Additionally, as in Bancroft, she involved herself with a Women's Sewing Group and with the local branch of the YWCA. She also helped to found a branch of the Red Cross and this of course entailed fund-raising. When the Mongu Agricultural Show took place in July, she was very busy with her friends sewing and making articles for sale at both the YWCA and the Red Cross stalls. And to her considerable surprise, she was asked to be one of the judges for the "Miss Mongu 1967" competition.

Sadly perhaps, she recalls very little of our time there to add to the above account – except the following anecdotes. One day she heard, far away across the old airstrip but drawing ever nearer, the sounds of a cow in anguish. It turned out to be a man playing a 'friction drum', rubbing his hands up and down a cane attached inside to the skin of the drum. She found the sound irresistible, and we still have the drum. On another occasion, when one expatriate lady wanted to decorate the church for Christmas with cotton wool balls to represent snow, Edward Robinson muttered to Wendy: "We should lock up a donkey and cow in the church for a week, to give it some **real** Christmas atmosphere!" She regrets that they resisted the temptation! Several of the old-timers when we first arrived were still reminiscing about the visit to Mongu of the Queen Mother in May 1960, when she had stayed with the then Resident Commissioner, Gervas Clay – "very best clothes had to be worn." In colonial days the PCs and DCs wore white uniform on formal occasions; I never possessed such a suit, nor wished to.

I was not sorry to leave Mongu, although much of my time had been a valuable experience and "interesting."

* * * * * * *

Thus ended my days in the PA and its successor, the P&DG. What changes had occurred in the P&DG and in the rest of the civil service by 1967, three years after Independence?

Perhaps I was lucky in my personal experiences, or was moved out of the P&DG at a favourable time. One legacy of 'good' PCs and DCs of pre-Independence days was, we appreciated, the way in which senior Zambian civil servants really kept an eye on the well-being and morale of more junior staff (expatriate and Zambian), as Michael Bwalya had demonstrated. The obvious process of Zambianization seemed to have gone steadily and smoothly. At a Copperbelt provincial meeting in early 1966 to discuss petrol rationing, I had noticed that all the DSs in that Province were still expatriates, although of course all Permanent Secretaries in Lusaka were Zambian. But in Barotse Province I was the sole expatriate DS and, at the 1967 Kitwe conference on the National Development Plan (see p155), I was one of only four expatriate DSs from the forty three Districts in the whole country. As I have described in my Chinsali chapter, the transfer after Independence of many responsibilities of former DCs to other departments had led to a decrease – almost an elimination – of junior officers such as DOs in the P&DG.

In September 1964, the month before Independence, the PA had become the P&DG and Resident Ministers had been appointed to each of Zambia's eight provinces. Resident Ministers were supported on the political side by at least one Political Assistant, recruited from the ranks of UNIP. On the administrative side, Resident Secretaries had replaced PCs and had become the senior civil service support for the Resident Minister. DCs had been renamed as, or replaced by, DSs. These changes in fact marked the new government's first moves towards political control of the P&DG.

Yet, initially, no politician was sent to replace the civil servant at District level, the DS. So the DS became more closely involved in political issues than the RS, his superior officer, and could be regarded as the political **and** administrative head of his District until mid-1967, when the UNIP Regional Secretary took over from him as Chairman of the District Development Committee (DDC).

By mid-1966 it was already clear to Government that the performance of the P&DG was not entirely satisfactory. In June of that year, the President issued a circular which attempted to raise the status of RSs and DSs, saying:

From now on I want it to be known and realised that Residential Secretaries and District Secretaries are, in their provinces or districts respectively, my personal civil service representatives

and charging them with certain specific responsibilities: to be the chief coordinating officers in respect of the work of economic development, to maintain the morale and well-being of the civil service, to ensure that government policies were understood by the people and that the presence of the Government was felt throughout the provinces and districts, and generally to supervise the functioning of other Government departments within their Provinces or Districts. But this presidential directive had little impact, and in January 1968 a Working Party of civil servants was set up to examine how the P&DG could be strengthened. Rapid Zambianization, it seemed, had not always been based on clear merit criteria, resulting in a fall in the average educational level of P&DG staff as well as a marked drop in the levels of experience. The standing of the DS fell drastically. He was no longer always the most powerful civil servant in the District or the highest paid or the most educated or the most experienced. Therefore many civil servants in the District ceased to respect him above others or to look to him for leadership. He thus ceased to be an effective coordinator of the different portions of the Government machine, and especially the Local Councils which were usually headed by the UNIP Regional Secretary.

To redress the situation, the 1968 Working Party's report included various proposals for strengthening the P&DG, giving more powers to the DS especially over Local Councils, a higher quality of staff (graduates), and freedom from political control. The President refused to accept most of these proposals, seeing in them a return to the colonial system of local administration. In the new reforms which took effect in January 1969, he not only rejected the call for freedom from political control but greatly increased this control by creating the post of District Governor. The DG was personally appointed by the President as the politico-administrative head of the District with overall responsibility for its good administration as well as for its political management. He was to be the chief Government coordinating officer in the district, with particular regard to the tasks of political and economic development. He took over from the UNIP Regional Secretary as chairman of the District Development Committee (DDC) and other district committees. Administratively he was served by the DS who assisted him in policy formulation and implementation of decisions.

Other important aspects of the President's 1969 reforms were the posting of a Cabinet Minister and Permanent Secretary to each Province (an upgrading of the Resident Minister and RS) and the merger at all levels of the P&DG and the Ministry of Local Government. By this stage and by these means the administration of Provinces and Districts had become more politicized, and Zambia had taken the initial steps towards operating as a one-party state. Valentine strongly objected both to the politicization of the civil service, of which he was the Head, and of the moves towards a one-party state. It may well have been the forthright expression of his objections which led Kaunda in 1970 to sack him from his Cabinet Secretary position and make him Minister of State for Technical Education. Like most of his senior Zambian colleagues, I of course shared his views that the impartial civil service system Zambia had initially inherited from Britain was, and would always be, preferable to the American system of changing the administration whenever a different party came to power.

Thirty years later, the 1995 Report of Zambia's Constitutional Review Commission made several recommendations which, implemented some years later, effectively reconstituted the PA, with the roles and titles of PCs and DCs reinstated (more recently, the title of PC has been changed to Permanent Secretary for the province, to work with the province's Minister – the title DC remains) . I think all this would have pleased John Hudson and others, as the belated recognition of the PA's merits would gratify all those who had served in it. The Commission's recommendations are given in **Appendix 3**.

The developments I have just described took place over the period 1964-69 and, yes, I think I was fortunate to have left the P&DG halfway through the process and merely to observe the second half from the side-lines. I never had to serve under a District Governor. In fact, the above changes hardly affected us at all. Our abiding impression of the post-Independence period was the almost total absence of any anti-European (anti-expatriate) feelings or actions.

10. LUSAKA AND KITWE, 1967-73

These six years, spent in urban environments, were very different for us from our earlier years. I was no longer in the P&DG. I had a series of four jobs, of varying interest. In some ways, although I did not shirk my work responsibilities – and could be accused of overworking for long periods – our family life became more dominant for me, particularly as our three children progressed in succession through nursery schools to Primary Schools and developed fast in their abilities and interests. If therefore my descriptions of details and anecdotes are more sparing in this chapter, this may reflect our genuine feelings at the time that by now life in Zambia was 'normal,' with fewer novelties than we had been fortunate to experience in our first five-and-a-half years. But it was still exciting and far from humdrum and, in retrospect, we seem to have packed in a tremendous amount of activity.

Lusaka itself had changed significantly since 1964. Independence naturally entailed the establishment of dozens of foreign embassies, and much of the area between the main Government offices and Longacres was now occupied by their buildings. Every self-respecting country must have its own university and an international airport; the University of Zambia opened its doors to its first students in March 1966, and about the same time construction of the new airport beyond Chelston was completed. A new Parliament building arose, just off the Great East Road. New large hotels were opening too. Numerous black Mercedes limousines were everywhere, carrying top politicians or civil servants. We had the impression that, despite UDI, the country was very prosperous. Independence had brought its material rewards for many of those who had been prominent in the struggle to achieve it. In Lusaka, at least, there was now a large and growing Zambian middle class, relatively well-to-do and well educated; this was as it should be, and welcome. On the other hand, little had changed in the lives of rural villagers; the poor and the unemployed were still poor and unemployed. The oft-misquoted promises by local politicians in 1963 of "jobs for all" and "money growing on the trees" had not materialised, and I remember in 1968 finding it extraordinary that there had as yet been no violent reaction to those broken political promises while the gap between rich and poor Zambians grew visibly wider day by day. One obvious symptom of this disparity was the continuing growth of squatter-settlements on the outskirts of the capital and the Copperbelt towns, as more and more migrants came in from the rural areas in search of paid jobs.

In the civil service the top jobs of Permanent Secretaries had been given in 1964 to the brightest and, like Valentine and Dominic Mulaisho, they were all in their early 30s. In theory they all had another thirty years of active working lives ahead of them. By 1970 it was recognised that they could not stay where they were forever; they were blocking the promotion of the next age-group of bright young administrators. Most of them therefore moved, or were moved by the President, to become chairmen of the large nationalised companies and industries which had been established at about that time.

Very little of the above affected my work or our family lives. Even the effects of UDI on, for instance, our shopping choices we now just took for granted. In the early 1970s the price of copper worldwide dropped sharply, from £600 to £40 per ton, largely because the USA had found a cheaper substitute they could use for weapons in the Vietnam War; it was an unhappy coincidence that this happened soon after UDI. Despite this, Zambia was holding its head up proudly and on the international scene was considered one of the most successful of the independent African states. Along with Botswana, it was regarded as a 'front-line state' in the fight against the apartheid regimes of Rhodesia and South Africa. In practical terms this seems to have meant that it acted as host to several freedom-fighting movements. We heard rumours of Mugabe's training camps in the wilderness east of Lusaka for the guerrilla war against Rhodesia (the unnecessary war and loss of life for which I have always blamed Britain's spineless acceptance of UDI), and it was said that Nelson Mandela had his ANC's headquarters-in-exile in Lusaka, as did the FRELIMO, UNITA and SWAPO freedom movements of Mozambique, Angola and Namibia respectively. As fact rather than rumour I was aware from Mongu days of the ways in which Zambia played host to thousands of refugees from neighbouring countries from 1966 onwards; starting with a modest 25,000 Angolans in that year, the numbers swelled in later decades from the continuing wars in Angola and the Congo (after we had left Zambia) so that UNHCR estimates have given a figure of 300,000 in 2001, housed in at least eight sites. Given her own economic difficulties arising from UDI, Zambia can be proud of this record of assistance. We were proud of it at the time, too.

* * * * * * *

Ministry of Local Government & Housing, November 1967 to August 1968

On transfer from Mongu we stayed for the first few days in the two-storey Government Rest House of Highlands House on Ridgeway (now called Independence Avenue) before being allocated a house out at Chelston, near the new international airport. It was here that we met up again with Jeremy and Margaret Collingwood from our Mporokoso days and made lasting new friends in Jim and Ena Robertson (see below) and John and Janet Housden. We all lived in the same little residential road, we were frequently popping into each other's houses; all our children played together and their lasting friendships of today date from that time.

I was now Senior Principal (Housing) in the Ministry of Local Government & Housing. This promotion put me on the bottom of the civil service upper salary grade, 'superscale 8'. (A DC's grade was normally the equivalent of a Principal, while DCs with long experience were often promoted to the Senior Principal grade. The position of PC or Resident Secretary, in which I had for a short time been acting, was at the higher grade of Assistant Secretary, 'superscale 6'.)

The offices were a short way down Church Road beyond the Cathedral. My main tasks covered the partial funding of all the city and town councils in the country for their development of various housing schemes. I effectively controlled a budget equivalent in those days to c.£3 million (£35.7 million in today's terms, by an RPI inflation measure, = K408 million), which seemed an enormous amount to somebody of my innocence. Strangely I did little touring around the municipalities to monitor the progress of their schemes, but there must have been some checking system from which I could authorise the release of the next instalments of funds! Most of the work, so far as I can recall, was in encouraging a particular town council to do more, or by correspondence to discuss plans and township sites and funding. I liaised closely with a friend, Jim Robertson of the Zambia Housing Association 'quango'. He was more involved than I with house designs; we certainly worked together on the new site and service schemes, in which the city/town council laid out the roads, water and sewage for an estate and then provided building materials on loans, so that the individual could then build his own house according to an approved design. In mid-1968 the Ministry's portfolio was changed to "Works and Housing" – Local Government became a division of the Office of the President, to be more closely allied to the P&DG in Kaunda's 1969 reforms (see the end of the previous chapter).

At one stage my immediate superior went on leave and I had to take his place as Acting Assistant Secretary for a short time. One of my staff was a female statistician who fed me with endless figures on houses built or to be built in the public sector. She meant well, but didn't give me the buzz for statistics which I had earlier or later in life. Another of my responsibilities was overseeing the 'Lusaka Housing Pool' office, to which every civil servant applied for a house allocation. I inherited the 'points' system on which it operated (much the same as housing waiting lists in UK Local Councils) and made no changes; I think it worked fairly. I stood well aside when, in mid-1968, I myself applied for a move to a more central location and we were allocated our second house, in Maybin Avenue (now Ngumbo Road) – almost opposite our ex-Cambridge Course friends, the Lavenders.

In about July 1968 I was approached by a senior colleague in the Secretariat with a hush-hush proposition. How would I like a new, exciting job, with plenty of travelling? "It might have political dangers attached; your name has been put forward to the President who would approve your appointment if you were willing." I was doing my best in the housing job, but it was not the most interesting or challenging that I'd had. I said Yes to a move.

* * * * * * *

Cabinet Office: Elections Office, August 1968 to 22 July 1969.
So, by some head-hunting system, I was appointed Assistant Director of Elections (Senior Principal grade) in the new sub-department set up in the Cabinet Office to run the first national elections in independent Zambia. The

elections were to be held on 19th December 1968. The Elections Office consisted of a Director and Deputy Director, my old friend Angus McDonald, myself, two young Zambians of 'executive' grade and two mini-skirted expatriate secretaries. Angus was Secretary to the Electoral Commission set up to oversee the operations and ensure they met international standards in fairness. The Commission was chaired by Judge Pickles (with whom Angus had worked on the Commission of Inquiry into the Lumpa Church, and who knew me from my testimony to that body); one member was a distinguished local barrister, Eddie Shamwana.

Our offices were in an annexe of the Secretariat, the grand 1932 building in the most prominent position on Ridgeway. Before Independence this had housed all the important departments of Government, as well as the chamber of the Legislative Council. Now it housed the Cabinet Office, the Office of the President (which included the P&DG, in which I had served for five years), the Establishments Division and the Audit Office. Various 'experts' and special advisers also wandered around, much as I imagine they do in Downing Street, London.

Once we had as a team worked out precisely how the elections would be run, the Deputy Director spent much of his time with a Parliamentary Draftsman in the long process of preparing the necessary Bill and Statutory Instruments. My main jobs, helped by the two executive officers, were: to select, appoint and train all the Returning Officers and Election Officers throughout the country; to write an Election Officers' Handbook which told them precisely what to do and covered every foreseeable problem; and to assemble and distribute all the equipment and small items needed for every polling station – and, at the last stage, the ballot papers themselves. It was a massive job to be completed in four months. We had the trust of the Electoral Commission, and of Kaunda himself who was obviously keen to enhance further his international reputation by ensuring these would be the best-run and fairest national elections in Africa.

Each DS was ex-officio appointed as the Election Officer for all the constituencies in his District; the number of constituencies in a single District might vary, from one to six. That job entailed choosing premises for all the polling stations, appointing all the election staff to man these on polling day, later dividing up and locally distributing all the equipment and supplies I would deliver to them for their District, collecting it all back afterwards, and dealing with all the travel/subsistence claims for payments by those involved. The logistics of all this in a rural District were considerable. A Returning Officer's duties were less onerous, but absolute integrity was required both on Nomination Day and at the close of the poll. All the Election and Returning Officers were summoned to Lusaka where I trained them in their duties, going carefully through the contents of the Handbook. I like to think my Handbook was a success; my colleagues all complimented me on it. It was published by the Government Printer – my only publication to date.

By November and early December I was dashing madly round the country, visiting every District headquarters including those (in Eastern, Southern and North-Western Provinces) which I had not previously seen. I could not take Wendy with me on any of these trips. The initial visits would have been to check progress on the preparations being made by Election Officers; on later ones, shared with the executive officers, I would be delivering election materials. It was all challenging but most enjoyable and I met many interesting DSs (all Zambian by this date).

For Nomination Day we foresaw the likelihood of political troubles, especially in Eastern Province. So I flew there, picking up a 'pool' landrover in Chipata for driving round the Province. Rob Molteno, a researcher in Political Science at the University of Zambia, came there too but under his own steam. Come Nomination Day itself, I set off with a driver for Lundazi, which embraced three constituencies. On the road we were confronted by three roadblocks, set up by local UNIP activists and clearly intended to prevent any candidates from the other parties getting to lodge their nomination papers at Lundazi Boma. We had to crash our way through these barriers, and a man at one of them fired his muzzleloader at our rear as we left – he missed, but dented the landrover. I was furious: I don't like being shot at! Rob Molteno had meanwhile gone the shorter distances to Chadiza and Katete and experienced similar roadblocks.

I flew back to Lusaka, grabbed a secretary and dictated a "strictly confidential" report immediately. By the evening this had been read by the Judge and passed at once to the President. The outcome was that the "unopposed election" of MPs in seven constituencies where there had been such roadblocks "be declared null and void". Kaunda, even without any pressure from the Electoral Commission, had no choice if he wished the elections to be seen to be fair. It was all so silly of UNIP, as they were bound to win all the Eastern Province seats anyway. The seven seats included those of three Cabinet Ministers. By-elections had to be mounted.

Despite that incident, the management of these first national elections was regarded as a great success. For the record, the political results were:

Presidential election:

Kenneth Kaunda	UNIP	1,079,970 votes	81.8%
Harry Nkumbula	ANC	240,017 votes	18.2%

National Assembly elections:

UNIP	657,764 votes	73.2%	81 seats
ANC	228,277 votes	25.4%	23 seats
Independents	12,619 votes	1.4%	1 seats

Voter turnout was 82.5% in the parliamentary election, but 87.1% in the presidential election. The Mpika Returning Officer (the DS) was the last to get his polling results, poor man: it took three days for D/Messengers to carry the ballot boxes up from a polling station down by the Luangwa River and for others to come by canoe across the Bangweulu Wetlands to the Boma!

But I was aware that in due course my name might be associated with the report which had triggered the need for seven by-elections. Action came fairly fast. In January 1967 Kaunda went off to a Commonwealth Prime Ministers' Conference, leaving Simon Kapwepwe as Acting President. I received a letter dated 23rd January from the Establishment Division saying that "in six months you are required to retire in the public interest." Sacked! – and, I quickly discovered, on Kapwepwe's instructions.

I had crossed swords with Kapwepwe twice before: he would have known that the report on his speech of incitement against the ex-Lumpas at Mulanga Mission in August 1964 (see Chapter 6) came from me; and then there had been the 'open arrest' following the Provincial Development Committee meeting in Mongu (see Chapter 9). Kaunda might well have told him I was the author of the report on the Eastern Province roadblocks, and for Kapwepwe this was surely the last straw. Bond must go. The Judge and the rest of the Electoral Commission rushed to my defence, as did the Expatriate Civil Servants' Association; I have on file a series of long letters on the subject, in which the Association claimed that Kapwepwe and Establishments had acted "ultra vires" in using the pejorative reason of "in the public interest" without going through the due process of disciplinary hearings. Had they used the reason of "in the interests of Zambianizing that part of the service", this would have been acceptable; but they couldn't initially change the reason to that, because they had immediately designated another expatriate as my successor – my old friend and ex-Cambridge Course colleague, Malcolm Mitchell, who later took over as Director of Elections. I understood that when Kaunda returned he would have supported me (and the Electoral Commission), but to overturn Kapwepwe's decision now would have created for him a massive political row.

While others fought on my behalf, I considered my next career step. Without my asking, the British Foreign & Commonwealth Office (the Colonial Office was by now dead) wrote to offer me a post in the Solomon Islands – after experiencing independent Zambia I felt that would really be putting the clock back! I wrote to the Overseas Services Resettlement Bureau in London, half-heartedly, and they kept sending me notices of various advertised posts, but none of these interested me. I did apply to UNHCR for some work with refugees, in view of my Chinsali experiences. Indeed, I had often wondered whether my posting to Mongu at that particular time in 1966 was in any way connected with my experiences with the Lumpa resettlement schemes in Chinsali in late 1964 or my very limited involvement with the passage of Belgian refugees through Bancroft. Anyway, I was put off by UNHCR's attitude. All UN organisations observe a quota system of recruitment – a kind of positive discrimination in favour of less developed member states – which makes it hard for a UK officer to find a position in them. When I went for an interview in Lusaka I remember being asked by a man of Middle Eastern origins, in what I thought was a supercilious and arrogant way, what books I'd written on refugee work; I replied: "None, I've just done it in practice" and walked out in disgust.

At the prompting of an old College friend, a World Bank representative visiting Lusaka asked me to a meal at the Hotel Intercontinental and seemed quite interested in recruiting me; but when I was asked what salary range I was looking for in US$, having no idea of New York salaries I completely undersold myself with a figure they would consider ludicrously low (three years later the World Bank offered me quite an attractive position in Ethiopia, but by then I had re-settled in the UK). But really neither I nor Wendy wanted to leave Zambia. Then Eddie Shamwana of the Electoral Commission invited me to take the position of Company Secretary in his furniture firm and, as this was a means of staying put, I accepted.

Meanwhile, I was seeing out my six months in the Elections Office. Our next task was to prepare, similarly, for a national constitutional referendum. This was held on 17th June 1969, on a proposal to remove the requirement for future amendments of clauses in the Constitution protecting fundamental rights to go to a public referendum, and instead to require only a two-thirds majority in the National Assembly. With hindsight this objective might have been seen as a warning of more autocratic systems of governance ahead, but I didn't recognise this at the time. The referendum was passed with 85% in favour of the change. Voter turnout was 69.5%.

Very belatedly, in October 1969, I received another letter from the National Assembly Establishment Division amending the one of January. It read:

In the light of representations received from the Zambia Civil Service Association it has been agreed, with the consent of the Public Service Commission, that your retirement from the Zambia Government was for the purpose of facilitating improvements in the part of the public service to which you belonged, by which greater economy or efficiency might be effected.

This was the standard wording for "Zambianization," much more acceptable than "in the public interest" which suggested a disciplinary measure. It also meant that I would now retain or regain my rights to retirement compensation, pension and passage entitlements as an expatriate.

* * * * * * *

From Northern Rhodesia to Zambia

Willykit (Zambia) Ltd, Lusaka, 2 October 1969 to 13 March 1971.
We went on 'leave pending retirement' in July 1969. We found and bought an old stone farmhouse in Northumberland, and had sufficient renovations done to be able to let it out while we returned to Lusaka in the October. In fact, I went first, with just young Alastair who had to go back to school, while Wendy finished off the work on the farmhouse. We moved into a house provided by Willykit for its senior staff, in Handsworth Park off the Great East Road.

My time at Willykit was the worst period in my whole life. The company produced wooden and upholstered furniture and prefabricated housing panels. My main task was to oversee the accounts and to bring these up to trial balance stage. A qualified accountant came in every month to deal with the higher levels of company accounts; he was a refugee from Biafra, where the war with Nigeria had recently finished. It was only after I had started with the company and had been able to see the books that I realised what financial problems it had. Basically, it was under-capitalised. And I quickly saw that Bond and the profit motive are incompatible. More and more I found I had to do debt collection, driving round to the larger customers (companies) to get prompt payments out of them in order to meet our salaries and wages, while at the same time putting off creditors. It was hard work, and demeaning. But I felt a loyalty to Eddie Shamwana and, having put my hand to the plough, I knew I must do all I could to help him and to make the company break even. I was so grateful to him: he had helped us to stay in Zambia as we had wished, and had given me a salary commensurate with my civil service level – plus a free house.

Meanwhile our family life increased in its excitements and the children were at an interesting stage of development. Alastair (aged six-seven) was now in Grade 2-3 at Northmead school, happy and doing well. Ruth had been a popular figure in the newly formed International Nursery School run by volunteers, down the road from Mulungushi House when we'd lived in Maybin/Ngumbo Road. Wendy as a volunteer became Treasurer at that school, and then became involved in running the YWCA Craft Shop. When we'd moved to the house in Handsworth Park she carried on with YWCA work. More importantly, she undertook a Postgraduate Certificate in Education (PCE) course at the nearby University of Zambia – a useful qualification for later life – and at the same time started *Orbit* (see below).

In September 1970, Zambia hosted the Conference of Heads of State of some fifty countries of the Non-Aligned Movement (NAM). This was of course a great honour for Kaunda personally and for Zambia, and enhanced the international status of both. For this event a grand new conference centre had to be constructed over the preceding year (Mulungushi Hall, next to the Parliament building), plus of course a whole new village to house the VIP visitors and their entourages – much like a village for Olympic Games – and this was almost opposite our estate in Handsworth Park. Alastair used to cycle along to see the conference centre as it neared completion. He became an expert on the flags of every country, which flew on poles beside the approach avenue, and on a couple of occasions had the nerve to point out to the policeman at the gate that certain flags had been hung upside-down!

Ruth started at Northmead school, and Eleanor finally qualified to start at Nursery School when she reached the age of three. Through her dancing class Ruth took part in a production of "The Sound of Music." My mother-in-law came out for Christmas and, apart from trips to Victoria Falls, seemed to spend a lot of time sewing sequins on costumes for that youngster! It was a delight to have her, and she fitted in so well with our circle of friends and our domestic life; on her side she was able to appreciate at first-hand what we had been describing in our weekly letters over the years, and to understand fully why we so loved our life in Zambia.

Meanwhile, on the political front Kaunda was beginning to appear too autocratic to some of his UNIP colleagues and his grip on a united Cabinet was perhaps slipping. Early in 1971 Simon Kapwepwe accused Kaunda of treating the Bemba unfairly, so he and Justin Chimba formed a rival party, the United Progressive Party or UPP, based among the Bemba. Kaunda feared that his two rivals, the ANC and the UPP, would form an alliance to fight the 1973 election. So in 1972 he banned opposition parties; as they were regionally based he accused them of being 'tribalist' (i.e. of putting tribal interests before national ones). Some opposition leaders were imprisoned. This was the start of the period of a one-party state, to which Valentine and his senior colleagues so strongly objected.

But in February 1971, almost as soon as UPP was formed, Kapwepwe fell from grace, and was actually imprisoned on Chilubi Island in the middle of Lake Bangweulu for a short time. My fortunes changed as a result. Out of the blue I received a call from an expatriate colleague in the Establishments Division: "Mick, should you wish to come back into the civil service, now Kapwepwe's gone, I think we have the ideal position for you, in the new Zambia Institute of Technology (ZIT) in Kitwe." This came under the Ministry of Technical & Vocational Education, of which Valentine Musakanya was now Minister of State; so it was fairly clear from where the suggestion for my appointment had come. After sixteen months at Willykit I felt I could resign without dishonour, and Eddie understood.

* * * * * * *

Wendy's *Orbit* Magazine, Lusaka-Kitwe, 1970-73.
Orbit deserves space for its own story. When Valentine became Minister of State for Technical Education, the man who as a boy had endless curiosity about how things worked and constantly experimented seized the opportunity to develop technology in Zambia for everyone, beginning by learning to fly an aeroplane himself! The Zambia Institute of Technology was set up to train young Zambians for an industrial future. But he wanted to lay a really secure technical foundation for **every** child. Wendy was summoned to recommend to him a good science magazine for circulation in schools. It very quickly became clear to her that no one in Europe was producing such a thing, at least not one that could make sense to Zambian children, including those in villages whose only experience of electricity, for example, was at most in a torch.

Valentine said: "When science and technology replace witchcraft here, as they must, everyone should have the knowledge to understand them and not just to believe blindly, replacing one superstition by another." This, then, became her brief for the new Zambian science magazine she created for children, with his encouragement. Valentine negotiated with Geminiscan in London, whose art expert Peter Clark became the third member of the team. They wanted to raise the expectations and ambitions of the young readers of the magazine, so its front cover had a space adventure serial starring two young Zambians! No one was left in any doubt that this was **the** magazine to be reading, because it was so exciting. The "Ackson" stories, contributed by Robert Baptie, were about a much more believable and highly enterprising young Zambian boy and made readers laugh. There were science experiments, a detective story, puzzles, wildlife articles, competitions (including the notable Best Wire Car competition), etc. And Wendy was the editor.

The quality was very high with a standard of colour illustration rarely seen in Africa, and there were no advertisements in the 32 pages. Soon she was asked by other Ministries to include (for example) a Young Farmers' page and a series on African history, as there was a new syllabus in the schools but as yet no materials. The middle-page spread on the waterborne disease, bilharzia, was notorious for its graphic illustration, but effective. The greatest success was the page where, after consulting all kinds of experts, she answered readers' questions which arrived literally by the sack-load at her tiny *Orbit* office. Young people all over the country were eager to get answers to all sorts of questions.

Valentine and Peter must have done a lot of work in the background as the team soon acquired an energetic recruit from the Voluntary Services Overseas (VSO) organisation who took over the magazine's countrywide distribution in a small van. They would also have arranged the details when two young competition prize winners were sent over to the UK, and when Wendy (with the rest of the family in tow) went to Nairobi to exhibit *Orbit* at the All-Africa Trade Fair. There she tried in vain to persuade other countries to use her material for magazines of their own – but Zambia remained unique in having *Orbit*! And somewhere there must surely remain a store of re-usable material. *Orbit* continued to be produced for about forty years – long after we had left Zambia.

There was another spin-off. The Wildlife Conservation Society of Zambia started clubs in schools across the country to interest young children in all aspects of their wildlife, and to encourage these the *Chongololo Magazine* soon took shape, with Wendy's help – and Chongololo Clubs continue to this day in many parts of the country.

Obviously *Orbit* absorbed almost all Wendy's time and energy when she was awake – and her dreams at night. She still found time to engage our children in all sorts of activities and to make clothes for them. But she was not always available for them when they wanted her and, one could say, they learnt the skills of independent living at an early age! However, the family was, and has remained, immensely proud of her achievements as the founder, editor and driving force of *Orbit* and *Chongololo* for those years.

* * * * * * *

Zambia Institute of Technology (ZIT), March 1971 to April 1973
Technical Education was Canada's form of aid to a developing Commonwealth country; the senior staff at the Department's HQ in Lusaka, ZIT's Principal and all its heads of department were Canadian, while most of the lecturers were British.

My position was as Registrar & Administrative Vice-Principal of ZIT. I seemed to work a 7-day week of some 80-100 hours usually, but it was enjoyable even in the details: e.g. controlling the accounts, all the personnel work, smoothing relationships between the overpaid Canadian staff and their relatively underpaid British counterparts, the planning of staff and student numbers, and (through a former Bancroft friend I recruited) overseeing all student affairs including catering, accommodation and social/sports activities. I used to visit the other campuses regularly, at Luanshimba and Luanshya, where the main courses in various technologies were delivered, and at Kitwe centre (the Secretarial College).

Courses in each of the main subjects – Electrical, Electronic, Mining, Architecture and Civil Engineering – were run at two levels. The basic level was for technicians; the more advanced level was for technologists, a label that was not fully understood everywhere but implied an academic standard closer to that of a degree course. For three months each year the students went on placements with the mining companies or other industries on the Copperbelt to gain work experience. Fairly soon, as I recognised the practical content and quality of these courses, I came to the view that, while the University's production of graduates was extremely important, ZIT's output was at least as valuable in terms of the skilled manpower the country needed at this stage in its industrial development – for example, in speeding the process of Zambianization in the mining and engineering sectors.

Lusaka and Kitwe, 1967-73

Our administrative offices were in a former Baptist church on the outskirts of Kitwe. We used the main church as an open-plan room for the clerks; the office of the Principal had a baptismal pool in it, although we were never aware of him using this facility. Behind these offices the new Institute was being built while I was there, and of course I was much involved in its planning and made frequent visits to watch its construction. In December 1987, well after we had left, the Copperbelt University was established by Act of Parliament and ZIT became an integral part of this successor establishment as its School of Engineering & Technology.

My memories of Kitwe are generally positive. We had arrived there on 15th March 1971 and, after a short time in a small house, were allocated a very pleasant house, 6 Hartford Avenue, within walking distance of the city centre. In the front garden was a huge monkey-puzzle tree, and we were once somewhat alarmed to find young Ruth (six and a half years old) had climbed to the top and was merrily waving to us without any fear. Along the side of the house was a row of small mango trees; the game of all the neighbourhood's children was to swing along the branches from one tree to another without touching the ground – to her everlasting regret, Eleanor was not big enough to achieve this feat before we left. Our dog Robbie, the small puppy from Limulunga, was now a very large Alsatian. Apart from chewing stones, he used to chase butterflies (or just their shadows) round the front garden; although he was quite harmless and friendly, these antics obviously terrified people passing by. At the end of the Avenue was one of the large 'slimes dams', created by dumping the unusable extracts from the Nkana mines. This was the favourite place for our children and their friends to play – dusty but wonderful for imaginative adventures.

Wendy, from a room in our house, continued to work on her great *Orbit* magazine, which she had started in Lusaka. With her conspicuous little blue van she used to travel a lot, both to Lusaka and around schools, and developed further all her practical skills in composing, editing, publishing and distributing this incredibly successful children's educational magazine.

We used to visit the Mindolo Ecumenical Centre quite often. Muriel Sanderson, our friend from Kitwe UCZ Church, was at that time the treasurer and accountant at Mindolo and continued to be so for at least another thirty years before she retired to Gaberone. She was the sister of Ruth Khama and hence sister-in-law of Seretse Khama, Botswana's distinguished President. At Mindolo pool our children were taught to swim, and of course Wendy swam too.

Kitwe Primary School was only a two hundred metres walk from the house. Alastair had had eighteen months at Northmead School in Lusaka and Ruth had had six months there too. Now they were both at Kitwe Primary, and Eleanor too started there after a pre-school year next door to us. They were all very happy and had many friends: Eleanor was diving into Mindolo pool at age four, Ruth learnt to bake at the Brownies, and Alastair was well known in every township. I am not sure that they suffered too much from the lack of constant parental presence as they grew more skilled in independent living, though they will doubtless disagree!

My sister came over from New York in August 1971. We met her in Dar-es-Salaam, and this gave us the opportunity to drive back through the exciting scenery of southern Tanzania and also to revisit parts of Mporokoso District for the first time since 1964. My mother-in-law came out for a second visit from the UK in May 1972 and, among other delights, was able to spend a few days in the Kafue National Park. We also had two wonderful family holidays in Malawi, visiting Livingstonia, spending a few memorable days and nights on Nyika Plateau, climbing a little way up Mt. Mlanje, and of course swimming at many spots along the Lake.

In April 1973 my initial contract with ZIT (or the Ministry of Technical Education) was coming to an end, and it wasn't clear whether they would definitely offer me a further contract. I was now thirty five and, conscious of our original recognition of a 'suicide career', felt I should postpone no longer the hassle of finding employment for the first time back in the UK. Alastair was now ten and we had to think of a secondary school for him. A ZIT friend drew my attention to a suitable advertised post at Newcastle University, where she had been an undergraduate, and while on leave I applied for it and was successful. So our severing of ties with ZIT was mutually convenient.

As for leaving Zambia, of course we were very sad. But we had seen or heard so many other expatriates become embittered and looking over their shoulders to the apparently 'good old days'. We avoided that, deliberately. We could honestly say we left with the happiest memories of the country intact for all of us.

11. CONTRASTS AND RETROSPECT, SEEN FROM 2012

Apart from two two-day quick liaison visits I made to the University in Lusaka on behalf of Newcastle University, I did not set foot in Zambia again until April/May 2012. The spurs for revisiting then, with Wendy, were purely personal: to celebrate both our Golden Wedding Anniversary in a far more memorable way than just having a party, and the fifty years' anniversary of our first arrival in the then Northern Rhodesia.

It turned out to be a most glorious journey of a lifetime. We hired a 4x4 with a tent on its roof, being unsure what accommodation we might find on our month-long tour and anyway hoping to camp in the bush sometimes (in the event we only used the tent for six nights). We drove to Livingstone, to see the Falls and the Museum; then to Sesheke, aiming to go via Senanga and see Mongu again – but the Kalongola pontoon was closed as the Zambezi floods were still too high, so we had to backtrack and go via Mulobezi to Kaoma and Kasempa, missing out Mongu entirely. Next we visited our old haunts in Chililabombwe, Chingola and Kitwe before heading up the Great North Road. The Mutinondo Wilderness area, Kundalila Falls, Nsalu caves, Kasanka National Park and Livingstone's grave at Old Chitambo were all sights we had not seen in the old days. New, too, was the so-called 'Chinese road' running from the Great North Road to Samfya and Luapula Province. After Mbereshi and Kawambwa we travelled around almost the whole of Mporokoso and Kaputa Districts, our favourite areas and still feeling so very familiar, and spent two nights relaxing at Ndole Bay on Lake Tanganyika. Then we revisited Kasama, Isoka, Chinsali and Shiwa Ngandu before returning to Lusaka for the final three days.

A major objective of this trip was to revisit in particular the rural areas of Zambia which we had known and loved the best, and out of curiosity to find out what differences men and women in those areas thought had been made to their lives since the 1960s with the advent of Independence, democracy and various development schemes. We did not expect to find any of our friends still there. We hoped that by talking to village headmen, women, old men telling stories in their *insakas*, Chiefs, local councillors and politicians, government officials, teachers and pupils, fishermen and farmers, craftsmen and traders, we'd be able to identify the main changes they saw in their lives and experiences since the 1960s – changes to traditional village life and customs, local government and politics, customary law, education, health and hygiene, cash crops or subsistence farming, marketing of rural crafts, communications and so on. Who now made the decisions at the local level? What were the opportunities nowadays for a bright child in the village?

These aims proved to be over-optimistic because we were moving on too fast with too many kilometres to cover. We did indeed wander around a few villages and chat to their headmen and groups of women – mostly in Mporokoso District but also in Kasempa, Chinsali and Mpika. We did have talks with three of the present Chiefs (Nsama, Mporokoso and Mukupa Kaoma), and had long and easy discussions with the managers or staff at most of the guest houses and lodges at which we stayed – some of them gave us most perceptive comments on how they saw the country's present political and economic situation. But we were aware that the impressions we gathered could be no more than superficial. However, we did happily renew our acquaintance with the typical sights and sounds of village, township, birds and waterfalls, regaining strong impressions of the diversity of the country and some awareness of the lives of real people. Our first stretch of driving on a dirt road gave us a real sense of homecoming!

It was wonderful to renew our friendship with Flavia Musakanya. Over lunch at her farm outside Lusaka she recounted to us aspects of Valentine's imprisonment in 1983-85 (along with Eddie Shamwana he had been convicted of treason but eventually released because the sole evidence against him was a confession extracted after torture). She remains as strong, fierce and full of humour as ever. We were also able to have a half-hour audience with ex-President Kaunda, now eighty eight but still with his friendly smile – and he remembered me; with him was his charming daughter, Cheswa, one of the twins whom in 1964 Mama Kaunda and Wendy had briefly exchanged with our baby Ruth for cuddles!

And a moving highlight for us was the very emotional reunion with James, who had looked after us from 1962 to 1969, now retired and in his home village of Lupungu, plus his wife Daviness and their now middle-aged children who used to play with ours. We could recall how helpful and loyal

James had always been, and could remind Daviness how much she had done in the past to teach our children good African manners when they had spent time with her and her children at their end of the garden.

We found we were both still sufficiently fluent in ciBemba to be quite relaxed in any company, and this language facility opened many doors for us. It was admittedly flattering to hear how astonished people were that we could remember so much ciBemba after an absence of thirty nine years. At least the use of it immediately established our credentials as 'old-timers' who had once belonged there, not *basungu* in the sense of 'foreigners'. With Chiefs, with James and Daviness, and with villagers we certainly used ciBemba almost exclusively. I was pleased to find that very quickly I was thinking in ciBemba again, not having to translate into it; and so often it expressed my thoughts more naturally than an English version would, anyway.

* * * * * * *

So what **were** our impressions? What had we learnt from the visit? We certainly wanted to avoid making judgemental comparisons with the past from our expatriate standpoint and to try to see things from a Zambian perspective. What changes did we find in the Zambia of today compared with 1962-73? I would say these could be considered in terms of five main categories: rural development, trade and commerce, governance, wildlife and natural resources, and people.

We had to remind ourselves of the fact that Zambia's population has grown from 3.4 million in the 1963 census to more than 13 million in the 2010 census. The only comparable statistics I can easily get of the breakdown have to take the figures for Lusaka plus the Copperbelt towns as proxy for the total urban areas, and show:

	1963	2010
Lusaka + Copperbelt (≈ urban?):	601,900 (17.6%)	4,110,000 (31.6%)
The rest (≈ mainly rural?):	2,809,300 (82.4%)	8,890,000 (68.4%).

That means the rural population has increased by 316% while the urban has grown by 683%. Lusaka's expansion was most noticeable, but we were aware that every small town has probably doubled in size over the period. We did not, however, see the kind of large squatter settlements (Nairobi-style) on the town fringes as we had in the 1960s; most urban development seemed to be in large estates of well-built housing. But, to be fair, we did not explore many of those areas.

The most noticeable positive developments in the rural areas since our days, particularly in the old Northern Province which we knew best, were the profusion of schools and hospitals, the provision of electricity and telephones in the towns, and the improved communications.

We were impressed by how many more schools we found in the rural districts than in the 1960s. That means, among other things, that children on average do not have to travel quite so far to get to school as they used to. 'Basic' schools seemed to be the most common, taking children from Year 1 up to Year 9, halfway through Secondary school grades, and these are mainly in areas with no secondary schools. Primary education had been free in the Kaunda years, but not during Chiluba's presidency. Since 2002 it has, thankfully, been free again and apparently the statistics suggest that all children do go to school; yet the number of schools still does not appear to keep pace with the population growth and some children cannot find places. Parents have to pay for uniforms plus books and pencils, and the cost of these items for a family with several children could be a crippling burden. We noticed that at the beginning of the new term each child takes to school a hoe or a slasher and puts in time sprucing up the school grounds – good practical experience! – and we even saw parents at one bush school joining in the work. We learnt that English is now no longer the usual medium for teaching as from day 1, and the results are sadly clear: Zambians of the youngest generation seem to have poorer fluency in this language than their older counterparts. As in the past, the life of a rural teacher, working two shifts a day and very isolated, continues to be hard. New to us were both the practice for every school to have a motto (e.g. 'Work Diligently'), displaying this proudly on the signpost to it, and the posters seen in most rural schools (even Primary Schools) warning against unsafe sex. The buildings, too, are all good; I don't think we saw any of the old type built with Kimberly brick and thatched roofs – although we did not see any of the 'community schools' which I suspect were built in the old style, less permanent materials.

The many large rural hospitals we saw all looked from their outsides to be well-sited, well-maintained and clean. How different this is from our days in Mporokoso, with its nearest hospital at Kasama! I only hope the present ones are all adequately staffed too, and that high standards are maintained in staff training (as e.g. for nurses at Mukinge Hill and Chitambo Mission). The HIV/AIDS problems were of course new to us: we noticed the isolation blocks for the sufferers, but we didn't notice people in the villages obviously affected.

Of course, to support the operation of the new hospitals and the many new Government offices in rural townships, there has had to be a massive investment since Independence in providing electricity and telephone landlines. Zambia's geographical position, largely on a mid-continent plateau enclosing the headwaters of so many rivers, gives it more opportunities than neighbouring countries have for developing hydro-electric schemes – quite apart from the huge Kariba and Kafue Dams which we did not revisit. We did not consciously look out for these schemes but we sensed that there had been quite a proliferation since our day (e.g. Musonda and Chishimba Falls, Shiwa), and rightly so. There are lines of electricity pylons through rural areas (I think Kaputa was the only township we noticed which still only had a diesel generator). This spread of electric power has transformed much of the country and people's ways of living in the townships. What we observed, with some pleasure, were the solar panels beside or on the roofs of so many houses in quite remote villages – again, such an obvious development should be expected. We also saw swathes of bush beside the roads cleared for lines of telephone poles but, we heard, the landline network is overloaded and unreliable. New to us, too, if to be expected in modern times were the abundance of mobile phones and of the transmitting masts positioned on the hills to support them; in all the larger villages there were stores offering facilities to recharge cell phones. The proliferation of cell phones does suggest that more cash is now available in the remotest villages than previously.

As for transport, I noted with some nostalgia that the bicycle remains the most useful possession for anyone living in the bush. We began to record the great variety of loads carried by bicycle: eight fish traps, as many as three heavy bags of charcoal or mealie-meal, sheets of corrugated iron for roofing, goats, a bed, and of course women and children, etc.

So many roads have now been tarred. If I compare the distances we drove on tar and dirt in 2012 with the same roads in 1964 I get the following statistics:

    1964   tar   1,213 kms (18%);   dirt/laterite   5,439 kms (82%)
    2012   tar   4,319 kms (65%);   dirt/laterite   2,333 kms (35%).

This road development has certainly opened up parts of the North-Western, Luapula and Northern Provinces and improved the access to markets, and I was pleased to see that the upgrading process was continuing in the Northern and Muchinga Provinces. The 'Chinese Road' bypassing the Congo Pedicle is a great benefit, as are the new bridges built or planned across the Zambezi, Luapula, Kalungwishi and Chambeshi Rivers. However, we were disgusted at seeing the appalling treatment of local labour by Chinese contractors on their road projects, e.g. on the Sesheke-Sioma road (the workers' shacks seemed to me far worse than I've seen in Nairobi's squatter settlements or the Bophutatswana 'homelands' of apartheid S.Africa!).

Both population growth and the improvements in communications by road have had their effects on trade. In urban areas the huge increase of trading and industrial estates, though these were unsightly, was a positive sign of economic growth. Zambia is now clearly exporting a lot: we found lorries stretched in lines at every major pontoon and border, laden with outgoing goods. It was hard to see what the loads were, except at Kashiba on the Luapula where sacks of mealie-meal were being loaded into barges for ferrying across to the Congo to be exchanged for beer and *citenge* cloth – *ubwali* for *ubwalwa*. The lorry route through Botswana seemed to be the most favoured one going south. Zambia has experienced a series of good harvests and that year's was no exception. It was sad to see that virtually nothing was going by rail, and when I chatted to railway officials at both Kasama and Kapiri Mposhi stations they confessed that TAZARA was bankrupt; certainly no passenger trains were running to or from Dar-es-Salaam, and no current timetables were displayed in the vast empty waiting halls.

Contrasts and Retrospect, Seen from 2012

Commerce seems to be thriving. But we experienced several differences in the shopping situation. It took some time for us to find out in Lusaka where to shop for supplies – no longer simply at CBC in Cairo Road! There was a small supermarket at Longacres, but this was clearly not where the well-off went now. In Chililabombwe the shop was the same but the goods on the shelves were few and uninspiring. We thought the South African chain of huge supermarkets called Shoprite would soon kill off all other groceries wherever they were established, although the imported goods they stocked were often of poor quality. Sesheke still had tiny grocery stores, staffed by overqualified young men. Best of all were the rural bakeries with delicious smells of new bread and often doughnuts. Mporokoso market was an eye-opener – quite apart from the great stacks of dried fish, there were mountains of big round cabbages, spinach and chinese leaves, all fresh, whereas in our day the only greens came when the one local farmer visited in his landrover or when we had grown our own in the Boma garden. There were shops of all sizes and colours in the larger villages selling specialities like *citenge* or pans or a mixture of small goods (e.g. soap) in neat stacks. A retail urge seemed to have gripped the nation. And always there were roadside stalls with tomatoes, melons or charcoal.

How the Civil Service was now operating was obviously of great interest to me, although a month's tour was too brief to get a full picture. Several people told me, to my quiet pleasure, that the impartial British-style civil service system, in contrast to an American-style party-based system, was regarded as one of the best colonial legacies. But this view was only realised after the two decades of Kaunda's 'One Party State'. It was one of my worries in the 1970s, and even more Valentine Musakanya's, that the one-party system would inevitably lead to a politicization of civil servants – they would cease to be impartial, and would protect their careers by doing just what a politician asked them to, whether it was right or wrong. Actually, when I visited Lusaka briefly in 1992, Valentine (by then released from prison and regarded by some as an elder statesman) tried to persuade me to return to Zambia to undertake a retraining of civil servants in the former style of strict impartiality, now that the one-party system had gone; it was an interesting proposal, but I was not prepared to give up my secure job at Newcastle for this pipe-dream – even for a friend. During our stay this time at Shiwa Ngandu we were privileged to meet and to talk at length with two Permanent Secretaries, one of the new Muchinga Province and one from Lusaka. They were highly intelligent, articulate, open-minded, very professional top civil servants, absolute workaholics, presumably incorruptible, and most impressive. We felt that, if all senior civil servants were of the calibre and enthusiasm of these two, the future for Zambia looked rosy.

In the Provinces the return of the DC post instead of the political District Governor, following the Constitutional Review Commission's report in 1995 (see **Appendix 3**), seemed to be welcomed and a success. It was interesting to meet several female DCs; the demands of the job are different from those of my day, and more women in key positions is obviously a good step forward. But I wondered whether the divisions of some Districts into two and the proliferation of Government departments' offices in every rural Boma was fully justified by actual developmental activity and the increase in population. One lodge manager told us firmly that he thought the creation of so many new Districts (e.g. now Kaputa, Mungwi, Nakonde, etc.) – and now a new Muchinga Province – was 'jobs for the boys'. In colonial days the Government provided housing with hard furniture, and this was justified because most officers were expatriates who were moved frequently; when Chiluba became President these assets were abolished and all civil servants had to buy their houses – I did not find out how easily this operates in practice, when I assume civil servants are still frequently moved between stations.

As for District Messengers, it is hard to avoid comparisons between the 1960s and now. It should be clear from earlier chapters that our D/Ms in pre-Independence days were not only a DC's eyes and ears but the outward and visible signs to everybody of the authority of the DC and Government. Even in times of trouble they were universally respected. They were absolutely honest, loyal, friendly and courteous, and very hard-working – often being sent off on their bicycles for days on end (in all weathers) to organise bridge or road repairs. They were expected to use their initiative, which they invariably did. But those I talked to in 2012 were very different. With their smart white shirts and long trousers or skirts (yes, some were women!), their jobs seemed confined to errands around the offices. One at

Mporokoso confessed that he only went anywhere in the District by landrover when accompanying the DC. It is not my right to criticize – if that's how Government wishes to use its messengers, so be it. But the contrast with the magnificent D/M force of the past saddened me.

I only met (had audiences with) three Chiefs: one pompous and self-important, one most unimpressive, one an absolute gentleman. Everybody I asked confirmed my hope that Chiefs generally still enjoyed people's respect as their traditional leaders, presided in the local courts and maintained tribal customs. The more proactive (better educated perhaps?) had more influence, as we saw in the varying standards of village layout, neatness and maintenance. I was also pleased to note that the House of Chiefs, established in 1963, has been revitalised in recent years after a period of stagnation, and that a whole section is devoted to its powers and responsibilities in the proposed new Constitution. What I could not find out clearly was the Chiefs' relationships with the local District Councils which we had formed a year before Independence; for instance, were any Chiefs members of such Councils ex-officio, sitting alongside elected members? The various road signs we had seen to a Chief's 'palace' did indicate a very positive attitude to these leaders.

I wanted to meet Bruce Munyama, but failed. Bruce had been Permanent Secretary, Ministry of Justice, in the early days of Zambia (1964-1973), a jovial and highly intelligent friend of Valentine through whom we met. I had discovered that President Chiluba had set up a Commission in 1993, headed by Bruce and hence called the Munyama Commission, "to investigate human rights violations by past governments". This Commission had exposed the use of torture in prisons and secret detention camps throughout the country, and its report led to a permanent Human Rights Commission being established under the Constitution in 1996. This HRC was tasked with "investigating human rights violations, proposing remedies to prevent abuses," mediating for victims of human rights abuses and acting as a spokesperson for detainees. This seemed to me a great leap forward for any country, and I should have liked to discuss all this with Bruce. In particular, I wondered whether the admitted torture of our friend Valentine in the treason trial of 1983 had in any way influenced the setting up of the Munyama Commission.

From Northern Rhodesia to Zambia

The National Monuments Commission became the National Heritage Conservation Commission by an Act of 1994. We met a most well-informed and enthusiastic officer of the Commission working in the Northern Province (we were even surprised and delighted to find that our last old house at Mporokoso, together with the DC's house of our day, being built before 1914 had been designated as "national heritage buildings"!) The number of national monuments or sites has increased tremendously over the last forty years; we only saw seventeen, but we were most impressed by the pride the caretakers generally had in restoring and maintaining the old buildings and their gardens, and the natural sites such as the waterfalls.

The importance of wildlife and its impact on other aspects of life deserve serious consideration. The game we saw in the wild on our trip was minimal but exciting: not only impala, puku, vervet monkeys, baboons and hares, but (far less common) a honey badger, a silver-backed jackal, a monitor lizard, sitatunga and red lechwe. But it was very sad to hear that not a single native rhino of either species was left alive anywhere in the country. The almost complete disappearance of game animals except in the major National Parks might be due to the pressures of increased population in the rural areas, deforestation, hunger in the bad times, or simply poaching to supply the insatiable overseas demands. The effects on tourism must be to restrict its potential for future expansion, if game-viewing is to be confined to Kafue, Luangwa, Lochinvar and the Lower Zambezi Parks, i.e. for only the rich safari tourist. However, animals are being imported to stock or re-stock some small parks, e.g. Sioma; protection might bring them back to others, such as Kasanka and Lavushi Manda. There are also the private parks where some owner-managers are trying against the odds to protect game. We noticed two other effects of the lack of game, though these were more mundane: no tsetse-fly control gates (and no such flies meant more cattle were kept); and we saw no spears! In our day it would be unthinkable for a lone villager to go off into the bush, even to his distant garden, without a spear for either self-protection or the legitimate catching of dinner. I even doubted whether they still had the odd muzzle-loader in a hut. Could they, these days, handle such basic weapons? What particularly surprised and concerned us was the almost total absence now of small reptiles, such as chameleons, the once very common blueskop lizards, centipedes (*chongololo* – we saw one) or snakes.

The other very visible differences we noticed in rural areas since the 1960-70s were the widespread deforestation, and the related massive increase in the production and sale of charcoal. I thought these were very negative aspects of modern Zambia. True, we now had some superb long-distance views because of the lack of trees, views which in the old days we did not know existed, but that is no justifiable consolation. All along the Great North Road were hundreds of bags of charcoal waiting for collection. It was confirmed to us in Chinsali that bags were being illegally exported via Tanzania to Saudi Arabia; their price went up through all the middle-men until they cost a small fortune in Saudi Arabia. Apart from the deforestation issue, the Muchinga Permanent Secretary was concerned at the economics: none of the vast profits came back to the local Zambians who had made the charcoal. We found it at least reassuring to hear both Kaunda and the Permanent Secretary taking these issues very seriously, not only in their internal effects but even more regarding the illegal export of charcoal.

I would add a quote, from the plaque on the Chichele Tree.

The Tree's Prayer:
Ye who would pass by and raise your hand against me, hearken ere you harm me. I am the heat of your hearth on the cold winter nights, the friendly shade screening you from the summer sun. And my fruits are refreshing draughts quenching your thirsts as you journey on. I am the beam that holds your house, the board of your table, the bed on which you lie and the timber that builds your boat. I am the handle of your hoe and the door of your homestead, the wood of your cradle and the shell of your coffin. I am the gift of God and the friend of man. Ye who pass by, listen to my prayer. HARM ME NOT.

The Chichele Mofu Tree was declared a National Monument by Kaunda on March 21st 1976 to celebrate World Forestry Day. "It symbolizes the need to conserve trees and use them wisely." It seems a pity that this message no longer resonates. Wendy herself invented an adage: "if the people look after the trees, the trees will look after the people". We were doubtful whether there is any longer a Minister in the Government taking active responsibility for the environment.

As for rosewood and teak, we were upset to see much evidence of the indiscriminate logging of these valuable species, on the road from Mulobezi to Kaoma. We knew that the export of rosewood and teak from Zambia was illegal: the villagers probably did not. They merely felled the huge trees (and some very young ones), used donkeys or ox-carts to drag the logs to the roadside, and were ignorant and innocent of what happened to the wood thereafter. It seemed likely to us that there was a big 'scam' here: some middlemen in Lusaka were making a killing by collecting the timber and passing it on to be exported to China or an Arab country at an exorbitant price – just like ivory and rhino horn, and equally highly valued. We were disgusted, not only because the trees are 'protected' and their felling is illegal but because of the inferred corruption in high places associated with their export.

With regard to natural resources and the awareness people should have of them, it was gratifying for Wendy to hear how so many people could remember reading *Orbit* in their youth and/or being in a Chongololo Club. As for the clubs (or lack of them) now, she was able to identify the main obstacles in rural areas: over-worked teachers, poor communications, only a monthly postal service, poor radio reception, and lack of radios or access to the internet. Town children were as addicted to their cell phones as children in the UK, and rural children rarely had books to read. But it was disappointing for her not to be able to trace the forty years' worth of *Orbit* material, which should be largely reusable even though *Orbit* had long since ceased to be a science magazine using eye-catching graphics. But on the plus side we were pleased to hear at Shiwa Ngandu that all the children at its estate school were taught to know the names and behaviours of all the animals (wild and domestic), and encouraged to report any problems they might notice among them, and that some 4,000 children passed through the estate each year on educational or family visits. So Shiwa was playing a role in wildlife awareness. We hope similar projects are going on elsewhere.

Contrasts and Retrospect, Seen from 2012

My observations on people were varied. Zambian women, in the towns at least, were now clearly taking on a wide variety of roles, many of them in leadership positions. There was a confidence and ease about them, most visible in the care and attention they paid to their appearance and especially to their hair; this was now worn long, in an astonishing range of styles, and was supremely elegant. In the villages of the rural areas, however, there were the much more familiar (to us) scenes of women surrounded by children, and still able to carry a load on their heads these days! Cooking was still being done with charcoal just as it always had been and we saw fires in the evenings. The villages themselves retained their characteristic styles in the different areas, but many more houses were now built of burnt bricks and had corrugated iron roofs; these improvements, plus the occasional village well, seemed the main contributions to easing the workload of the women after fifty years.

We were really surprised how few Europeans we met or even saw. Apart from in Lusaka and Livingstone, they totalled twenty eight only throughout our month's tour and they were mostly at the lodges! And we saw no others on the Copperbelt or in any other town. Why? There must be thousands of people of European origin and expatriates working on fixed contracts. As for foreign tourists, outside of Livingstone we were the only two from the UK. Of course our tally would be completely different if we had visited the major National Parks of Kafue or Luangwa. Asian Zambians were also very thin on the ground now. Then there were the Chinese. Nobody really had a good word to say for them, especially when they refused to speak either English or a local language and simply used gestures. Yet they continued to secure contracts. We hope Zambia will keep the Chinese presence within reasonable limits and avoid economic exploitation or excessive infiltration; its wealth in natural resources makes it vulnerable. As for domestic security, while we used to lock our doors at night, in none of our houses did we have gates or fences. It is a pity to see that in Zambia today most houses in the low density areas of towns are thought to need these protections; it must surely make it less easy for informal neighbourly visits, and give children the sense of unknown dangers surrounding them. We did notice the large numbers of unemployed youths but, when the subject was raised (as it often was), we found we had to explain that this was a serious problem worldwide these days, not confined to Zambia.

"You are a living part of our history, a part we know nothing about! You must tell us what it was like" (see Foreword). Yes, this genuine plea to hear us talk about our past was flattering but, more seriously, deserves to be addressed. I noticed with some sadness that in the history section of the otherwise fascinating Livingstone Museum there was plenty of material on the nationalist struggle for Independence, and then a complete gap until the 1990s. This gap does need filling, and not just in school education. We were given the impression, happily, that the UK is now regarded as just a good friend of Zambia but no more so than any other western country, and that the colonial connections have been almost completely forgotten – except for a few comments on the positive sides of the legacy (e.g. education, health, law, the civil service, and some buildings); I gained no idea, for example, whether the British Council has any influence.

* * * * * * *

So, putting aside our visit of 2012 and returning mentally to our 1962-73 period, how would I summarise our experiences over those eleven years? How and why did we enjoy that period so much?

We were extremely lucky in many ways. One obvious example was the friendship with Valentine, which had started when he lived with us in Cambridge. I never abused this; he was still, for me, the top civil servant and then the Minister of State for Technical Education and to be given full respect accordingly. But behind the scenes he had obviously initiated favourable moves for me of which at the time I was totally unaware – the move from Mongu, probably the next move into the Elections Office, certainly the move to ZIT, and equally certainly asking Wendy to start *Orbit*. We owed him more gratitude than we perhaps realised at the time. And it was probably more through our friendship than because of my position as a middle-ranking civil servant that we also came to know several Permanent Secretaries and their wives. To Eddie, too, I owed much, for giving me a job which at least allowed us to stay in Zambia after 1969.

Contrasts and Retrospect, Seen from 2012

We were so lucky, too, to be posted in the first instance to Mporokoso. It was such a wonderful District not just for its variety and places of interest but for the warm and caring friendship of all the people we lived among or worked with. Our colleagues helped us to adjust quickly to our new experiences, always ready with advice and encouragement for us; our DCs in particular were generous, and good at giving us (and others) breaks when these were needed to keep up the morale. When I became more senior I hope I treated my staff in a similar caring way, but I doubt it. I also hope that that caring attitude continued in the Zambian Civil Service after I left it.

Additionally, I felt lucky – and privileged – to have the variety of jobs and postings that came my way. In spite of all its difficulties, I am so glad to have had the experiences of that exhausting year in Chinsali; I'm sure it made something of me.

With the advantage of hindsight, I would identify and summarize all the benefits we gained, and the good lessons we learnt, from those eleven years in the country in the following paragraphs.

We experienced at first-hand, and therefore could understand, the last two years of the British colonial system. Of course we recognised this had to be replaced, and we sincerely felt we were playing a very small part in helping to achieve a smooth preparation for, and transition to, Independence. While to a great extent we found the system racial, class-ridden and out-of-date, its arrogance had also at times some amusing aspects for us. I could not change the history of the previous eighty years, but I could still appreciate the many benefits colonial civil servants had strived to bring, with considerable success, to the Protectorate of Northern Rhodesia; and they had done so on a shoestring, on tiny budgets – if we in 1962-64 had had the size of post-Independence budgets, I can only imagine the greater developments we should have been able to achieve! Many features of the British legacy do not cause me to be ashamed.

To have lived and worked through the periods of Internal Self-Government and of Independence, and to have witnessed the impact of these events on the different categories of Zambian society – from the leading politicans and civil servants to the ordinary villagers, as well as expatriates of various hues – was a privilege not granted to many of my associates in later life. To that extent I am proud to have been "a living part of the history of Zambia" through those momentous years.

I was able to maintain my original principle of following a 'suicide career' and of therefore readily accepting my role as an expatriate, whose services Zambia could dispense with as and when it wished. One aspect of this was the need at times to adopt a protective role towards my Zambian counterparts in the late 1960s: for example, they might feel timid about voicing their serious objections to some actions or policies of Government for fear of jeopardising their career prospects, while I could act as their voice because I had nothing comparable to lose – as an expatriate I had somewhere else to go. There have been several occasions later in life when I have similarly found myself in the position of whistle-blowing on behalf of, and to protect, others. Both in Zambia and in the UK I would like to think this kind of action has earned me some trust and respect for perceived integrity.

We became used to change, and learnt to adapt quickly and cheerfully to new or changing situations, however unexpected or worrying they might at first seem. This often entailed a measure of self-confidence, and certainly of mutual trust between members of the family. It also requires a positive philosophy – "it'll all be for the best in the long run." We lived in sixteen different houses over the eleven years, so we became accustomed to change at the domestic level! On a wider scale, I can boast in the UK that we had experienced more rapid changes in Zambia (in developments and in ways of living) over eleven years than most European countries have been through in the course of a century.

Our children grew up in an atmosphere of freedom, warm friendship and racial equality – and value those concepts today, passing them on to their children too. They could wander freely to play, usually going barefoot, mixing easily and unselfconsciously with children of different races and social backgrounds. I must add that the excellent educational grounding they received at Northmead and Kitwe Primary Schools (with fifty children in every class) put them far ahead of other children when they came to the UK. And the bullying and cruelty they came across in UK schools contrasted harshly with their experiences of the great mutual support all Zambian children naturally give each other.

Initiative was welcomed and encouraged. Again, there was a measure of luck, but I wonder in what other situation or country Wendy could have had similar opportunities to develop her successful *Orbit* magazine. And all her other activities (Women's Welfare, YWCA Craft Shop, children's nurseries, etc.) were so well received and welcomed. We have as a result not been shy of pursuing initiatives in later life.

We learnt, too, to endure and adapt to shortages, and to expect and enjoy a life without luxuries. In Chapter 8 I mentioned the first effects of UDI, but it should be remembered that shortages of many basic foodstuffs and of other domestic requirements continued on and off for the rest of our time. For the children's birthdays and Christmas presents we mostly made toys or sewed dresses and other items of clothing. So our practical skills increased – "necessity is the mother of invention."

I had witnessed extreme poverty, hunger, destitution, deaths from violence, etc. (especially in Chinsali) which made me that much more conscious of my own luck and privileged lifestyle and the unfortunate fate of my fellow human beings. In spite of all their registered Charities, UK residents do not see at first-hand or comprehend the plight of such people. Our experiences have been humbling.

We have also learnt that material possessions can be very pleasant but are not to be valued as much as human interactions. Perhaps the abiding memory of our days in Zambia is characterised by the word *"ubuntu"* – an abstract concept common to all the Bantu-speaking languages – usually translated into English (inadequately) as "a sense of humanity" but perhaps best captured as follows:

> "No man is an island" – John Donne, 1624, together with
>
> "A man's a man for a' that." – Robert Burns, 1790.

This we enjoyed in our dealings with almost all Zambians, of whatever social standing.

Yes, those years in Northern Rhodesia and Zambia were the happiest and spiritually most rewarding or enriching of my whole life.

Appendix 1
My First Tour Report: Chief Mukupa Kaoma's area, 1963

Set out below is a copy of my first Tour Report in full. My DC would make comments on each annexure before forwarding a copy of the report to the PC. At the end of my Report are my hand-drawn map of the area and statistical tables; the latter were of great use to the 'Native Authority' for tax purposes, and gave us a clear insight on male migrant labour – most went to the Copperbelt for employment. I have retained copies of my second and third Tour Reports, whose length and contents (including statistics and maps) are similar.

The Report's inclusion in this book is intended to answer an average reader's queries as to what pre-Independence DOs did on tour, why they went, and what were their interests and objectives.

NORTHERN PROVINCE   MPOROKOSO DISTRICT
TOUR REPORT No. 1 OF 1963.
AREA: CHIEF MUKUPA KAOMA

Touring Officer:	Mr M.A.H.Bond, District Officer (Cadet).
Area toured:	Chundu and Malaila Parishes, Chief Mukupa Kaoma's.
Object of tour:	Routine administration.
Date left station:	Tuesday, 26th February, 1963.
Date returned to station:	Sunday, 10th March, 1963.
Number of days on tour:	13.
Miles travelled:	112 by vehicle; 225 on cycle and on foot.
Number of villages visited:	37.Administrative Secretary, Gracewell Sikazwe; Court Clerk, Henry Chongo; Court Members, Alexander Kombe and John Musonda; District Messengers, Kapasus, carriers. (District Commissioner, Mr Alan McGregor, for three days only).
Previous tour reports on the area.	No. 3 of 1960, No. 3 of 1961 (part).

Annexures:
- I General
- II The Native Authority, and Tax
- III The Native Court
- IV Agriculture
- V Education
- VI Development
- VII Communications
- VIII Health
- IX Game
- X Population
   Map and statistics

MPOROKOSO M.A.H.BOND
13. 3. 63 DISTRICT OFFICER (CADET)

ANNEXURE I; GENERAL.

Chief Mukupa Kaoma's area, lying directly to the south of Mporokoso Boma, is mostly high plateau rising to over 5,000 feet in many places. It encompasses the headwaters of three large rivers and their tributaries: the Kalungwishi, Luangwa and Lukulu. The Musumba is sited on the crest of an escarpment, with a fine view to the south-east over the upper basin of the Lukulu. The two parishes toured were Chundu in the north-east and Malaila including the Musumba in the south-east; they form the larger and more interesting part of the Chief's area, but had not been toured by a Boma officer since 1960. A number of changes have taken place since then.

The Lungu area, comprising Chiefs Mukupa Kaoma and his cousin Chitoshi, is very much the Cinderella of Mporokoso District. There is little or no trade, and hardly any labour except that provided occasionally by the poor Native Authority or recently by the small Agricultural Department sub-station. At first sight it has little to offer in its natural resources, and certainly nothing to compare with the fish industry of the Tabwa to the north. The Native Treasury struggles; without a generous deficiency grant at the end of last year, its head would scarcely be above water.

The people are very friendly, contented and for the most part easy-going, and this impression is given by the Native Authority staff as well as the villager. Some effects of this attitude may be noticed in other parts of this report. At

Appendix 1

any rate, for all its deficiencies, this is a most happy area to visit and work in. The touring party was well received in all but a few villages and, although times have changed, the older people still observe some of the elaborate etiquette of greeting the touring officer. At most villages, and more especially in the north, food was provided for the party. The villages were generally of a high standard, clean and well laid out, although small. The Chief obviously takes a pride in the condition of the villages, and when a village moves he personally chooses the new site and plans the layout; in this and in other ways he keeps in close contact with the people. He himself was unfortunately not able to accompany me on tour, as he had only returned from a session of the House of Chiefs when I was half-way through, and then he was preparing to follow up his work there by visits to his fellow Chiefs in this and neighbouring Districts. However, he took great interest in the progress of the tour and at the end we had long discussions on matters arising.

Politically the whole area is quiet. They had their troubles in 1958 and 1961, just like everybody else; road blocks were constructed, the school staff were in fear of their lives, and the Chief was threatened by a mob with spears. At election time last year I presided at the polling station here and nothing could have been more peaceful. There are few branches of political parties here compared with the rest of the District, and local opinion is that most trouble-makers that do appear come from the neighbouring area of Chief Shibwalya Kapila. During the course of the tour a political meeting was held at the Musumba, and one of my Messengers went to attend. From his report I gathered that, in spite of distances, more than half of the 450 audience had come from the areas of Chiefs Chitoshi and Shibwalya Kapila, and nearly all those locally resident came from the Musumba itself. In the villages we toured that day only three people had gone to attend that meeting. My general impression is (and here, as in most of my report, I make the distinction between the Musumba with its environs and the rest of the outlying villages) that in the villages the people are not madly interested in politics; they just wish to live, to let live, and to be left alone. The same easily contented and unambitious attitude may be noticed in their relationships with the Native Authority, the Boma, and other Government Departments; they respect them all, so long as they don't trouble them.

The theme of the talks we gave to the villagers while on tour included an explanation of the new Government, in what ways it has not changed, the forthcoming census, the House of Chiefs, and identity certificates. Audience response was always polite and they seemed to agree with all that was said. I would have liked plenty of questions and arguments, but got none. I also tried to enquire more informally what they expected from Government in return for their taxes and so on, and again I got the impression that for the most part they were either content that Government knew what it was doing (why meddle in such celestial matters?) or content that progress should pass them by. No party posters or other signs of political activity were seen in the whole area.

The religion of the area is almost entirely Roman Catholic, and the schools here are run by the White Fathers. There is, however, no Mission in the whole of the Chief's country. Worship takes place in the houses, and very few churches were found; in one village an excellent new church has been built in the last few months in Kimberley brick and the old one is being turned into a cattle shed. There are a few Watchtower adherents in the vicinity of the Musumba and they too have a Kimberley brick church, close to the road. Some of the farmers are Watchtower, and have in the past allowed their religious convictions to play a part in their relations with the Agricultural Department and with the schools, but no such trouble is apparent now. The Administrative Secretary is a lone Seventh Day Adventist, and consequently does not work on Saturdays.

The touring party visited the "Ngulu shrine" near Chongo Chibimbi. This is a natural outcrop of granite rocks, about five in number, the largest of which measures some 35 feet in height and 50 feet in width and is so striking in its solitary grandeur and unexpected position that it naturally contains a powerful spirit. The spirit of the Ngulu is said to live in a python which guards the rocks and the spring which emanates from the base of them. I had read of this python from earlier reports but we saw no sign of him. This used to be the shrine of the Chief's hunting spirit, and had to be invoked before the Chief set out on a hunting expedition. Superstition with regard to it is dying fast; the villagers and ourselves climbed all over the rocks without thought of sacrilege and the present Chief often visits it as a tourist attraction.

Five exemption certificates were issued, no new identity certificates. A total of 64 guns were recorded in the two parishes, including 7 shotguns.

Comments on Annexure I above by the District Commissioner,
This was Mr Bond's first village-to-village tour and he has clearly made the most of his opportunities.

As he says, the Lungu area of this District does not offer any very obvious channels of development but the Chief is a notable figure both locally and in the wider sphere of the House of Chiefs.

A.N.McGregor

ANNEXURE II: THE NATIVE AUTHORITY, AND TAX

Chief Mukupa Kaoma is progressive and ambitious for the welfare of his people. He keeps himself well informed and is in close touch with what is going on in his area and in his people's minds. I shall not forget my first meeting with him when I found him working in the Administrative Secretary's office during the latter's absence and dealing most competently with the day-to-day administration. He is an easy person to work with, has definite opinions of his own, and deliberates carefully on all sides of a problem before making up his mind. He never seems to bully his staff or be overbearing towards his people, and obviously commands their affection and respect. He is to be congratulated on his recent election to the House of Chiefs, an honour which he undoubtedly deserves and a responsibility which he takes very seriously. Unfortunately the facilities are not readily at hand in his area to be equal to his high hopes, but one could not say that he would fail for want of trying. He became Chief in 1950 and, from what I can gather, has matured greatly in wisdom and experience since he took office.

The Administrative Secretary, Gracewell Sikazwe, is again a delightful personality, and runs the Native Authority with reasonable efficiency. He has not been in this District for many years, having spent most of his service under Senior Chief Tafuna in his home area. On tour he was competent and cheerful, but I was sometimes surprised to notice how unacquainted he was with the villages and the people. He has been on two training courses at Chalimbana and one at Mungwi, some time ago; he did reasonably well but not as well as perhaps he thinks. What he would like now is to go on a course to England (in place of the Chief who had similar hopes but has since postponed them), but perhaps what is needed is an assessment of his abilities at one of the new Mungwi courses.

Anthony Chipasha, who has been Treasury Clerk since 1956, is Standard VI but of not high material. He is slow and hard-working, but on a number of occasions has got himself into great difficulties with his accounts. At the end of the tour I inspected his books and his February Trial Balance, and after the necessary amendments they were found to be correct. The Native Treasury is poor, and is not helped by the fact that nobody at Mukupa Kaoma has a firm grasp of financial matters. It is a pity that the pleasant and friendly attitude which one finds among the staff cannot compensate for this unfortunate deficiency.

There remain the Kapasus, a smart and hard-working force. I was particularly impressed on tour with the new Head Kapasu who, though young, showed great authority and efficiency and was at all times helpful and thoughtful.

The Native Authority building programme has been going ahead well. The office block was built in 1961 and there are now nine staff houses, the last of which should be completed and inhabited this month. There is also a house for a Dispensary Assistant which is just ready for occupation. The Administrative Secretary is undoubtedly a good builder, whatever his other failings, and supervises the construction closely with the eye of an expert. Transport of materials and labour problems made progress last year rather slow, and the delay in the release of money from loans and grants was partly the cause for the Native Authority staff to exist for four months without salary, a hardship they endured with customary cheerfulness.

Tax collection is a more serious reason for the impecunious state of the Lungu Treasury. So often the excuse for low tax revenue is that the bulk of the taxpayers are on the Copperbelt and beyond the control of the home Treasury. With a few rough figures I should like to prove that this argument has no basis. Briefly, in the Lungu areas of Mukupa Kaoma and Chitoshi during 1962:- estimated taxable rate £1,205; amount received, £180 locally

Appendix 1

and about £600 from the Copperbelt (due allowance being made for those employed elsewhere); taxable population estimate, 980 local and 1,825 on the Copperbelt; conclusion, only 40% of those locally resident paid tax, while 55% of those on the Copperbelt paid tax! The political uncertainty last year and elections undoubtedly had their effect on tax collection, but if this effect was at all widespread it makes little difference to the disparity between these figures. Of course we here can do little about the other 45% on the Copperbelt but there is little excuse for collecting from only 40% within one's own area. Another reason for this position is, I feel, the easy-going attitude of the Native Authority staff, to which I have referred earlier. If they go without their salaries for failure to collect levy, that is principally their own affair, but failure to collect tax is a serious neglect of their duty to Central Government.

While on tour, about £30 was collected in tax and the same amount in levy. All of it was 1962 tax or even 1961's. There is thus no reason why in the current year, collecting for 1961, '62 and '63 plus a sizeable amount in late payments, they should not exceed their present estimates. This was pointed out to them and a careful watch will be kept on their collection figures. They must show they mean business, once the months of grace have expired, or they will lose their authority over the people – which in this respect is very low anyway at present. In two distant villages I visited almost all the taxpayers had deserted over the border into Chief Munkonge's area on our approach; the Native Authority had to be told to send back Kapasus the following week to collect defaulters. The Chief, however, takes a much firmer hand, and his recent tour in another parish may have spread rumours and had its effect on other tax defaulters.

The system adopted last year with many tax defaulters was to confiscate their bicycles, and the idea was to sell these later and recover tax from them. A dozen bicycles were found still in the lock-up. The disadvantage of this system is to deprive a man of one of the means of finding labour through which to pay his tax. Many people would gladly have served as carriers on tour, but they had no bicycles.

Comments on Annexure II above by the District Commissioner.
I agree with Mr Bond's comments on the staff of this Native Authority

which serves as the Headquarters for the two Lungu Chiefs.

The tax figures are worse than I had expected for, although until the end of 1962 the Chief was very loth to take vigorous action, there have been recent signs that he realises his Treasury's need for the revenue. His absence at two meetings of the House of Chiefs has since delayed things but I think we shall see considerable improvement in the months ahead. His staff very definitely need his driving force behind them before they can achieve much.

The seizure of bicycles is a difficult point and the Authority's legal powers in this matter have been explained to it in detail. This is one case in which the staff show no lack of enthusiasm! It may be as much the relative lowness of the pay offered as lack of bicycles which discouraged potential carriers, and it is for consideration whether the extra 3d per day should not be introduced in this District – a carrier's day is certainly a more strenuous one than the average road labourer's.

A.N.McGregor

ANNEXURE III: THE NATIVE COURT

Chief Mukupa Kaoma has a Grade D Court with power to impose a maximum sentence of £15 fine or three months imprisonment. At present the Lungu native Rules and Orders give an alternative sentence in most cases, of £1 fine = one month or £5 = 3 months, but the Chief is considering putting forward an amendment to raise fines given, on the basis that if a labourer these days earns 3/- per day a month's imprisonment is equivalent to at least a £4 fine. A drawback to this plan was pointed out to him, that more people would opt for a prison sentence, since they have little money and would be as willing to work in prison as spend the time sitting at home with no work – and, besides, the conditions at Mporokoso prison are not unattractive (and at Milima are luxurious, I am told); consequently the Court might well lose an important part of its revenue.

Appeals go to the superior Court of Senior Chief Tafuna in Abercorn District. There have been no appeals recently, which perhaps indicates the fairness of judgements in the eyes of the people.

Appendix 1

The Chief himself is clearly experienced and very well acquainted with the law, and hears most of the cases himself. This may be necessary at the moment, since his two Court Members are both new to the job, but under pressure of other commitments he is naturally anxious that they should cope with most of the work by themselves. The Court Members, Alexander Kombe and John Musonda, were appointed in January 1962 and January 1963 respectively. Their appearances (a cowboy and a prize-fighter) do not do justice to their obvious potential abilities. They seem to command great respect and authority among the people, and they are both conscientious in studying the law.

The office of Court Clerk has also changed hands recently. Henry Chongo, son-in-law of the ex-Head Kapasu, took over in November 1962 and again is busy learning the law. Although on probation at present, the Chief has high hopes that he will gain sufficient experience in the next six months to be an asset to the Native Court. He is Standard VI and a former temporary Kapasu. At first acquaintance he appears conceited and insolent, but until I know him better I would say it is only a mannerism.

At the end of the tour the Court Clerk's books and case records were checked, and a number of skeletons in the cupboard were found, left over by his predecessor who was not famed for his accuracy or legibility. About 120 cases were heard in the Court during the last twelve months, with no prize for popularity going to any particular type. What was alarming was the number of outstanding fines:- 93 for a total of £109-6-6, the majority pending since 1962 and some being outstanding for well over a year. In its present financial state especially the Native Authority and Court cannot afford such inefficiency in the execution of justice, and the Court Clerk has been warned (though his predecessors may be more to blame) to take immediate steps to recover these fines. The trouble partly lies, I think, in the Court Room itself; the case records have shown no date by which the fine must be paid and on which the alternative of imprisonment will be imposed, and Court Members have now been advised to include this in their judgements so that firm action may be taken immediately the deadline is reached. In the last month or so this system has been observed, but it does not lessen the task of catching up on 1962 defaulters.

No cases were heard on tour, in spite of my encouragement to do so when an obvious instance presented itself. I was informed that, with regard to the normal offences one meets on tour, it was the custom for the Native Authority to tour all areas in April for tax collection and village hygiene inspection, and that villagers were given grace until the end of the rains to put their houses in order. I feel that on this subject, as on that of my previous paragraph, too much grace is given, and the Native Authority will suffer for its easy-going attitude.

<u>Comments on Annexure III above by the District Commissioner.</u>
The previous Court Clerk was very definitely at fault on the collection of fines and compensation outstanding. I had cause to bring this forcibly to his attention when going through the books with him and his successor at the end of last year. Several of the people concerned have left the District since fines were imposed but every effort will be made to collect the rest. Two men have recently been committed for contempt of Court in such cases and the Chief himself is well aware of what is needed.

A.N.MacGregor

ANNEXURE IV: AGRICULTURE
The villages continue to practise shifting cultivation, and the staple produce is cassava, with maize and finger millet. Down in the valleys below the escarpment, where the soils seem more fertile, cassava matures in two or three years, but in some of the higher parts it was observed to take as long as four years sometimes. At this time of the year (early March) most of the villagers were engaged in fencing their gardens; some were already beginning to lop branches for October burning, which seemed a little early. In first year gardens we often saw sweet potatoes and cucumbers, and in a second year garden usually beans and groundnuts. Occasionally pumpkins were seen. Mushrooms are now out of season. I had the impression that the relish part of the diet was poor and not varied enough, but it is difficult to judge without closer study.

As the country lies at the headwaters of the rivers there is virtually no fish

Appendix 1

and, with lack of meat in many parts, this is a serious deficiency in the diet. Only in the lower Luangwa in the extreme north-west, outside the area toured, are fish caught. There have been several suggestions in the past for trading with the Tabwa for fish, but so far nothing has happened and it is difficult yet to know what to give the Tabwa in return. At the Musumba there are a number of small fish ponds which have been started under the encouragement of the Agricultural staff, but this is on too small a scale. The Chief has a larger fish pond, about one square mile of marsh near Vincent Bulaya, which is fed by a furrow. This has not been a great success yet as the first load of fish to be deposited there died on the journey, but with the help of the Agricultural Assistant he is still hopeful for better results this year.

The main development activity is concentrated around the Musumba and is under the general management of a quiet but most helpful Agricultural Assisitant and his Demonstrator. The Assistant has been here since 1959, and has a fine large house which is very much the envy of the Native Authority staff. Improved farming methods and the introduction of cash crops such as tobacco and coffee have been the achievements of the last few years. Tobacco is now in its third year. After a poor start, when the growers were discouraged by the return from their first attempts, the area under tobacco cultivation has risen from 2½ acres last year to about 9 acres this year. It is all the 'samsun' variety of Turkish tobacco. In all there are 21 growers, including the large individual farmers. At first the Agricultural Department gave the growers the seedlings and fertilizer ("V" solution containing plenty of nitrogen for the young plants), but as the growers become more successful they will have to pay for these items. The crop is harvested from April to June, baled and labelled on the spot after two weeks of drying and curing; the marketing problem is handled by the Department at present, who transport the bales to Lusaka for collection by the Salisbury manufacturers, but again it is hoped that in the near future the growers will be sufficiently prosperous and competent to carry on the marketing by themselves.

There is an excellent coffee nursery run by the Department with sufficient seedlings for the bedding of about 50 acres. As coffee needs a fair amount of mulching, napier grass is grown in the rotation system for this purpose. Here again the produce is marketed by the Department, but they plan to provide a small pulping plant at Mukupa Kaoma soon and buy the beans from the growers.

Sites are being prepared for twenty small farms close to the nursery, of about four acres each, divided by windbreaks down the slope and served by a furrow along the contour. Three of these farms are already under cultivation, and a few more on the same pattern at nearby Kalimanshila. The finished farms will have an orchard and house plot (½ acre each), coffee and napier grass (1 acre each), and a final acre divided into six plots for crop rotation. Though this neat plan is the usual one, it is outside the previous experience of the small farmers and will require constant patience and instruction on the part of the Department to ensure its success. All round the Musumba methods of crop rotation are being introduced, on the five-year system of finger millet, tobacco, groundnuts, maize, and finally sun hemp (as green manure). As with tobacco, fertilizer (sulphate of ammonia) will be provided at low cost; the Agricultural Officer is going to experiment and demonstrate with one farmer, giving him the fertilizer free and encouraging others with the success of the first man. In this area it is essential to employ scientific methods and get away from the *citemene* system, since the population around the Musumba is already too high to be supported by the land available for wasteful *citemene*.

Villagers sometimes allow only eight years regeneration before re-cutting, unless dissuaded; just here there is scarcely enough land for this undesirable rate of felling, let alone for the more fastidious demands of the Forestry Department for at least 20 years of uninhibited growth. Generally this point is appreciated by the local inhabitants and response to scientific rotation is good, especially from the older men which is somewhat surprising. The Agricultural Department's policy is to persuade them to make the transition rather than compel them, and it has no doubts that by these means farming development will be achieved which will fit in with the general plans for improving the Musumba's environs.

There are three large farmers in the vicinity, each with about 12 acres. Two of them have been on a farmers' course at Mungwi for six months, and they all took up farming only a couple of years ago. They received the usual loan in kind to start their ventures – 4 oxen, 2 cows, 2 ploughs and labour for stumping the land – and are repaying in £12 per annum instalments. They too are growing cash crops but also go in for larger amounts of staple

Appendix 1

food produce on a rotation system. One of these, Philip Mukupa, has not been co-operating with the Department and his fertilizer loan has not been provided; he is not growing tobacco this year. Farms of this kind are large by Mporokoso District standards, and every encouragement should be made to interest others in similar enterprises, both for the agricultural development of this area and to alleviate the unemployment problem.

In the last two months a Local Farmers' Committee has been formed under the guidance of the Assistant and the chairmanship of the Administrative Secretary who takes a keen interest in agriculture. The various farmers with large or small interests have been divided into four groups which each send a representative to the committee. The committee's aims are to discuss new techniques and development in their own plots, but I hope that as they become more firmly established themselves they will give thought to the need for agricultural progress in other parts of the Chief's area than just in the vicinity of the Musumba.

A rainfall gauge has recently been installed, mainly for observation of the coffee's rain supply. In the last two calendar months 17 inches were recorded, compared with 24 inches at the Boma.

The figures for livestock in the area toured are as follows:

	Bulls & Oxen	Cows	Sheep	Goats	Pigs
(a) Villages					
Yowane Lupiya	-	-	30	-	-
Others, Chundu Parish	-	-	22	8	15
Chongo Chibimba	1	1	42	18	-
Timothy Chiinga	-	-	23	-	-
John Mwamba	-	-	10	13	-
Others, Malaila Parish	2	3	40	6	-
(b) Farmers					
Philip Muswilwa	6	2	-	-	-
Philip Mukupa	4	4	-	-	-
Frank Enga Enga	4	5	-	-	-
Mark Enga Enga	4	1	-	-	-
Total	21	16	167	45	15

There is no tsetse fly in the Chief's area, and good natural grazing ground in many parts. I feel that villages particularly should be encouraged to breed and keep more livestock to supplement their own diet and as a possible source for local income. Cattle of course are expensive to obtain, but the problem should not be dismissed. On this point the Assistant said he hoped to introduce rotation grazing in the next year or two, to build up the number of sheep in the villages and on farms, and eventually to produce a butchery.

In conclusion it must be stressed that agriculture is the key to development in this poor area, and co-operation from all sections of the community must be given to the Agricultural Department staff who are doing a fine job. People are learning slowly by watching the success of a few. I should like to see more happening in the villages and hope that the Department's staff will be able to spread their influence there, once the initial hard work near the Musumba has established firm roots.

Comments on Annexure IV above by the District Commissioner.

The Parliamentary Secretary to the Ministry of African Agriculture on his recent visit expressed optimism for the future of both coffee and tobacco in the District. He paid a short visit to the Mukupa Kaoma sub-station. It is cheering to know that the older men are prepared to take advice on rotation, and I underline the touring officer's hope that the extension staff will be able to spend more time beyond their sub-station.

A.N.MacGregor

ANNEXURE V: EDUCATION

The area is not well covered by schools. There are only three in the whole of the Chief's area, two of which were visited during the tour. In the north the closing down of Pemba School, over the border in Chief Shibwalya Kapila's area, has not helped the situation. Further over to the north-west, in an area not visited this time, most of the children go to Sunkutu School in Chief Mporokoso's area. In the south, where there is a large child population, Mukupa Kaoma can obviously not cope with the number of applicants for Sub A level, and the children go to Chitoshi or Lubushi when they cannot find room at home.

Appendix 1

At the Northern Province Education Authority's 17th meeting it was proposed that provision should be made in the five-year Primary Schools Development Plan for the upgrading of Mukupa Kaoma School, and that a Standard III class should be opened in 1965. This is certainly required as soon as possible. Equally urgent is the provision for another Lower Primary School to serve the border areas of Mukupa Kaoma and Chitoshi, and Mutoba Kaibele has been put forward as a suggested site, in Chitoshi's area. In the area toured there were 1,319 children resident, excluding those at school in other areas, perhaps equivalent to some 600 of Primary School age; there are 440 school places at home, of which not a few are taken by children from outside the area as will be seen. Thus, given the possible inaccuracy of my statistics, a third of the children go without education of any kind.

Vincent Bulaya:-
This is an Upper and Lower Primary School in the north of Mukupa Kaoma's area, only five miles from the border with Bemba country. It is run by the White Fathers and comes within the circuit of the Manager of Schools at Kapatu Mission. There is one Headteacher, Mr.Ndakala, in charge of both parts of the school, but he finds that he does not have enough opportunity for proper supervision of the Lower School, and in the foreseeable future the schools may be run separately under two Headteachers. Topographically, however, the two sections form one unit, sited in a rough circle with a diameter of only 200 yards between the Upper and Lower buildings. There is a staff of eight, including one female teacher, and all appear to be quite satisfactory. Father Bedard visits the school frequently, mainly to supervise the building programme, and the new Provincial Education Officer visited it only a week before my tour.

The roll and attendance statistics are as follows:

	On Roll		Attendance		Full Boarders	Weekly		Daily	
Std	Boys	Girls	Boys	Girls	Boys only	Boys	Girls	Boys	Girls
Sub A	20	20	19.9	19.2	-	5	7	15	13
Sub B	20	20	19.8	19.9	-	7	4	13	16
I	27	13	25.4	12.5	-	9	6	18	7
II	26	14	25.9	14	-	12	6	14	8
III	31	10	30.5	9.8	-	19	4	12	6
IV	27	9	25.8	9	-	21	5	6	4
V	36	-	34.9	-	31	-	-	5	-
VI	40	-	37.6	-	31	-	-	9	-
Totals	227	86	96.8%	98.1%	62	73	32	92	54

Standard V and VI boys living more than a mile from the school automatically become full boarders. On the day I visited the school, the grounds were littered with the senior boys with their books, swotting hard for the Secondary School selection examination which was to take place the following week. There are no Standard V or VI girls, it will be noticed; they go from here to Chilubula Mission School in Kasama District (also White Fathers'). The standard of education in the school is high, and well above the Provincial average, as shown by these 1962 Standard VI results:-

Entered	Passed	% Pass	Prov. average	Prov. position: 1962	1961
37	34	92%	74.6%	5th	8th

From here the majority of the boys (97% in 1962) go on to the Secondary School of St.Francis, Malole, in Kasama District. The feeder schools for Vincent Bulaya Upper School, apart from its own Lower Primary School, are Mukupa Kaoma and Chewe. A second intake at Standard V comes in from Kapatu and Kalabwe Mission Schools which both go as far as Standard IV. Apart from Chewe, these schools are all about 30 miles away.

Appendix 1

In the current school year there were more than 80 applicants for Sub A, so that half the local children are deprived of education from the very start.

A heavy building programme has been going on in the last year, and has nearly been completed:

1 x 2-classroom block: needs only furniture for the teachers;
2 teachers' houses: one needs doors, the other only to be painted;
1 dormitory for 20 children: needs paint only;
1 store room: needs doors, windows and whitewash.

All these buildings were inspected and I found a good job has been made of them all. The White Fathers have not stinted where a little extra money would provide better results, but they are running into a little financial difficulty in this final phase. One of the teachers is a trades instructor and has closely supervised the actual construction; both he and the boys seem naturally very proud of their new buildings. It is hoped that the next stage in the programme will be the demolition of the old thatched classroom block in the Upper Primary School, once they can move into the new one; in its place or just behind will then, perhaps, be built a dining room block with a kitchen attached.

Vincent Bulaya is always a joy to visit. The site is good (though too close to the village, but the Chief wants the village to move soon), the staff are very helpful and co-operative, and there always seems to be some activity going on. Sports include the usual items: football and athletics twice a week, stoolball, volleyball, netball and rounders. Football fixtures with other schools present the usual problems of lack of transport; if the senior boys had not been studying hard when we visited the school I should have liked to challenge them to a match against the touring party – any fixture would be most gratefully received. They have a Scout troop, too, of about 32 (not enough girls to form Guides), but they lack the leadership to be a first class troop at the moment. We met their patrol leaders at their camp near Mporokoso last October. Their religious society, the Saverian Movement, though less practical in application, is an indoor equivalent to scouting in its aims and is well supported.

The Headteacher is very proud of their combined debating society and drama group, and in spite of obvious lack of amenities for the latter section, these activities are also enthusiastically supported. I should like to see them in action, in either capacity. The school is most fortunate in having a well-stocked library, containing 608 books on subjects of every variety. These books are bought by the White Fathers on a £5 per annum grant – a system which, with the present appetite for anything in print, must give the advantage to their schoolchildren in competition with others. The children themselves run the library, under the direction of an assistant teacher.

On the ground sloping down to the river the school has a fine garden and orchard. This again is entirely managed and worked by the boys; they sell their produce of cassava or vegetables to the teachers and the rest goes to the school for their own maintenance. The orchard is quite large, and full of bananas, oranges, lemons, guavas, mangoes and so forth,

Mukupa Kaoma:
After Vincent Bulaya, this school is a bit of a disappointment. It is a Lower Primary School only, run by the White Fathers from Lubushi. The Headteacher indicated that he would appreciate more frequent and regular visits from the Manager of Schools. The usual statistics are:-

	On Roll		Attendance		Weekly Boarders		Daily	
Std	Boys	Girls	Boys	Girls	Boys	Girls	Boys	Girls
Sub A	24	16	22.95	15.7	18	8	9	8
Sub B	26	11	25.6	9.7	13	4	13	7
I	22	18	21.1	16,4	11	7	11	11
II	28	12	27.52	12.0	16	5	12	7
Totals	100	57	97.2%	96.1%	58	24	45	33

This is a feeder school for Chitoshi and secondarily Vincent Bulaya, both 28 miles away. Last year 24 children passed their Standard II but only 14 of these were able to find places at the other schools and the rest had to return to their villages. They had over 100 applicants for Sub A this year, which meant turning away three-fifths. These facts speak for themselves and, I hope, in support of the upgrading of the school.

The staff consists of the Headteacher and his Assistant, of Standard VI and V respectively and both studying for higher qualifications themselves.

Appendix 1

There is also a female Assistant Teacher. As is generally found in schools of this grade, the teaching day is divided between work with the upper two and lower two standards, and the teachers do their best in the circumstances to keep the children well occupied when not in the classroom.

The buildings consist of one old-type classroom block, two teachers' houses and several dormitories. The classroom block is re-thatched every year, but the walls and primitive desks are in bad condition; their maintenance is a Native Authority responsibility, but the Administrative Secretary seems more inclined to find fault with the original construction than to make the necessary repairs. The teachers' houses, in permanent materials, were built in 1958; for some reason they still have no internal doors, and the Headteacher is at last thinking of getting help from learner carpenters at the nearby Rural Development Extension Team. The dormitories are small pole-and-dagga huts that have to be destroyed and rebuilt each year. After a year they accumulate ticks and bed-bugs, but the Provincial Medical Officer has said that this is the school's affair. If this is not due to poor hygiene methods, the problem will not be solved until a dormitory block is built in permanent materials. It is encouraging to note that the parents have already burnt the bricks and provided the timber to start on such a venture, and again carpentry and semi-skilled labour may be available from the extension team; all that is needed are the other materials. Watchtower and local politicians did cause trouble in 1960 and 1961, but no interference is felt now.

There is a small orchard and garden, and a fish pond that is well stocked. The teachers keep rabbits, which are breeding furiously.

Comments on Annexure V above by the District Commissioner.

The Lungu area has suffered from being on the fringe of various Missions' spheres of influence. Kapatu, Lubushi and Luwingu are all stations of the White Fathers, some 60, 53 and 60 miles respectively from the Musumba, but they have all tended to concentrate upon the Bemba on their doorsteps. But the position is improving. Munshimbwe in the north-west corner of the Chief's area is due to open as SubA this year and Mutoba Kaibele is on the District list though no date can be given for its opening. Once Mukupa Kaoma School is upgraded the Lungu will have three schools providing

Standards III and IV. The Administrative Secretary is a lively member of the District Education Authority and can be relied on to ensure that the interests of this area are not overlooked.

A.N.MacGregor

ANNEXURE VI: DEVELOPMENT

Enough has already been said on agricultural development, which must remain the lynch-pin of overall development here. All other plans are, rightly, concentrated on Mukupa Kaoma Musumba.

For some years there have been vague ideas for the construction of a proper neatly laid-out township at the Musumba, and the Chief has kept a close eye on the erection of permanent or semi-permanent buildings so that their sites fit into the general plan. Permanent buildings are for the most part Native Authority staff houses, the offices, and public amenities such as a tea-room, bottle store, market and new dispensary. There is a line of stores and private houses built on a self-help basis with the aid and encouragement of the extension team. Township Rules have been drawn up and submitted to the Governor for his approval.

The extension team under Duncan Banda is a great asset. It is doing good work in spite of the uphill grind of trying to keep the interest of the local population – particularly difficult during the rains. The annual report of the Community Development Officer, Mungwi, spoke most favourably of the group and he is considering its upgrading to a community development sub-centre. Carpentry classes are going well, and some bricklayers and carpenters have been sent on courses to Mungwi. The staff are being encouraged to minimise their dependence on Mungwi as a parent body and, as they become more firmly established, to make their present site a base for development work in the field throughout this Lungu area. Difficulties were encountered at first in the self-help housing scheme as some private jealousies affected mutual co-operation, but the aims are now understood and successful results have begun to unite the people in a working spirit. It is hoped to build a Community Development Assistant's house in the near future.

Appendix 1

The Chief envisages his Musumba as an attraction to traders and that the proposed township will be the next stage in the progress towards economic take-off. One cannot but admire his enthusiasm and ambition, but there are too many difficulties. Communications and the new road to Chikwekwe are dealt with elsewhere (Annexure VII). Trade is at present negligible. There are exceptionally few stores in his area – 5 at the Musumba and only 9 in other parts – all of very low standard; none of them ever had anything I wanted, but I am not judging them by this criterion alone! The basic need is for a wider circulation of money, for at present there is insufficient money in the villages to make any general trading store a going concern.

With regard to traders from outside there is nothing to attract them except in the local agricultural produce. One cannot base a local economy entirely on tobacco and coffee, and thought should be given to the export of groundnuts also, which could be grown on a larger scale and for which I am told there is a market as close as Kasama. Livestock could also be considered in the same context. The Kasama Marketing Union did come here last year to buy local produce but the villagers, unaccustomed to sales, expected a fortune at their first attempt and refused the reasonable buying prices of the Union. I noticed this myself on tour, that they had no experience of outside price values. If the people of the Musumba area could concentrate on cash crops for sale outside the area this might help; as this area is too heavily populated for *citemene* (see Annexure X) staple foods could be bought from the outlying villages. This at least would circulate money from outside through the Musumba to the villages (and back to the Native Treasury in tax!); but the prospects are not good.

The only other ideas put forward in the recent past have been the sale of work from the women's welfare and home-craft section of the extension team's activities, and furniture. There is not likely to be much market for the woollen garments and the output would be minimal, but it is better than nothing and anyway the women should be encouraged in these affairs as much for their education as for trade. There are insufficient sawyers and carpenters in the area for furniture or any other product of timber at the moment, but it is of course hoped that the extension team will improve this situation. Again there remains the problem of finding an outside market. On tour I noticed that the area, being at the headwaters of many rivers, is very rich in *mishitu* in which there appears to be plenty of excellent timber. Although these must of course be rigorously protected, I feel that there may be possibilities for controlled exploitation of their resources if closely supervised by the Forestry Department. Transport difficulties would not be great as the main road along the watershed is within easy reach of the mishitu.

The bottle store, market and tea-room are not very successful. There is not enough money to provide them with custom and the bottle store has only been used once since it was a polling station for the elections in December.

ANNEXURE VII: COMMUNICATIONS

This area is served by one spinal road running north-south to link the Mporokoso-Kasama and Luwingu-Kasama roads. It also serves as a short-cut between Luwingu and Abercorn and between the two divisions of Lungu territory. It is a very well-built District road, following the line of the watershed all the way, and needs very little maintenance. An all-weather road, it has survived the rains better than any other in the District, owing to its good siting and lack of traffic. Two cul-de-sacs leading off it are Native Authority responsibilities: the two miles to Vincent Bulaya and the three miles to Mukupa Kaoma. The 15-mile road to Chewe School has not yet been gazetted. Two culverts on the main District road were repaired at the end of the tour, with local labour. They need only more ballast.

Village paths were all in good condition, and here again the Chief insists on a high standard. Rains have naturally taken their toll on a number of bridges and these will be rebuilt in April. There is a fair amount of cycle traffic (traders and others) between Mukupa Kaoma and Kapatu and Shibwalya Kapila, and also southwards from Mukupa Kaoma to the Lubushi vicinity.

The Central African Road Services (CARS) bus runs twice a week in each direction between Kasama-Kapatu-Mukupa Kaoma-Chitoshi-Luwingu. It carries little traffic. In 1960 a service was started between Abercorn and Luwingu, but last year owing to lack of custom this service was suspended and passengers travel via Kasama. Mukupa Kaoma has no postal service,

Appendix 1

although the bus calls there. There is a private bag at Chitoshi, and a Kapasu has to be sent there every week to collect and deliver. The Native Authority clearly needs a second private bag at the Musumba and this is included in this year's estimates.

For many years it has been proposed to build a road from the Musumba to Chikwekwe in Chitoshi's area, where there is already a road leading to the main Luwingu-Kasama thoroughfare. This will shorten the route to Kasama by nearly 30 miles and is primarily designed to encourage trade. It is planned for 1964, and the touring party considered the general line of the new road and the possible siting of the two bridges needed.

ANNEXURE VIII: HEALTH

The general health in the villages toured is good. The number of cases of total blindness in the area could not have been more than half-a-dozen, and only two lepers were noted, both of whom had been treated at Kabalenge in Kawambwa District. Instances of malnutrition or protein deficiency among the children were minimal, which was surprising in view of one of my comments in Annexure IV. There have been no known cases of smallpox since 1958.

Two outbreaks of measles were encountered during the tour. At one village we found all the children present were suffering from it and had been treated with local *muti*; three had died. I was shown with some pride by an old matriarch how she had soaked *kangwa* leaves and applied the solution to the eyes and into all the orifices of the body. Though ignorant of the properties of the *kangwa*, I could see the effect on the children: one was already half-blind and was sent to Luwingu immediately, and all the others were badly affected in their eyes. The local medicine-man still very much exists; some charge fees and are therefore thought more skilled.

Hygiene in the villages was generally good, and the Chief is keen on a high standard in this. Every house and latrine was inspected by a Kapasu and notes were made. I have already indicated (in Annexure III) that, on occasions when hygiene was obviously below standard, no action was taken apart from a reprimand and the matter was left for future inspection.

The new Dispensary at Mukupa Kaoma is almost complete and only needs plastering and painting. The Native Authority received a grant of £200 from the Provincial Native Treasuries Fund for roofing the building. All the labour on this project has been voluntary, and has been provided either by learners from the nearby Rural Development extension team or by villagers – brick-burning, bricklaying and carpentry. The Administrative Secretary is planning the finishing touch which will be a 10'x16' kitchen behind. A dispensary has long been needed in this area where the nearest medical services are either at Luwingu (63 miles) or Mporokoso (72 miles). The Provincial Medical Officer has approved in principle the posting of an Assistant to Mukupa Kaoma, and a house has just been completed for him.

The Native Authority has a drug box which contains only bandages, plaster, iodine and Epsom salts. One Kapasu has been trained as an itinerant Medical Orderly but is very unsatisfactory. A more useful person is the new Court Member, John Musonda, who has been training and working for 14 years as a medical orderly in Tanganyika and S.Rhodesia, is qualified to give injections and might be of some assistance in the new Dispensary.

<u>*Comments on Annexure VIII above by the District Commissioner.*</u>
The matriarch mentioned in the second paragraph would presumably be liable to prosecution under Section 16 of the Blind Persons Ordinance, but education is clearly the best way of dealing with such practices. It is hoped that the Provincial Information Officer will run a campaign later in the year, to follow up a previous campaign of 1960 and to promote the work of the Mporokoso Blind School.

The Provincial Medical Officer has regretfully announced his inability to staff the new Dispensary in the next financial year. The Native Authority plans, however, to employ a man who resigned from the Territorial service rather than be transferred to Federal terms, and the PMO has agreed to give him refresher training. Once the Dispensary is complete, a Special Warrant will be submitted to cover this unforeseen commitment. The new Dispensary will meet a long-felt need.

A.N.MacGregor

ANNEXURE IX: GAME

Hardly any game was seen during the tour. However, there was reported to be a lot in the extreme south-east of the area, which perhaps accounts for the reluctance of small villages there to move to otherwise preferable sites. Lions frequent the central area and one village had to move because of their incursions. Monkeys are a nuisance around the gardens in certain parts, and numerous traps for them were seen, as well as small camp sites for the more systematic drives against them.

There is an abundance of game in the uninhabited western part of the Chief's area, outside the area toured, by the headwaters of the Kalungwishi and opposite Kawambwa District. The Chief was keen that this area should be demarcated as a Game Reserve and, after discussions in the full Lungu Council at Abercorn, the idea was put to the Game Dapartment. I understand that the Department considered that it would have to be run by the Native Authority as their own affair and, since they had no funds to maintain the necessary staff, the idea was temporarily dropped. The Chief is still very keen on this matter, remembering how well stocked his whole area was in his not so distant youth, and would welcome an opening for fresh discussions on the topic.

Comments on Annexure IX above by the District Commissioner.

I am passing a copy of this Annexure to the Game Officer, Mporokoso, and the possibility of a Private Game Area will be discussed with him. The Native Treasury is certainly in no position to provide funds at present but future developments may make it possible to employ some Game Kapasus. It would be unfortunate if the Chief's enthusiasm were frustrated for this reason alone.

A.N.MacGregor

ANNEXURE X: POPULATION

The population of Chief Mukupa Kaoma's area is concentrated in the extreme north along the tributaries of the Luangwa and in the south-east in the upper basin of the Lukulu. As a whole, this is the most thinly populated of the Chiefs' areas in Mporokoso District, with 3.7 persons per square mile; but within a four mile radius of the Musumba there was found to be a resident population of about 700. That is 14 persons per square mile. The centre and west are entirely uninhabited, so that a natural population division can be made between the Luangwa and Lukulu sections.

The statistics for the two parishes visited are attached; a reasonably accurate assessment of the resident population has been attempted. A half of the taxable males are working on the Copperbelt, and Chingola hits the top of the popularity poll. It is noticeable, as always, that each village has connections with one particular urban centre and most of its men will go there to seek work. As expected, the figures for the Congo and Tanganyika have completely slumped; this Lungu area has always had more connections with Tanganyika for employment (probably due to tribal history) while the Bemba of the District have favoured the Congo for similar ancestral reasons.

Most villages have moved site since the area was last toured, and one had even moved into Chief Chitoshi's area. There is a general trend noticeable for the people in the south-east to move out of their present area over the border into Chitoshi's or Munkonge's areas where trade and communications are much better. The Chief recognises this but is not unduly perturbed; he is senior to Chitoshi in rank and regards them as still in "his Lungu area". Emigrants to Munkonge are beyond his control.

In spite of the increase in houses of semi-permanent materials villages will continue to move too often for them to be accurately sited on a map. However, for present information a map is attached.

The forthcoming census and its aims were explained to every village.

A few villages are too small in total population, let alone in the number of taxable males resident. The Chief rightly favours amalgamation in these cases, and in general is keen to concentrate the people into fewer and larger villages for administrative reasons. But he will take no autocratic step against the wishes of the villagers, and is finding it hard to persuade them to his views.

Appendix 1

MAP OF AREA TOURED

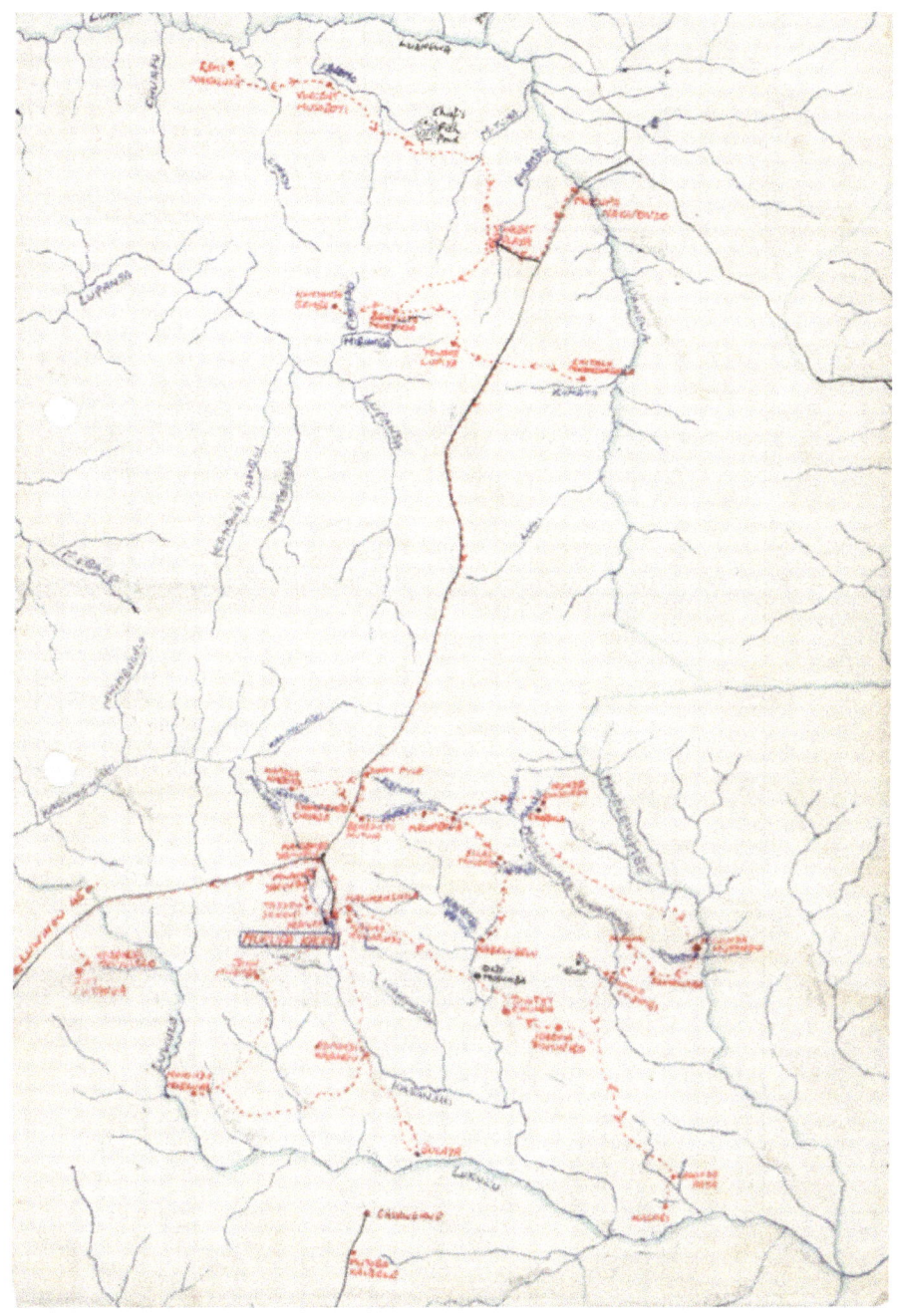

Tour report No.3 of 1963
CHIEF MUKUPA KAOMA'S AREA: POPULATION & LABOUR STATISTICS

(Figures in brackets indicate those resident in Chief's area)

Village	Adults M	Adults F	Children M	Children F	TOTAL	Exempt males	At Home	N. Prov.	Copper belt	Other	Total
CHUNDU PARISH											
Mukupa Nakapondo	15(5)	14(9)	16(12)	17(12)	62(38)	4	1	3	6	1	11
Chaiwa	11(7)	13(11)	10(9)	14(12)	48(39)	3	4	2	2	-	8
Inasho Mulonga	24(7)	20(13)	20(14)	21(13)	85(47)	2	5	3	14	-	22
Vincent Musoboyi	20(11)	19(6)	38(34)	33(30)	110(91)	4	7	4	5	-	16
Remi Nakaluka	23(6)	15(11)	7(13)	15(12)	70(42)	5	2	3	13	-	18
Sikapembwa	12(5)	11(7)	13(10)	14(10)	50(32)	2	3	2	5	-	10
Vincent Bulaya	48(18)	39(28)	52(38)	47(37)	186(121)	8	10	4	24	2	40
Kanyanja Bemba	21(7)	21(13)	17(12)	13(11)	72(43)	4	4	1	9	3	17
Benelito Musonda	18(5)	17(9)	19(9)	23(12)	77(35)	3	2	1	12	-	15
Yowane Lupiya	58(24)	61(39)	74(47)	86(52)	279(162)	8	16	12	21	1	50
Chitalu Mwansanshila	21(5)	16(8)	15(11)	17(8)	69(32)	3	3	2	13	-	18
Saferi Musonda	21(11)	20(16)	29(23)	29(23)	99(73)	3	8	-	10	-	18
Total	**292**	**266**	**320**	**329**	**1,207**	**49**	**65**	**37**	**134**	**7**	**24**
Resident	111	180	232	232	755						
Non-resident	181	86	88	97	452						
MALAILA PARISH											
Champembe Chisube	14(9)	17(16)	17(13)	65(55)	2	7	1	3	1	12	11
Benedicto Mutuka	13(8)	14(9)	17(10)	18(15)	62(42)	2	6	-	5	-	11
Dixon Pule	13(7)	18(13)	23(19)	16(12)	70(47)	2	5	-	6	-	11
Kapasa Kabota	18(9)	18(11)	31(23)	20(12)	87(55)	1	8	1	8	-	17
Malupenga	32(15)	39(32)	24(12)	27(15)	122(74)	6	9	8	9	-	126

Appendix 1

Kabelubelu	13(6)	12(8)	11(8)	9(5)	45(27)	2	4	-	7	-	11
Nonde Chisongo	19(9)	8(10)	18(13)	20(14)	75(46)	4	5	3	7	-	15
Chabula 23(12)	24(18)	28(19)	32(22)	107(71)	3	9	1	10	-	20	
Musonda Mutengo	16(6)	13(7)	19(7)	11(3)	55(23)	1	5	5	5	-	15
Mukumi	17(7)	13(7)	13(9)	13(9)	56(32)	4	4	4	5	-	13
Chongo Chibimbi	25(11)	27(21)	32(20)	26(18)	110(70)	6	6	4	8	1	19
Kasonde Pata	9(4)	7(2)	8(4)	12(3)	36(13)	3	1	1	4	-	6
Kasabi	19(4)	12(7)	10(4)	10(4)	51(19)	3	1	5	9	1	16
Kaoma Dominico	14(6)	17(12)	25(10)	26(16)	82(52)	2	4	2	5	1	12
Timothy Chiinga	53(10)	40(22)	42(19)	53(25)	188(76)	3	7	12	26	5	50
Jim Matanga	11(3)	12(8)	17(8)	13(9)	53(28)	2	2	2	5	-	9
Kansembe Yamwelu	19(7)	22(17)	147(7)	20(19)	78(60)	3	5	3	7	1	16
Mwamba Yamwelu	11(7)	12(10)	18(18)	16(16)	57(51)	2	5	2	2	-	9
Taddeo Sokoni	28(13)	28(19)	39(29)	30(20)	125(81)	5	9	4	10	-	23
John Mwamba	16(5)	23(14)	25(13)	21(9)	85(41)	41	4	7	-	12	19
Musonda Nseluka	20(5)	20(8)	23(9)	37(11)	100(33)	1	4	8	7	-	19
Edmondi Kabungo	11(11)	13(12)	15(13)	12(12)	51(48)	4	7	-	-	-	7
Bulaya	20(4)	21(9)	21(10)	29(12)	91(35)	2	2	9	6	1	18
Kalimanshila	30(11)	30(17)	37(14)	38(22)	135(64)	2	9	6	13	-	28	
Mafuta	19(3)	21(7)	22(4)	24(8)	86(22)	4	1	5	9	-	15
Nsama Nakapondo	12(7)	11(7)	24(18)	15(9)	62(41)	1	6	-	5	-	11
MUKUPA KAOMA	113(44)	109(67)	139(74)	142(89)	503(274)	14	31	17	49	1	99
Total	**608**	**611**	**711**	**707**	**2,637**	**88**	**163**	**107**	**237**	**5**	**520**
Resident	243	390	433	422	1,488						
Non-resident	365	221	278	285	1,149						

(Figures in brackets indicate those resident in Chief's area)

Appendix 2
Rules of the Lumpa Church

(Appendix to a lengthy, 88-paragraph, report to the Central Intelligence Committee, dated 5 September 1959; translated from ciBemba)

1. The Lumpa Church is a church in which God and His Son Jesus Christ are to be praised. It is an organisation that has no connection with Government.
2. In our congregation there is no citizen or foreigner, black or white, man or woman, but we are all of the same family; therefore we must love each other.
3. A Christian must take no part in:
   (a) Backbiting, (b) Cursing, (c) Lying, (d) Pride, (e) Selfishness, (f) False evidence, (g) Anger, (h) Harshness, (i) Hatred, (j) Harmful words and actions, (k) Disobedience, (l) Cunning, (m) Stealing, etc.
   Therefore he must be truthful, kind, faithful, happy and obedient.
4. A Christian must avoid covetousness, witchcraft, stealing, adultery, witch-hunting, killing, drunkenness and bawdy songs, dancing and other pagan things.
5. Every Christian must be of good character, whether in private or public, when eating or going to sleep, waking from sleep or when starting or ending his work, while at play or in times of sorrow or trouble. When he is on a journey a Christian must pray to his Father.
6. There must be no beer or pagan dances during a Christian wedding. If they have these things, those who are being wed will be punished by the Commandment of Jesus. They must not be separated from each other until they die.
7. It is the duty of a Christian to go with others to prayers from time to time, and on every appointed day of worship.
8. A widow must not be punished by being prevented from re-marrying. She must only wear a string of white beads. If she wishes to re-marry she must be allowed to do so.
9. A Christian must not be a polygamist.
10. A Christian must not eat food prepared for the dead, and there must be

no witch-hunting for the killer of the deceased person after the funeral.
11. At the time of worship no one should smoke cigarettes or a pipe or take snuff. They must not take any of these things into the church.
12. If anyone has taken some beer he must not come to worship in church, though he has taken only a little.

Any person who disobeys these rules is the one whom the Lord Himself came to seek. That is why God the Father says "Give up all things leading to witchcraft, and live in my love." Anyone who is fond of bewitching, when his time comes to an end, will suffer because he will be troubled greatly.

These are the Rules of the Lumpa Church.

Lenshina Mulenga.

Some Lenshina Hymns

1.
Nefwe nga tukatulwa lilali?
Fwebatemwa Calo ca mfifi,
Fwebatemwa Calo ca busha.

Natemwa sana nemunenu
Pakumona maluba yandi yasanika;
Nelyo mwaya mubulwani mwisakamana nelyo cimo,
Kabiyeni kalangeni abanenu abashama.

Mwebashuka bonse mwebo Tata fikilila,
Nelyo mulwani aicushe twakula imba,
Fwebapelwa pakameko.

Mulemona kubanenu abashama,
Balemona imilimo ya Mfumu ye ibi,
Abo Satana akulila nganda pa mutwe;
Twiba nga balwani bakale balya baipeye Katula.

Pakwabukila peshilya kano imitima yasambwa,

When shall we be saved?
We who love the country of darkness,
We who love the country of slavery.

I your friend am very glad
To see my flowers bloom;
Although you go to encounter enmity do not worry at all,
Go and show your less fortunate brethren.

Blest are all who have received the Father.
Though the enemy troubles us, we shall still be singing, we who are given pride.

See your unfortunate (unconverted) friends,
Those who set no store by the Lord's work,
On whose heads Satan has built a house;
Let us not be like those enemies of old who killed the Saviour.

When you cross that river, if your hearts are cleansed,

Appendix 2

Ngo kamona Mwana Lesa nga kafika
    na kucinso.

Mwebanandi mwebomfwa ifyo nanda
Moneni kubanenu abashala ku cibolya
Balefwaya babile, kuleni mwandi pakalisha

2.
Mwe Shikulu tulangeniko inshila
Yakupita palusale pakwabuka iyakufika
Kuli Imwe Bakatula.

Shikulwifwe natulangila, no mulwani
Naseba inshila moneni kubasuminisha
Ebaleya mu cibolya mububi.

3.
Welupili kamutola wewaimikwa pano calo,
Welupili kamutola wewafilwa ukunina
Kamutola waputulwa pakati waimwena,
Wewafilwa ukunina kamutola.

Mwebanina kamutola sekesheni,
Yauleni mwalishuka, mwebanina kamutola

4.
Abakengila mu Sion mupya
Tebalwambo tebalubuli iyo.

Nobe we munyima ne nkashi yandi
Tamwakengile mu Sion mupya
Pantu mwasula umupusushi Yesu.

Mwebashasumina, nimwe mwalenga
Yesu Klistu ukukokola ukwisa.
Alisosele ku Basambi bakwe ati
"Naya mumulu, nkabwela kabili."

We cipumbu, butuka lubilo. Umulilo
Naupalama. Noma mwibukishe

Then you will see the Son of God, He will
    appear before you.

All my children who understand my words,
Look to your friends who have stayed in a
    ruined place; they are near to crying.

Our Heavenly Father, show us the way
To lead us across the other side so that we
Arrive at your Kingdom in Heaven.

Our Lord has shown us the way, but the
Enemy has paved the way too wide. See,
Those that follow him go to the desolation of
    deserted homes.

You the highest mountain on earth,
Whoever fails to climb the highest mountain
Will be cut off from the Kingdom of Heaven,
He who fails to climb you.

You who have climbed the highest mountain
Rejoice unto the Lord, you fortunate ones,
Who have climbed the highest mountain.

Those who will enter into the new Zion
Are pure in all ways.

My brothers and sisters,
You will not enter into the new Zion
Because you despise your Saviour Jesus.

You unbelievers have caused
Jesus Christ not to come soon.
He said to his disciples
"I go to Heaven, I shall return again."

You sinners, hasten (to believe).
The fire of destruction is nigh.

From Northern Rhodesia to Zambia

Sodom na Gomorrah.
Yesu aponeshe umulilo. Bapwa bonse.

5.
Ifyo natemwa Ing'uni shandi ngashaisa,
Ifyo natemwa Ing'uni shandi ngashaisa;
Kabiyeni kashimyeni ifyushi fyafula.

Ndelumba ndetasha ndelumfya kuli Tata
Mwe Ng'uni shandi mwinaka.

6.
Tata natantika bulalo bwakwe,
Tata natantika bulalo bwakwe.
Bukabukapo abashuka,
Uwashama akawila mu cilindi ateya.

Cishibo ca balwani,
Cishibo ca balwani,
Ukacula ngafilwa bacushishe Satana.

7.
Akulatulanga Shikulu, akulatulanga
Pa citamba maluba.

Uluse lwakwe lusuma elukatutwala
Ukusuma, elukatutwala kuli Tata waluse

Remember Sodom and Gomorrah.
Jesus destroyed them with fire, all died

How I rejoice when my lost sheep return,
How I rejoice when my lost sheep repent.
Go and quench the fire, there is too much
   Smoke.
I am praising and rejoicing unto the Father.
You my followers, do not tire.

Our Lord has built a bridge,
Our Lord has built His bridge.
The blessed, they will cross it;
Sinners will fall into a pit and perish.

The sign of the enemies,
The sign of the enemies,
You sinner will suffer as Satan did.

Our Lord will show us, He will show us,
All the signs to His Kingdom in Heaven.

His kindness is very great; it will lead us
To the good life, to our Father of grace.

Appendix 3
Structure of Government Administration at the Local Level
(Recommendations of the Constitutional Review Commission, 1995)

"Overwhelmingly, petitioners throughout the country wanted to see an effective well constituted local government structure, which is readily responsive to the needs of the people. The present structure in their view was totally ineffective.

They looked forward to a structure which would operate smoothly from province downwards to district level. Petitioners felt that in order for the needs of the people at the lowest level to be adequately addressed by the administration, there was a need to devise a clear, workable and dynamic administrative structure. For instance, they point out that there existed no competent office at the district level to co-ordinate government affairs. Thus the problems at grass roots could not be resolved or properly addressed.

Therefore the Commissioners recommended that, in addition to the office of the Assistant Minister for the province, the offices of the Provincial Commissioners be established with full powers and defined responsibilities aimed at yielding results. The Provincial Commissioner will be a senior civil servant appointed by the Civil Service Commission. He should co-ordinate the activities of all the Districts and Sub-Districts in the Province as well as linking the activities of the Provincial Government with those of Central Government.

The petitioners equally supported the idea of the office of District Commissioner at district level. There was universal agreement that the administrative power vacuum presently being experienced by the people at district level could be filled by the establishment of the office of the District Commissioner.

The Commission recommends the establishment of the office of the District Commissioner. As with the Provincial Commissioner, the District Commissioner should be a civil servant appointed by the Public Service Commission.

In order to fill the perceived power vacuum at the district level in the post-One-Party era, the Commission recommends that the functions of the

District Commissioner should include the supervision of the general administration of the district and councils, as well as the co-ordination of government and civic activities as between district and province."

Lightning Source UK Ltd.
Milton Keynes UK
UKHW020825040220
358104UK00004B/48